# ASIAN ECONOMIC AND POLITICAL ISSUES

# VOLUME IV

# ASIAN ECONOMIC AND POLITICAL ISSUES

# VOLUME IV

### FRANK COLUMBUS
### EDITOR

**Nova Science Publishers, Inc.**
*Huntington, New York*

**Senior Editors:** Susan Boriotti and Donna Dennis
**Coordinating Editor:** Tatiana Shohov
**Office Manager:** Annette Hellinger
**Graphics:** Wanda Serrano
**Book Production:** Matthew Kozlowski, Jonathan Rose and Jennifer Vogt
**Circulation:** Cathy DeGregory, Ave Maria Gonzalez and Raheem Miller
**Communications and Acquisitions:** Serge P. Shohov

*Library of Congress Cataloging-in-Publication Data*
*Available Upon Request*

ISBN 1-59033-115-X.

Copyright © 2001 by Nova Science Publishers, Inc.
   227 Main Street, Suite 100
   Huntington, New York 11743
   Tele. 631-424-6682 Fax 631-425-5933
   e-mail: Novascience@earthlink.net
   Web Site: http://www.nexusworld.com/nova

*Printed in the United States of America*

# CONTENTS

# PREFACE

In spite of economic bubbles, meltdowns and a variety of current financial hiccups, Asia remains an economic powerhouse.

The articles presented examine the current political and economic situations in nations across Asia, particularly focusing on the south and east of the continent. Noted scholars present and analyze a wide range of issues -- from Chinese business to politics in Bangladesh as well as original research on crucial issues in the trade dynamics of China.

# Chapter 1

# STOCK MARKETS AND FOREIGN DIRECT INVESTMENT: AN EXTENSION OF TOBIN'S Q THEORY[*]

## *Yue Ma*

Department of Economics
Lingnan University
Hong Kong
Tel: +(852) 2616 7202/Fax: +(852) 2891 7940 Email: yuema@ln.edu.hk
Internet: http://www.ln.edu.hk/econ/staff/yuema

## A SHORT BIO OF DR YUE MA

Dr Yue Ma obtained his BSc in Optimal Control Theory from Xiamen (Amoy) University at China in 1985, Certificate of Graduate from Sino-American Economic Training Centre sponsored by Ford Foundation at People's University of China in 1986, and PhD in Economics and Econometrics from Manchester University in 1991. He is currently an Associate Professor at Lingnan University, Hong Kong, where he lectures Money and Banking, International Finance, and Chinese Economy. Dr Ma has more than 30 publications in international refereed journals. He is specialized in international macroeconometric modeling, forecasting and policy analysis. His research interests include economic modeling of exchange rate and banking, as well as international policy co-ordinations, with particular reference to the economies of mainland China and Hong Kong. He is also a Concurrent Professor at Lingnan College, Zhongshan University, China, and was a Reader at Stirling and a Senior Research Fellow at Strathclyde, UK. He has been working for Hong Kong Institute for Monetary Research (an affiliation of Hong Kong Monetary Authority), Princeton University, Oxford University, National Institute

[*] The author is grateful for the helpful comments from Koichiro Morikawa on the earlier draft of this chapter.

of Economics & Statistics (INSEE in Paris), Hong Kong Baptist University, European University Institute (Italy), London Business School, Manchester University under various research projects. He is a member of the editorial board of the *Scottish Journal of Political Economy*.

For details, please see Dr Ma's personal website: *http://www.ln.edu.hk/econ/ staff/yuema/*

## ABSTRACT

Financial economic theory suggests that the investment and financing decisions are closely related. This has been recognised in most of the literature on *domestic* investment process. However, research on the foreign direct investment (FDI) are usually focused on those determinants excluding the financing factors. This paper studies financial dependence of the dynamic allocation of investments between domestic and foreign destinations. We developed an intertemporal optimisation theoretical model of foreign direct investment which is an extension of Tobin's (1969) q theory and Goldsbrough's (1979) static model on the production allocation. The optimal foreign direct investment is determined mainly by the difference between domestic q and overseas q in the new model, which indicates the relative market-value of a multinational corporation in domestic and foreign financial markets. The model is developed in such a general framework that it also incorporates imperfect competition in domestic and overseas markets. Furthermore, it can evaluate the effects of the real exchange rate, the corporate tax rates and investment credits on the FDI.

**Keywords**: foreign direct investment, financial markets, Tobin's q theory
**JEL codes**: F23, F21, F15, C22

## 1. INTRODUCTION

There is a strong growth in foreign direct investments (FDI) in the late 1990s (see Table 1). The FDI phenomenon is also worldwide happening in both developed and less-developed countries (see Table 2).

**Table 1. Indicators of FDI and international production in 1990s**

|  | Value at current price (billion dollars) | | | Annual growth rate (%) | | |
|---|---|---|---|---|---|---|
|  | 1996 | 1997 | 1998 | 1996 | 1997 | 1998 |
| FDI inflows | 359 | 464 | 644 | 9.1 | 29.4 | 38.7 |
| Gross product of foreign affiliates | 2026 | 2266 | 2677 | 6.7 | 12.8 | 17.1 |
| Employment of foreign affiliates (millions) | 30941 | 31630 | 35074 | 4.9 | 2.2 | 10.9 |

**Source:** United Nations (1999) p.10.

**Table 2. Regional distributions of FDI inflows and outflows in 1990s (%)**

|  | Inflows | | | Outflows | | |
|---|---|---|---|---|---|---|
|  | 1996 | 1997 | 1998 | 1996 | 1997 | 1998 |
| Developed countries | 58.8 | 58.9 | 71.5 | 84.2 | 85.6 | 91.6 |
| Developing countries | 37.7 | 37.2 | 25.8 | 15.5 | 13.7 | 8.1 |
| Central and Eastern Europe | 3.5 | 4.0 | 2.7 | 0.3 | 0.7 | 0.3 |
| World | 100 | 100 | 100 | 100 | 100 | 100 |

**Source:** United Nations (1999) p.18.

Financial economic theory suggests that the investment and financing decisions are closely related. This has been recognised in most of the literature on *domestic* investment process (see, e.g. Sensenbrenner, 1991; Ma, 2001). However, research on the FDI are usually focused on the international competition to reduce the production costs (Caves, 1982, Dunning, 1985), technology and management expertise transfers (Helpman and Krugman, 1989; Hu and Ma, 1999), the avoidance of tariff and efficient sales and service network around the world (Ma, Morikawa and Shone, 2000), the diversification of real exchange rate risks (Cushman, 1988, Ma and Kanas, 2000), the government policies that attract FDI (Ma, Tsang and Tang, 1998; Tsang and Ma, 1997; Tsang and Ma, 2000), and other determinant factors of FDI (Drake and Caves, 1992). They did not intend to give a general modelling framework of FDI activities of the multinational enterprises that incorporates the important relationship between FDI and finance[1].

In this paper, we develop an intertemporal optimisation model of FDI which is an extension of both Tobin's q theory (Tobin, 1969) and Goldsbrough's (1979) static model on the production allocation. Tobin's q theory can be derived from the profit maximisation approach with capital installation costs. The optimal investment is a function of q, the ratio of the stock market valuation of a firm's securities to the replacement cost of the physical assets they represent. The original idea of the q-theory was come from Keynes's (1936) arbitrage principle. When private businesses intend to expand their capital, they either purchase them from the market, or produce them by arbitraging between its market demand price and supply price.

The earlier applications of Tobin's q theory suggested the lack of empirical evidence to support the theory (von Furstenberg, 1977, Summers, 1981). However, these findings are subject to at least two major problems. Firstly, the Tobin's q model is not directly implementable, since the marginal q is not observable (Hayashi, 1982). Other papers have been inclined to use the average q, which is the ratio of the market value of the capital to its replacement cost, to approximate the marginal q in most of the empirical work. This practice in fact implicitly imposes the assumption of perfect competition in the product market to the q model, since the average q and marginal q is equivalent under this assumption (Hayashi, 1982). The empirical rejection of the q theory based on this assumption therefore does not necessarily refute the q theory *per se*.

---

[1] The only exception perhaps is Gilman (1981), who, however, considers the financing of FDI as a portfolio management problem rather than a process of joint production and finance decisions.

The second problem is related to the econometric technique. The possible existence of heteroscedasticity and serial autocorrelation in residuals as well as the problem of the simultaneity invalidate the ordinary least square and conventional instrumental variable estimators. Indeed, recent empirical works have been in favour of the q theory after the above-mentioned two problems have been overcome. Aggregate time series analyses include Schiantarelli and Georgoutsos (1990) for the UK industrial and commercial companies and Galletti and Schiantarelli (1991) for the US manufacturing sector. Panel data research works include Blundell *et al* (1992) for the UK companies whose main activity was manufacturing, and Hayashi and Inoue (1991) for a panel of Japanese manufacturing firms.

The q theory is understood to be applicable to the aggregate investment behaviour. However, Goldsbrough (1979) developed a static allocation model of FDI. In his model, a multinational firm locates its production facilities among different countries to maximise its total profits. Our model is an attempt to unify the two approaches of *dynamic* profit maximisation and allocation decisions in a single model. The model is developed in such a general framework that it also incorporates imperfect competition in domestic and overseas markets; the hypotheses of the competitiveness can be tested independently for the domestic and international markets. Our model can also analyse the effects of both the tax rate and investment credit differentials between domestic and foreign governments on the domestic investment and FDI.

The structure of this chapter is organised as follows. Section 2 develops our dynamic FDI model and explores the theoretical implications. Finally, Section 3 concludes the chapter.

## 2. STOCK MARKETS AND FDI

Consider an intertemporal optimisation model of a multinational corporation which attempts to maximise the present-value of its net cash flow over an infinite horizon by allocating the exogenously determined total investment, $\bar{I}(t)$, between domestic and overseas production[2,3]:

$$\bar{V}(0) = V(0) + V^*(0) \qquad \int_0^\infty [\, R(t) + R^*(t) \,] \exp\left[-\int_0^t r(s)\, ds\right] dt \qquad (1)$$

where a variable with superscripted by an asterisk is associated with the activity of the foreign affiliates, domestic variables are without "*". r(s) is the nominal borrowing rate of interest. $\bar{V}(0)$ is the aggregate market-value of the multinational corporation, which

---

[2] This paper focuses on the optimal *allocation* of total investment. The total investment is assumed to be exogenously determined due to the financial constraint - to endogenise it is beyond the scope of this paper (see Takenaka, *et al*, 1989).

[3] In reality, the foreign direct investment should also consider the country specific characteristics such as distance, country risk, etc. However, this is left for further research.

consists of its domestic market-value, V(0), and its overseas market-value, V*(0). V(0) and V*(0) are the present-value of the net cash flow R(t) and R*(t), respectively. The net cash flow at time t, R(t), is defined as profits after tax minus costs of investment goods plus investment credits:

$$R(t) = [1 - \tau(t)]\pi(t) - [1- \varphi(t)] \, p_I(t)[ \, \bar{I}(t) - I^*(t)], \tag{2}$$

and in parallel:

$$R^*(t) = [1 - \tau^*(t)]\pi^*(t) - [1- \varphi^*(t)] \, p_I^*(t)I^*(t), \tag{2'}$$

where $\bar{I}(t)$ is the exogenously determined total investment, which consists of $I^*(t)$ as FDI and I(t) as the domestic investment. That is, $I(t) = \bar{I}(t) - I^*(t)$. $\tau(t)$ is the corporate tax rate, $\varphi(t)$ is the rate of investment tax credit, $p_I(t)$ is the price of new investment goods. $\pi(t)$ is profits before tax, which is defined as:

$$\pi(t) = p(t) \, F(K(t), L(t)) - w(t)L(t) - p(t)G(I(t), K(t)), \tag{3}$$

and in parallel:

$$\pi^*(t) = p^*(t) \, F^*(K^*(t), L^*(t)) - w^*(t)L^*(t) - p^*(t)G^*(I^*(t), K^*(t)), \tag{3'}$$

where p(t) is the output price, F(.,.) is the production function, K(t) is the capital stock, L(t) is the labour input, w(t) is the wage rate, G(.,.) is the adjustment cost function. The adjustment cost function G(.,.) depends on both K and I because the cost of installing I units of investment goods depends on the size of I relative to K. The capital stock accumulation constraints are given as:

$$dK(t)/dt = \bar{I}(t) - I^*(t) - \delta \, K(t) \tag{4}$$

$$dK^*(t)/dt = I^*(t) - \delta^* \, K^*(t) \tag{4'}$$

where $\delta$ and $\delta^*$ are domestic and foreign capital depreciation rates, respectively. Rewrite (4) as follows:

$$dK(t)/dt = I(t) - \delta \, K(t) \tag{4a}$$

This shows (4a) and (4)' in a parallel way.

To solve the above dynamic optimisation problem, we apply the Pontryagin's Maximum Principle to our model. The current-value Hamiltonian is (omitting time subscripts for clarity):

$$H = R + R^* + q \, ( \bar{I} - I^* - \delta \, K ) + q^* \, ( I^* - \delta^* \, K^* )$$

$$= (1 - \tau)\pi - (1- \varphi)\, p_I\, (\bar{I} - I^*) + [(1-\tau^*)\pi^* - (1- \varphi^*)\, p_I^* I^* ]$$
$$\quad + q\, (\bar{I} - I^* - \delta K ) + q^*\, ( I^* - \delta^* K^* )$$
$$= (1-\tau)[\, p\, F(K, L) - wL - pG(\bar{I} - I^*, K)\,] - (1 - \varphi)\, p_I\, (\bar{I} - I^*)$$
$$\quad + \{\, (1-\tau^*)[\, p^*\, F(K^*, L^*) - w^*L^* - p^*G^*(I^*, K^*)] - (1- \varphi^*)\, p_I^* I^*\, \}$$
$$\quad + q\, (\bar{I} - \varepsilon\, I^* - \delta K ) + \varepsilon\, q^*\, ( I^* - \delta^* K^* ) \tag{5}$$

where q and q* are the shadow prices of the domestic capital stock (K) and capital stock of foreign affiliates (K*), respectively. They are in fact the Tobin's marginal q for domestic and overseas capital stocks.

To eliminate any bubble solution, we impose the transversality conditions:

$$\lim_{t\to\infty} q(t)K(t) \exp\left[ \int_0^t r(s)\, ds\right] = \lceil \lim_{t\to\infty} q(t) \exp\left[ \int_0^t r(s)\, ds\right] = 0 \tag{6}$$

$$\lim_{t\to\infty} q^*(t)K^*(t) \exp\left[ \int_0^t r(s)\, ds\right] = \lceil^* \lim_{t\to\infty} q^*(t) \exp\left[ \int_0^t r(s)\, ds\right] = 0 \tag{6'}$$

where $\lceil$ and $\lceil^*$ are the steady-state domestic and foreign capital stocks, respectively. The first-order conditions for optimality are given in the following:

$$\partial H/\partial I^* = (1-\tau)pG_I + (1- \varphi)\, p_I - q + \{-(1-\tau^*)p^*G^*_{I^*} - (1- \varphi^*)\, p_I^* \} + q^* = 0 \tag{7}$$

i.e.

$$q - (1-\tau)pG_I - (1- \varphi)\, p_I = q^* - (1-\tau^*)p^*G^*_{I^*} - (1- \varphi^*)\, p_I^* \tag{8}$$

Equation (8) sets the optimal levels of domestic and foreign investments at which the marginal profits from domestic and overseas production are equalised.

$$\partial H/\partial L = pF_L - w = 0 \tag{9}$$

$$\partial H/\partial L^* = p^*F^*_{L^*} - w^* = 0 \tag{9'}$$

Equations (9) and (9)' set the marginal revenue product of labour equal to the wage rate in the domestic and overseas markets, respectively.

The first-order conditions for the capital stock of domestic and foreign affiliates define the evolution of q and q*, the shadow prices of the capital:

$$dq/dt = rq - \partial H/\partial K = (r+\delta)q - (1-\tau)\, (1 - \eta)p(F_K - G_K) \tag{10}$$

$$dq^*/dt = rq^* - \partial H/\partial K^* = (r+\delta^*)q^* - (1-\tau^*)\, (1 - \eta^*)\, p^*(F^*_{K^*} - G^*_{K^*}) \tag{10'}$$

where $\eta$ and $\eta^*$ are the inverse of the price elasticities of output demand of domestic and overseas product markets, respectively:

$$1/\eta = -(\partial F/\partial p)(p/F) \tag{11}$$

and

$$1/\eta^* = -(\partial F^*/\partial p^*)(p^*/F^*) \tag{11'}$$

If the product market is perfectly competitive, it is expected that $\eta$ (or $\eta^*$) $=0$. Otherwise $\eta$ (or $\eta^*$) will not be zero. As we do not impose zeros for $\eta$ and $\eta^*$, our model does not assume the perfect competition in either the domestic product market or the foreign product market.

Rewrite (10) and (10)' as follows:

$$(r+\delta)q = (1-\tau)\,(1 - \eta)p(F_K - G_K) + dq/dt \tag{10a}$$

$$(r+\delta^*)q^* = (1-\tau^*)\,(1 - \eta^*)\,p^*(F^*_{K^*} - G^*_{K^*}) + dq^*/dt \tag{10a'}$$

Equations (10a) and (10a)' state exactly the Keynes (1936) capital market arbitrage principle. For example, the left-hand-side of (10a)' denotes the rental price of the capital of foreign affiliates, i.e., the costs incurred to the firm if it purchases capital from the market. The right-hand-side of (10a)' is the return on the foreign capital stock expansion, i.e., the tax-adjusted marginal product of capital, minus the marginal adjustment costs of FDI, plus the increase in the market-value of capital stock of foreign affiliates.

If (a) the firm reaches its steady state, $dq/dt = dq^*/dt = 0$, (b) there is no adjustment costs, $G(.,.)=G^*(.,.)=0$, and (c) the product markets are perfectly competitive, $\eta = \eta^* =0$, then we have the Jorgensonian neoclassical investment theory (Jorgenson, 1963) from (10) and (10)':

$$pF_K = (r+\delta)q/(1-\tau) \tag{12}$$

$$p^*F^*_{K^*} = (r+\delta^*)q^*/(1-\tau^*) \tag{12'}$$

which can also be obtained by maximising the following two profit functions, respectively (Lucas, 1967; Haavelmo, 1960):

$$\Pi(t) = (1-\tau)[\, p(t)\, F(K(t),L(t)) - w(t)L(t)\,] - (r+\delta)q(t)K(t) \tag{12a}$$

$$\Pi^*(t) = (1-\tau^*)[\, p^*(t)\, F^*(K^*(t), L^*(t)) - w^*(t)L^*(t)\,] - (r+\delta^*)q^*(t)K^*(t) \tag{12a'}$$

where $(r+\delta)q(t)$ and $(r+\delta^*)q^*(t)$ are defined as the rental price, or user cost, of capital of domestic and foreign affiliates, respectively. (12) and (12)' simply state that marginal product of capital equals user cost of the capital.

To derive the solution of the q and q*, we substitute (10) and (10)' into following equations:

$$d\left(q(s)\exp\left[-\int_0^s (r(u)+\delta)du\right]\right)/ds = \exp\left(-\int_0^s (r(u)+\delta)du\right)dq/ds - (r+\delta)q \exp\left(-\int_0^s\right.$$

$$(r(u)+\delta)du\right) = -(1-\tau)(1-\eta)p(F_K - G_K) \exp\left[-\int_0^s (r(u)+\delta)du\right] \tag{13}$$

Integrating (13) from t to infinity and using the transversality condition (6), we obtain (Abel, 1990)[4]:

$$\int_t^\infty \{d\left(q(s)\exp[-\int_0^s (r(u)+\delta)du]\right)/ds\}ds = -\int_t^\infty (1-\tau)(1-\eta)p(F_K - G_K) \exp\left[-\int_0^s\right.$$

$$(r(u)+\delta)du\right]ds$$

Hence:

$$0 - q(t)\exp\left(-\int_0^t (r(u)+\delta)du\right) = -\int_t^\infty (1-\tau)(1-\eta)p(F_K - G_K) \exp\left(-\int_0^s (r(u)+\delta)du\right)ds,$$

and

$$q(t)\exp\left(-\int_0^t (r(u)+\delta)du\right) = \int_t^\infty (1-\tau)(1-\eta)p(F_K - G_K) \exp\left(-\int_0^s (r(u)+\delta)du\right) ds.$$

That is:

$$q(t) = \int_t^\infty (1-\tau)(1-\eta)p(F_K - G_K) \exp\left(-\int_t^s (r(u)+\delta)du\right) ds \tag{14}$$

Similarly:

$$q^*(t) = \int_t^\infty (1-\tau^*)(1-\eta^*)p^*(F^*_{K^*} - G^*_{K^*}) \exp\left(-\int_t^s (r(u)+\delta^*)du\right) ds \tag{14'}$$

---

[4] This invokes the rational expectations hypothesis for the forward-looking agents. For a detailed discussion and derivation of general solutions for the discrete-time model, see Ma (1992) and Ma and Liu (1996).

We define q and q* as the generalised Tobin's marginal q of the domestic and overseas capital stocks, respectively.

However, only the average q is observable and the marginal q is not observable. We now derive the relationship between the two variables. Similar to Hayashi (1982), we make some simplifying assumptions about both the production and adjustment cost functions. We assume that production function is linearly homogenous in K and L, and the adjustment cost function is linearly homogenous in I and K. This implies that

$$I\, G_I + K\, G_K = G \tag{15}$$

and

$$K\, F_K + L\, F_L = F \tag{16}$$

Substituting (9) into (3), we have:

$$\pi = pF - wL - pG = pF - pF_L\, L - pG = pF_K\, K - pG \tag{17}$$

We substitute (4a) for dK/dt, (10) for dq/dt, (8) for q, (15) for I $G_I$, (17) for $pF_K K$, and (2) for R in following equation:

$$d\left(q(t)K(t)\exp\left[-\int_0^t r(s)ds\right]\right)/dt = [\, Kdq/dt + q\, dK/dt - rqK\, ]\, \exp\left[\int_0^t r(s)ds\right]$$

$$= [(r+\delta)qK - (1-\tau)(1-\eta)p(F_K - G_K)K\, qI - q\delta K - rqK]\, \exp\left[\int_0^t r(s)ds\right]$$

$$= [qI - (1-\eta)(1-\tau)\, p(F_K - G_K)K]\, \exp\left[\int_0^t r(s)\, ds\right]$$

$$= [qI - (1-\tau)p(F_K - G_K)K + \eta(1-\tau)\, p(F_K - G_K)K]\, \exp\left[\int_0^t r(s)\, ds\right]$$

$$= \{\, I\, [(1-\tau)pG_I + (1-\varphi)\, p_I + q^* - (1-\tau^*)p^*G^*_{I*} - (1-\varphi^*)\, p_I^*]$$

$$-(1-\tau)p(F_K - G_K)K + \eta(1-\tau)\, p(F_K - G_K)K\, \}\, \exp\left[\int_0^t r(s)\, ds\right]$$

$$= \{\, -(1-\tau)(pF_K\, K - pG) + (1-\varphi)\, p_I\, I$$

$$+ I\, [q^* - (1-\tau^*)p^*G^*_{I*} - (1-\varphi^*)\, p_I^*] + \eta(1-\tau)p(F_K - G_K)K\}\, \exp\left[\int_0^t r(s)\, ds\right]$$

$$= \{-(1-\tau)\pi + (1-\varphi)\, p_I\, I + I\, [q^* - (1-\tau^*)p^*G^*_{I*} - (1-\varphi^*)\, p_I^*] + \eta(1-\tau)p(F_K - G_K)K\}\exp\left(\int_0^t r(s)\, ds\right)$$

$$= \{-R + I\, [q^* - (1-\tau^*)p^*G^*_{I*} - (1-\varphi^*)\, p_I^*] + \eta(1-\tau)p(F_K - G_K)K\}\exp\left[\int_0^t r(s)\, ds\right] \tag{18}$$

Integrating (18) from 0 to infinity and using the transversality condition (6), we obtain:

$$\int_0^\infty \{d\big(q(t)K(t)\exp[-\int_0^t r(s)ds]\big)/dt\}dt =$$

$$= \int_0^\infty \{-R + I\,[q^* -(1-\tau^*)p^*G^*_{I^*} -(1-\varphi^*)\,p_I^*] + \eta(1-\tau)p(F_K -G_K)K\}\exp[\int_0^t r(s)\,ds]dt,$$

and,

$$0 -q(0)K(0) = -\int_0^\infty \{R -I\,[q^*-(1-\tau^*)p^*G^*_{I^*} -(1-\varphi^*)\,p_I^*]+\eta(1-\tau)p(F_K - G_K)K\}\exp[\int_0^t r(s)ds]dt.$$

Hence:

$$q(0)K(0) = V(0)$$
$$-\int_0^\infty \{I\,[q^* -(1-\tau^*)p^*G^*_{I^*} -(1-\varphi^*)\,p_I^*] + \eta(1-\tau)p(F_K -G_K)K\}\,\exp[\int_0^t r(s)\,ds]\,dt$$

$$\tag{19}$$

That is:

$$q(0) = V(0)/K(0)$$
$$-\int_0^\infty \{I\,[q^* -(1-\tau^*)p^*G^*_{I^*} -(1-\varphi^*)\,p_I^*] + \eta(1-\tau)p(F_K -G_K)K\}\exp[\int_0^t r(s)\,ds]$$

$$dt/K(0) \tag{20}$$

As $q(0)$ and $V(0)/K(0)$ are the marginal and average q, respectively, (20) gives the relationship between the two variables.

In parallel, we have:

$$q^*(0) = V^*(0)/K^*(0)$$
$$-\int_0^\infty \{I^*[q -(1-\tau)pG_I -(1-\varphi)p_I]+\eta^*(1-\tau^*)p^*(F^*_{K^*} -G^*_{K^*})K^*\}$$

$$\exp[\int_0^t r(s)ds]dt/K^*(0) \tag{20'}$$

If we assume a quadratic adjustment cost function[5], i.e.,

$$G(\bar{I} - I^*) = a_1(\bar{I} - I^*) + \tfrac{1}{2} a_2(\bar{I} - I^*)^2 \qquad \text{with } a_2 > 0 \qquad (21)$$

$$G^*(I^*) = b_1 I^* + \tfrac{1}{2} b_2 I^{*2} \qquad \text{with } b_2 > 0, \qquad (21)'$$

then we have linear marginal adjustment costs as follows:

$$G_I = a_1 + a_2(\bar{I} - I^*) \qquad (22)$$

$$G^*_{I^*} = b_1 + b_2 I^* \qquad (22)'$$

Substituting (22) and (22)' into (8), we have:

$$q - (1-\tau)[a_1 + a_2(\bar{I} - I^*)] - (1-\varphi) \, p_I = q^* - (1-\tau^*)[ b_1 + b_2 I^*] - (1-\varphi^*) \, p_I^*$$
$$\Rightarrow [(1-\tau^*)b_2 + (1-\tau)a_2] \, I^* = [q^* - q] - [(1-\varphi^*) \, p_I^* - (1-\varphi) \, p_I ] + (1-\tau)a_2\bar{I} - [(1-\tau^*)b_1 - (1-\tau)a_1]$$
$$\Rightarrow I^* = \{ [q^* - q] - [(1-\varphi^*) \, p_I^* - (1-\varphi) \, p_I ] + (1-\tau)a_2\bar{I} - [(1-\tau^*)b_1 - (1-\tau)a_1]\} / [(1-\tau^*)b_2 + (1-\tau)a_2] \qquad (23)$$

The economic interpretation of eq. (23) is now straightforward. The first term in the right-hand-side of (23) states that FDI (I*) depends upon the difference of overseas and domestic q, adjusted by the market imperfections ( $\eta^*$ and $\eta$) in the international and domestic markets and tax rates [c.f. (14) and (14)']. As the q and q* are the stock market values of capital stocks of domestic and foreign affiliates of the multinational corporation respectively, the FDI (I*) decision is directly related to its finance decision, a fact that has been neglected in most of the literature. Furthermore, an increase in the competition in the international market (a fall in $\eta^*$) would increase FDI. This is a well-known theory that FDI is the consequence of the international competition (Caves, 1982, and Dunning, 1985). On the other hand, a high monopolistic power possessed by the firm in the domestic market ($\eta$ is high) would also encourage capital outflow, since the investment in the domestic market would be low and the multinationals would relocate their activities to overseas market as the aggregate investment level ($\bar{I}$) is fixed.

The second term of the right-hand-side of (23) indicates the relative price (or, the real exchange rate) effect, which shows that if the overseas price is relatively lower than the domestic price then the multinational firms would increase the FDI. If there is an increase in the investment tax credits ($\varphi^*$) by the foreign government, or a fall in domestic $\varphi$, the FDI rises too. The third term of (23) states that if the aggregate investment level ($\bar{I}$) increases, then FDI will increase unambiguously[6].

---

[5] For simplicity, the adjustment cost does not include the cross-term between domestic investment and foreign direct investment in our model. To relax this assumption is left for future research.

[6] Ma and Morikawa (2001) applied a similar idea to test a small sample of Japanese FDI data and found strong empirical support of the extended q model.

However, the fourth term together with the numerator of (23) indicates an ambiguous effect of corporate tax rates ($\tau^*$ and $\tau$) on the FDI. There two off-setting effects if there is, say, a reduction of $\tau^*$. The expansion effect comes from the fact that a lower $\tau^*$ will increase the profitability of FDI, but the adjustment cost will also rise that generates a contraction effect of the FDI. As a result, the overall effect is ambiguous.

## 3. CONCLUSION

In this paper, we extended the traditional Tobin's (1969) q theory of aggregate investment behaviour to the dynamic allocation model of the production of multinational corporations. The new model has a number of appealing features. We find that both the domestic and overseas Tobin's q have very crucial role in determining FDI. This indicates one often ignored determinant of FDI: both domestic and foreign financial market values of a multinational corporation are equally important in decision process of FDI. Furthermore, the real exchange rate, not the nominal exchange rate, also appears to have a important relationship with FDI. This is consistent with the recent findings of Cushman (1985), Froot and Stein (1991), and Ma, Morikawa and Shone (2000). Finally, market structure in both international and domestic product markets also have effects on FDI, which is consistent with the conventional theory that FDI is the consequence of the international competition (Caves, 1982, Dunning, 1985). If it is possible to collect the panel data of FDI in the future, we can estimate and test our new model to explore its full implications.

## REFERENCES

Abel, A B (1990) Consumption and Investment, in B M Friedman and F H Hahn (eds) *Handbook of Monetary Economics*, Vol. 2, Chapter 14.

Blundell, R, S Bond, M Devereux and F Schiantarelli (1992) Investment and Tobin's Q, *Journal of Econometrics, 51,* 233-57.

Caves, R E (1982) Multinational enterprise and economic analysis, Cambridge University Press: Cambridge.

Cushman, D O (1988) Exchange rate uncertainty and foreign direct investment in the Unite States, *Weltwirtschaftliches Archiv, 124,* 322-336.

Drake, T A and R E Caves (1992) Changing determinants of Japanese foreign investment in the United States, *Journal of the Japanese and International Economies, 6,* 228-246.

Dunning, J H (1985, ed) *Multinational enterprises, economic structure and international competitiveness*, Wiley: Chichester.

Froot, K A and J C Stein (1991) Exchange rates and foreign direct investment: an imperfect capital markets approach, *Quarterly Journal of Economics, 106,* 1191-1217.

Galletti, M and F Schiantarelli (1991) Generalised q models for investment, *Review of Economics and Statistics, 73*, 383-392.

Gilman, M G (1981) *The financing of FDI: a study of the determinants of capital flows in multinational enterprises*, London: Frances Pinter Publishers.

Goldsbrough, D (1979) The role of foreign direct investment in the external adjustment process, *IMF Staff Papers, 26*, 725-754.

Haavelmo, T (1960) *A study in the theory of investment*, Chicago: University of Chicago Press.

Hayashi, F (1982) Tobin's average q and marginal q: a neoclassical interpretation, *Econometrica, 50*, 215-224.

Hayashi, F, and T Inoue (1991) The relation between firm growth and q with multiple capital goods, *Econometrica, 59*, 731-54.

Helpman, E and P R Krugman (1989) *Trade policy and market structure*, MIT Press: Cambridge, MA.

Hu, X and Y Ma (1999) The International Intra-Industry Trade of China, *Weltwirtschaftliches Archiv, 135*, 82-101.

Jorgenson, D W (1963) Capital Theory and Investment Behavior, *American Economic Review, 53(2)*, 247-259.

Keynes, J M (1936) *The general theory of employment, interest and money*, Macmillan: London.

Lucas, R E (1967) Adjustment Costs and the Theory of Supply, *Journal of Political Economy, 75*, 321-334.

Ma, Y (1992) Policy Measurement for the Dynamic Linear Model with Expectations Variables: a Multiplier Approach, *Computational Economics, 5*, 303-312.

Ma, Y (2001) The impact of financing the hi-tech industry on the banking sector in Guangdong, in M K Nyaw and G H Chen (ed) *The economic integration of Greater China*, Hong Kong: The Commercial Press, forthcoming (in Chinese).

Ma, Y and A Kanas (2000) Testing Nonlinear Relationship among Fundamentals and Exchange Rates in the ERM, *Journal of International Money and Finance, 19*, 135-152.

Ma, Y, and S Liu (1996) A Double Length Regression Computation Method for the 2SGLS Estimator of Rational Expectation Model, *Oxford Bulletin of Economics and Statistics, 58*, 423-429.

Ma, Y, and K Morikawa (2001) *Determinants of Japanese Foreign Direct Investment in Manufacturing Industry*, National Economy, Kokumin Keizai Research Institute, Tokyo, No.164, 1-13.

Ma, Y, K Morikawa and R Shone (2000) A macroeconomic model of direct investment in foreign affiliates of Japanese firms, *Japan and the World Economy, 12(4)*, 311-335.

Ma, Y, S Tsang and S Tang (1998) The Impact of China Factor on the Hong Kong Economy pre-1997: a macroeconomic modelling analysis, *International Review of Applied Economics, 12(1)*, 89-106.

Schiantarelli, F and D Georgoutsos (1990) Monopolistic competition and the q theory of investment, *European Economic Review, 34*, 1061-1078.

Sensenbrenner, G (1991) Aggregate Investment, the Stock Market, and the Q Model: Robust Results for Six OECD Countries, *European Economic Review; 35,* 769-825.

Summers, L H (1981) Taxation and corporate investment - a q-theory approach, *Brookings Papers on Economic Activity, 1,* 67-140.

Takenaka, H, R Senda, K Watanabe, and H Horioka (1989) *An econometric analysis of Japanese foreign direct investment,* Financial Review, pp.3-18, Institute of Fiscal and Monetary Research, Ministry of Finance, Tokyo, March.

Tobin, J (1969) A General equilibrium approach to monetary theory, *Journal of Money, Credit and Banking, 1,* 15-29.

Tsang, S and Y Ma (1997) Simulating the Impact of Foreign Capital in an Open-Economy Macroeconometric Model of China, *Economic Modelling, 14,* 435-478.

Tsang, S and Y Ma (2000) The Integration of China and Hong Kong into the World Economy: a Prototype Global Econometric Model, *Business Research Centre Discussion Paper No. CP 200007,* Hong Kong Baptist University.

United Nations (1999) *World investment report 1999: foreign direct investment and the challenge of development,* New York: United Nations.

von Furstenberg, G M (1977) Corporate investment: does market valuation matter in the aggregate, *Brookings Papers on Economic Activity, 2,* 347-408.

# Chapter 2

# REAL WAGE BEHAVIOR IN THE UNITED STATES, BRITAIN, AND JAPAN: AN ARCH APPROACH

*Shigeyuki Hamori*
Faculty of Economics
Kobe University
2-1, Rokkodai, Nada-Ku
Kobe, 657-8501
Japan

*David A. Anderson*
Associate Professor
Centre College
Danville, KY 40422
KY 40422
U.S.A.

## ABSTRACT

Using OECD data from the United States, Britain, and Japan, this research determines that ARCH-class models are valuable for the analysis of volatility in real wage growth rates. It also establishes that asymmetry exists in the response to positive and negative shocks in real wages. Such asymmetry is the strongest in Britain, weaker in the United States, and insignificant in Japan.

**JEL** classification number: J3
**Key Words**: real wage, ARCH model, risk

# 1. INTRODUCTION

This paper analyzes the volatility of real wages in the United States, Britain, and Japan using ARCH-type (autoregressive conditional heteroskedasticity) models. These models were developed by Engle (1982) and Bollerslev (1986), and have since become popular for the analysis of financial time series[1]. This research represents the first application of ARCH-class models to the volatility of real wages. If the volatility of real wages is constant, we can forecast volatility by calculating the sample variance or the sample standard deviation over a period of time. However, real wages experience not only periods of great fluctuation, as during the aftermath of the oil crisis, but also periods of more stable change. Since the volatility changes over time, it is important to clarify its characteristics in order to predict future volatility.

There are several reasons why the forecast of real wage volatility and related parameters might be valuable. First, a forward view of real wage volatility may be essential to appropriate risk management. For any given real wage rate and trend, volatility increases the risk of holding human capital, and investors are rational to respond to increased volatility with decreased investment. Second, forecast confidence intervals may be time varying, meaning that more accurate intervals can be obtained by modeling the variance of the errors. And third, more efficient real wage estimators can be obtained if heteroskedasticity in the errors is handled appropriately.

It has been widely observed that volatility in securities prices does not follow a random walk. In a phenomenon called volatility clustering, a period of high (or low) volatility is likely to persist for some time before transitioning into a period of low (high) volatility. Engle (1982) devised a volatility fluctuation model called the ARCH model, which takes the high persistence of volatility into consideration. This has since been expanded into the GARCH (generalized ARCH) model by Bollerslev (1986).

It has also been observed that in securities markets, a larger increase in volatility is likely to follow an unexpected decrease in prices than an unexpected increase in prices. This phenomenon cannot be grasped by ARCH or GARCH models. Glosten, Jagannathan, and Runkle's (1993) TARCH model and Nelson's (1990) EGARCH model respond to this shortcoming with the ability to measure asymmetric responses to good and bad news. This paper applies each of these ARCH-class models in the new context of real wage growth in the United States, Britain, and Japan to determine relevant characteristics of volatility and asymmetry.

# 2. ARCH MODELS

The ARCH models are designed to forecast the variance of a dependent variable. Under each model, the variance of the dependent variable is specified to depend upon

---

[1] See Bollerslev, Chou and Kroner (1992), Bollerslev, Engle and Nelson (1994), and Shephard (1996) for examples.

past values of the dependent variable according to some formula. The ARCH ($p$) model is specified as

$$y_t = x_t \pi + \varepsilon_t, \tag{1}$$

$$h_t = \alpha_0 + \sum_{i=1}^{p} \alpha_i \varepsilon_{t-i}^{2}, \tag{2}$$

where in the present adaptation, $y_t$ is the growth rate of real wages from time $t$-1 to time $t$, $x_t$ is a vector of wage determinants excluding news, $\varepsilon_t$ is a collective measure of news at time $t$, $h_t$ is the conditional variance of $\varepsilon_t$, and elements in the vector $\pi$ and the series $\alpha_0,..., \alpha_p$ are constant parameters. An unexpected increase in real wages ($\varepsilon_t > 0$) is read as the arrival of good news, while an unexpected decrease in real wages ($\varepsilon_t < 0$) suggests the arrival of bad news. The ($p$) in the ARCH ($p$) name refers to the order of the model, or equivalently, the number of ARCH terms summed in (2). As is clear from (2), the conditional variance is the weighted average of the squared values of past residuals.

Bollerslev (1986) developed the GARCH model as an extension of the ARCH model. A GARCH ($p$, $q$) model specifies that the variance depends only upon the past values of the dependent variable. The model for the variance is specified as

$$h_t = \alpha_0 + \sum_{i=1}^{p} \alpha_i \varepsilon_{t-i}^{2} + \sum_{i=1}^{q} \beta_i h_{t-i}, \tag{3}$$

where $\beta_1,..., \beta_q$ are constant parameters.

The variance at a given time depends on three factors: a constant, past news about volatility as represented by the squared residuals from previous periods (the ARCH term), and past forecast variance (the GARCH term). The expression ($p$, $q$) following the GARCH name indicates that there are $p$ ARCH terms and $q$ GARCH terms in the model. This specification can be applied in financial settings where an agent or trader predicts today's variance by forming a weighted average of past variances. If the most recent change in asset return was large in either the upward or downward direction, the trader will increase the variance estimate for the next day. This specification of the variance equation incorporates the familiar phenomenon of volatility clustering which is evident in financial returns data. That is, large returns are more likely to be followed by large returns of either sign than by small returns.

Consider the simple GARCH (1, 1) model:

$$h_t = \alpha_0 + \alpha_1 \varepsilon_{t-1}^{2} + \beta_1 h_{t-1}. \tag{4}$$

If equation (4) is lagged by one period and substituted for the lagged variance on the right hand side, then an expression with two lagged squared returns and a two-period lagged variance is obtained. Successive substitution for the lagged conditional variance yields the expression

$$h_t = \frac{\alpha_0}{1-\beta_1} + \alpha_1 \sum_{i=1}^{\infty} \beta_1^{i-1} \varepsilon_{t-i}^2 . \tag{5}$$

An ordinary sample variance would give each of the past squares an equal weight rather than declining weights. Thus, the GARCH variance is like a sample variance but it emphasizes the most recent observations. Since $h_t$ is the one-day-ahead forecast variance based on past information, it is called the conditional variance. The surprise in squared returns is given by $v_t = \varepsilon_t^2 - h_t$, which, by definition, is unpredictable based on the past. Substitution into (4) yields an alternative expression:

$$\varepsilon_t^2 = \alpha_0 + (\alpha_1 + \beta_1)\varepsilon_{t-1}^2 + v_t - \beta_1 v_{t-1}. \tag{6}$$

It can immediately be seen that the squared errors follow an ARMA (1 , 1) process which has severe heteroskedasticity. The autoregressive root is the sum of $\alpha_1$ plus $\beta_1$, and this root governs the persistence of volatility shocks.

So far, the effect of good news and bad news on predictable volatility have been treated as symmetric. However, as suggested by Black (1976) and verified by Engle and Ng (1993) among others, it is often the case that downward movements in the market are followed by higher volatility than upward movements of the same magnitude. The TARCH and EGARCH models are ways of describing such asymmetry. The TARCH or Threshold ARCH model was introduced independently by Zakoian (1994) and Glosten, Jaganathan, and Runkle (1993). The TARCH model for the variance is

$$h_t = \alpha_0 + \alpha_1 \varepsilon_{t-1}^2 + \gamma \varepsilon_{t-1}^2 d_{t-1} + \beta h_{t-1}, \tag{7}$$

where $d_t = 1$ for $\varepsilon_t < 0$, and 0 otherwise. Good news has an impact of $\alpha_1$, while bad news has an impact of $\alpha_1 + \gamma$. If $\gamma$ is significantly different from zero, then the leverage or asymmetric effect exists. If $\gamma > 0$, then bad news increases volatility by more than good news, as has been the case in securities markets. If $\gamma < 0$, then good news increases volatility by more than bad news.

## Table 1
## Results of Unit Root Tests
## The Real Wage Growth Rate
## January 1965 - November 1996: 383 Observations

|  | United States | Britain | Japan |
|---|---|---|---|
| Phillips-Perron w/o constant* | -19.946 | -25.9915 | -21.2553 |
| Phillips-Perron w/ constant** | -20.2258 | -25.9606 | -21.2563 |

* The Phillips and Perron unit root test statistics, where the regression excludes the constant term. Critical values are: 10%: -1.6161, 5%: -1.9403, 1%: -2.5710.

** The Phillips and Perron unit root test statistics, where the regression includes the constant term. Critical values are: 10%: -2.5709, 5%: -2.8693, 1%: -3.4495.

The Exponential GARCH or EGARCH model was proposed by Nelson (1990) in a somewhat earlier attempt to model asymmetry. The specification for the variance is

$$\log(h_t) = \alpha_0 + \omega_1 \left| \frac{\varepsilon_{t-1}}{\sqrt{h_t}} \right| + \omega_2 \frac{\varepsilon_{t-1}}{\sqrt{h_{t-1}}} + \beta \log(h_{t-1}), \tag{8}$$

which indicates asymmetry if $\omega_2 \neq 0$. Because of the log transformation, there is no possibility of a negative variance. The impact of the most recent residual is now exponential rather than quadratic. Other things being equal, if $\omega_2 < 0$, then bad news increases volatility by more than good news, and vice versa.

# 3. DATA

Monthly data on real wages in the United States, Britain, and Japan for the period from January, 1965 to November, 1996 were obtained from the Organization for Economic Cooperation and Development's Main Economic Indicators. Nominal wages for each country were divided by the wholesale price index to determine real wage rates. The values for each variable were seasonally adjusted. The growth rate of real wages was regarded as the proxy for the real return on human capital.

Table 1 provides the results of unit root test of the real wage growth rate for each country. We analyzed whether the real wage growth rate can be characterized by a unit root using the test developed by Phillips and Perron (1988). Table 1 shows the Phillips and Perron unit root test statistics that resulted when the regressors did and did not include a constant, respectively. The fifth degree was used for the Bartlett Kernel's lag truncation. The hypothesis that a unit root exists cannot be accepted with any reasonable degree of certainty for any of the countries studied.

## 4. EMPIRICAL RESULTS

Tables 2-1, 2-2, and 2-3 list the GARCH-model results for the United States, Britain, and Japan, respectively. A regression of the growth rate on a constant was used to estimate the mean in equation (1). A specification with a constant term and the unemployment rates was also tested, but the unemployment rates were not significant. Each possible combination of one or two ARCH terms and one or two GARCH terms was tested. Variance was regressed on a constant term to estimate the mean of the ARCH term in equation (3). As indicated in Table 2-1, the first-degree ARCH and GARCH terms are significant for U.S data. For example, under the GARCH (1, 1) model, the coefficients on the ARCH and GARCH terms are 0.236 and 0.584, with t-values of 4.733 and 7.660 respectively. However, as the number of lags increases, the likely influence of each term decreases in significance. This corresponds to the fact that the values of AIC and SBIC are minimized when $p=1$ and $q=1$. The same tendency can be observed for Japanese data, as illustrated in Table 2-3. A somewhat different scenario is presented for British data in Table 2-2. Here, the t-value on the GARCH-term coefficient is small and insignificant for $p=1$, $q=1$. However, all of the ARCH and GARCH terms are significant for $p=2$, $q=1$.

Tables 3-1, 3-2, and 3-3 present the TARCH-model results for the United States, Britain, and Japan, respectively. A TARCH (1, 1) model was applied, for which a value of $\gamma$ significantly different from zero indicates that an asymmetry effect exists. The $\gamma$ coefficient for variance in the United States is -0.654 with a t-value of -4.000, indicating the existence of an asymmetry effect. A similar result was found for Britain, where the $\gamma$ coefficient is -0.711 with a t-value of -3.772. In a departure from financial market findings, good news was found to have a larger effect than bad news on the variance of real wage growth. For the United States, we estimate that a unit increase in $\varepsilon_{t-1}^2$ leads $h_t$ to increase by 0.793, whereas a unit decrease in $\varepsilon_{t-1}^2$ leads $h_t$ to increase by 0.139. The analogous results of good and bad news on variance in Britain are estimated to be 1.033 and 0.322 respectively. In contrast, we could not conclude that an asymmetry effect exists in Japan, where the estimated $\gamma$ coefficient was a positive 0.098 with a t-value of 1.315.

Tables 4-1, 4-2, and 4-3 present the EGARCH-model results for the United States, Britain, and Japan, respectively. An EGARCH (1, 1) model was applied, for which a value of $\omega_2$ significantly different from zero indicates asymmetry. Asymmetry was not found in the United States or Japan, where $\omega_2$ values were 0.001 and -0.045 with t-values of 0.031 and -1.109 respectively. In Britain, however, the value of $\omega_2$ was 0.194 with a t-value of 2.951, again indicating not only that asymmetry exists, but that volatility increases more after good news than after bad news.

**Table 2-1**
**GARCH Model - United States**

$$y_t = \pi_0 + \varepsilon_t \ h_t = \alpha_0 + \sum_{i=1}^{p} \alpha_i \varepsilon_{t-i}^{2} + \sum_{i=1}^{q} \beta_i h_{t-i}$$

|  | $p=1, q=1$ | $p=2, q=1$ | $p=1, q=2$ | $p=2, q=2$ |
|---|---|---|---|---|
| $\pi_0$ | -0.161<br>(-3.666) | -0.163<br>(-3.752) | -0.160<br>(-3.662) | -0.160<br>(-3.675) |
| $\alpha_0$ | 0.157<br>(3.465) | 0.142<br>(2.602) | 0.191<br>(3.524) | 0.181<br>(2.025) |
| $\alpha_1$ | 0.236<br>(4.733) | 0.288<br>(3.765) | 0.298<br>(4.756) | 0.308<br>(4.049) |
| $\alpha_2$ |  | -0.076<br>(-0.714) |  | -0.026<br>(-0.156) |
| $\beta_1$ | 0.584<br>(7.660) | 0.627<br>(5.463) | 0.221<br>(1.022) | 0.278<br>(0.553) |
| $\beta_2$ |  |  | 0.265<br>(1.481) | 0.236<br>(0.772) |
| Log Likelihood | -497.161 | -469.886 | -496.404 | -496.382 |
| AIC | -0.008 | -0.003 | -0.003 | 0.002 |
| SBIC | 0.033 | 0.049 | 0.048 | 0.064 |

Note:
The numbers in parentheses are t-values.

**Table 2-2**
**GARCH Model - Britain**

$$y_t = \pi_0 + \varepsilon_t \ h_t = \alpha_0 + \sum_{i=1}^{p} \alpha_i \varepsilon_{t-i}^{2} + \sum_{i=1}^{q} \beta_i h_{t-i}$$

|  | $p=1, q=1$ | $p=2, q=1$ | $p=1, q=2$ | $p=2, q=2$ |
|---|---|---|---|---|
| $\pi_0$ | -0.056<br>(-0..940) | -0.062<br>(-1.076) | -0.075<br>(-1.241) | -0.049<br>(-0.805) |
| $\alpha_0$ | 1.384<br>(7.540) | 0.025<br>(1.435) | 1.029<br>(4.653) | 0.966<br>(1.581) |
| $\alpha_1$ | 0.685<br>(8.488) | 0.800<br>(8.795) | 0.620<br>(7.676) | 0.582<br>(7.803) |
| $\alpha_2$ |  | -0.773<br>(-8.159) |  | -0.079<br>(-0.300) |
| $\beta_1$ | -0.013<br>(-0.261) | 0.972<br>(60.474) | -0.017<br>(-0.432) | 0.119<br>(0.268) |
| $\beta_2$ |  |  | 0.154<br>(1.709) | 0.101<br>(1.250) |
| Log Likeloihood | -701.707 | -698.148 | -700.960 | -701.486 |
| AIC | 1.000 | 1.005 | 1.006 | 1.010 |
| SBIC | 1.041 | 1.057 | 1.057 | 1.072 |

Note:
The numbers in parentheses are t-values.

## Table 2-3
## GARCH Model - Japan

$$y_t = \pi_0 + \varepsilon_t$$

$$h_t = \alpha_0 + \sum_{i=1}^{p} \alpha_i \varepsilon_{t-i}^2 + \sum_{i=1}^{q} \beta_i h_{t-i}$$

|            | $p=1, q=1$ | $p=2, q=1$ | $p=1, q=2$ | $p=2, q=2$ |
|------------|------------|------------|------------|------------|
| $\pi_0$    | 0.163      | 0.171      | 0.174      | 0.164      |
|            | (2.105)    | (2.227)    | (2.367)    | (2.193)    |
| $\alpha_0$ | 0.451      | 0.257      | 0.617      | 0.491      |
|            | (2.292)    | (1.260)    | (2.489)    | (1.892)    |
| $\alpha_1$ | 0.186      | 0.284      | 0.301      | 0.333      |
|            | (2.952)    | (2.899)    | (3.433)    | (3.467)    |
| $\alpha_2$ |            | -0.170     |            | -0.099     |
|            |            | (-1.468)   |            | (-0.996)   |
| $\beta_1$  | 0.660      | 0.799      | -0.033     | 0.107      |
|            | (6.178)    | (6.061)    | (-0.395)   | (0.601)    |
| $\beta_2$  |            |            | 0.526      | 0.496      |
|            |            |            | (3.714)    | (3.768)    |
| Log Likelihood | -726.640 | -724.825 | -722.322 | -721.501   |
| AIC        | 1.119      | 1.125      | 1.125      | 1.130      |
| SBIC       | 1.160      | 1.176      | 1.176      | 1.192      |

Note:

The numbers in parentheses are t-values.

## Table 3-1
## TARCH Model - United States

$$y_t = \pi_0 + \varepsilon_t,$$

$$h_t = \alpha_0 + \alpha_1 \varepsilon_{t-1}^2 + \gamma \varepsilon_{t-1}^2 d_{t-1} + \beta h_{t-1},$$

where $d_t = 1$ for $\varepsilon_t < 0$, and 0 othwise.

|                |              |
|----------------|--------------|
| $\pi_0$        | -0.152       |
|                | (-3.555)     |
| $\alpha_0$     | 0.524        |
|                | (10.455)     |
| $\alpha_1$     | 0.793        |
|                | (5.131)      |
| $\gamma$       | -0.654       |
|                | (-4.000)     |
| $\beta$        | -0.017       |
|                | (-2.650)     |
| Log Likelihood | -490.495     |
| AIC            | -0.004       |
| SBIC           | 0.047        |

Note:

The numbers in parentheses are t-values.

## Table 3-2
## TARCH Model - Britain

$$y_t = \pi_0 + \varepsilon_t,$$

$$h_t = \alpha_0 + \alpha_1 \varepsilon_{t-1}^2 + \gamma \varepsilon_{t-1}^2 d_{t-1} + \beta h_{t-1},$$

*where* $d_t = 1$ *for* $\varepsilon_t < 0$, *and* $0$ *othwise*.

| | |
|---|---|
| $\pi_0$ | 0.057 (0.787) |
| $\alpha_0$ | 1.441 (7.462) |
| $\alpha_1$ | 1.033 (7.526) |
| $\gamma$ | -0.711 (-3.772) |
| $\beta$ | -0.023 (-0.441) |
| Log Likelihood | -698.254 |
| AIC | 1.006 |
| SBIC | 1.058 |

Note:
The numbers in parentheses are t-values.

## Table 3-3
## TARCH Model - Japan

$$y_t = \pi_0 + \varepsilon_t,$$

$$h_t = \alpha_0 + \alpha_1 \varepsilon_{t-1}^2 + \gamma \varepsilon_{t-1}^2 d_{t-1} + \beta h_{t-1},$$

*where* $d_t = 1$ *for* $\varepsilon_t < 0$, *and* $0$ *othwise*.

| | |
|---|---|
| $\pi_0$ | 0.135 (1.659) |
| $\alpha_0$ | 0.406 (2.300) |
| $\alpha_1$ | 0.119 (1.764) |
| $\gamma$ | 0.098 (1.315) |
| $\beta$ | 0.691 (6.992) |
| Log Likelihood | -725.769 |
| AIC | 1.124 |
| SBIC | 1.175 |

Note:
The numbers in parentheses are t-values.

**Table 4-1**
**EGARCH Model - United States**

$$y_t = \pi_0 + \varepsilon_t$$

$$\log(h_t) = \alpha_0 + \omega_1 \left| \frac{\varepsilon_{t-1}}{\sqrt{h_t}} \right| + \omega_2 \frac{\varepsilon_{t-1}}{\sqrt{h_{t-1}}} + \beta \log(h_{t-1})$$

| | |
|---|---|
| $\pi_0$ | -0.195 |
| | (-5.237) |
| $\alpha_0$ | -0.321 |
| | (-5.931) |
| $\omega_1$ | 0.372 |
| | (5.935) |
| $\omega_2$ | 0.001 |
| | (0.031) |
| $\beta$ | 0.880 |
| | (21.213) |
| Log Likelihood | -493.982 |
| AIC | 0.002 |
| SBIC | 0.053 |

Note:
The numbers in parentheses are t-values.

**Table 4-2**
**EGARCH Model - Britain**

$$y_t = \pi_0 + \varepsilon_t$$

$$\log(h_t) = \alpha_0 + \omega_1 \left| \frac{\varepsilon_{t-1}}{\sqrt{h_t}} \right| + \omega_2 \frac{\varepsilon_{t-1}}{\sqrt{h_{t-1}}} + \beta \log(h_{t-1})$$

| | |
|---|---|
| $\pi_0$ | 0.062 |
| | (0.892) |
| $\alpha_0$ | 0.242 |
| | (1.485) |
| $\omega_1$ | 0.799 |
| | (8.788) |
| $\omega_2$ | 0.194 |
| | (2.951) |
| $\beta$ | -0.015 |
| | (-0.111) |
| Log Likelihood | -699.672 |
| AIC | 1.006 |
| SBIC | 1.058 |

Note:
The numbers in parentheses are t-values.

**Table 4-3**
**EGARCH Model - Japan**

$$y_t = \pi_0 + \varepsilon_t$$

$$\log(h_t) = \alpha_0 + \omega_1 \left| \frac{\varepsilon_{t-1}}{\sqrt{h_t}} \right| + \omega_2 \frac{\varepsilon_{t-1}}{\sqrt{h_{t-1}}} + \beta \log(h_{t-1}),$$

| | |
|---|---|
| $\pi_0$ | 0.137 (1.736) |
| $\alpha_0$ | -0.139 (-1.923) |
| $\omega_1$ | 0.361 (3.466) |
| $\omega_2$ | -0.045 (-1.109) |
| $\beta$ | 0.847 (12.293) |
| Log Likelihood | -727.744 |
| AIC | 1.124 |
| SBIC | 1.175 |

Note:
The numbers in parentheses are t-values.

# 5. CONCLUDING REMARKS

In a new application of models typically used for the study of financial data, this paper presents evidence that ARCH-class models are useful for the analysis of volatility in real wage growth rates. The paper also demonstrates clear differences among countries in regard to the asymmetric effects of good and bad news on volatility. For Britain, both the TARCH model and the EGARCH model indicate significant asymmetry, with good news having a larger effect than bad news on the volatility of real wage growth rates. The same type of asymmetry was observed for the United States under the TARCH model, but the asymmetry was not significant under the EGARCH model. Neither the TARCH model nor the EGARCH model displayed significant asymmetry for Japan. Among other implications, this means that important adjustments must be made before applying research or policy conclusions regarding real wage growth rates from one country to another.

# REFERENCES

Black, Fisher. "Studies in Stock Price Volatility Changes." *Proceedings of the 1976 Business Meeting of the Business and Economics Statistics Section, American Statistical Association* (1976): 177-181.

Bollerslev T., (1986), "Generalized Autoregressive Conditional Heteroskedasticity," *Journal of Econometrics*, Vol. 31, pp. 307-327.

Bollerslev T., R. F. Engle, and D. B. Nelson, (1994), "ARCH Models," in R. F. Engle and D. M. McFadden eds., *The Handbook of Econometrics*, Volume 4, North-Holland

Bollerslev T., R. Y. Chou, and K. F. Kroner, (1992), "ARCH Modeling in Finance: A Review of the Theory and Empirical Evidence," *Journal of Econometrics*, Vol. 52, pp. 5-59.

Engle R. F. and V. K. Ng, (1993), "Measuring and Testing the Impact of News on Volatility," *Journal of Finance,* Vol. 48, pp. 1749-1778.

Engle R. F., (1982), "Autoregressive Conditional Heteroskedasticity with Estimates of the Variance of United Kingdom Inflation," *Econometrica,* Vol. 50, pp. 987-1008.

Glosten L. R., R. Jagannathan, and D. Runkle, (1993), "On the Relation between the Expected Value and the Volatility of the Nominal Excess Return on Stocks," *Journal of Finance,* Vol. 48, pp. 1779-1801.

Nelson D. B., (1990), "Conditional Heteroskedasticity in Asset Returns: A New Approach," *Econometrica,* Vol. 59, pp. 347-370.

Phillips P. C. B. and P. Perron, (1988), "Testing for a Unit Root in Time Series Analysis," *Biometrica*, Vol. 75, pp. 335-346.

Shephard N., (1996), "Statistical Aspects of ARCH and Stochastic Volatility," in D. R. Cox, D. V. Hinkley and O. E. Barndorff-Nielsen eds., *Time Series Models in Econometrics, Finance, and Other Fields*, Chapman & Hall.

Zakoian J. M., (1994), "Threshhold Heteroskedastic Model, " *Journal of Economic Dynamics and Control,* Vol. 18, pp. 931-955.

*Chapter 3*

# GLOBAL CAPITAL, CURRENCY CRISES AND DEVELOPMENT IN EAST ASIA

## *Tony Makin*
School of Economics
The University of Queensland
St Lucia
Australia 4072
email: makin@economics.uq.edu.au

## ABSTRACT

This paper highlights the macroeconomic implications of international capital flows for the emerging East Asian economies. Improved access to international capital has contributed significantly to the high economic growth rates of many economies in the region that allowed dramatic rises in living standards to occur over the course of a generation. Yet, the international capital flow reversals of the late 1990s also caused widespread financial distress and severe recessions in a group of these economies, prompting calls for the re-imposition of Bretton Woods style capital controls. The paper identifies unforeseen risk attributable to past exchange rate management and fragile financial systems, as well as the panic behaviour of resident Asian investors, as the main causes of the sudden collapse of currencies and asset prices in the East Asian region in the late 1990s. It concludes that exchange rate flexibility combined with ongoing reform of domestic banking systems and financial practices rather than limiting international capital mobility is the most appropriate policy response for safeguarding against future crises.

# 1. INTRODUCTION

The dramatic reversal of international capital inflows to previously fast growing East Asian economies in 1997-98 represents the most significant international adjustment to date in the relatively new era of globally integrated capital markets. A record capital inflow of US$93 billion to Indonesia, South Korea, Malaysia, Philippines and Thailand in 1996, became a net outflow of US$12 billion in 1997, a reversal equivalent to eleven per cent of the combined GDP of these economies. The economic crisis this caused in East Asia at the time will probably be remembered as the most important international economic event of the 1990s. Since then, global capital has returned to the region and economic and financial activity has again stabilised. Although the Asian economic and financial crisis affected all key macroeconomic variables in the stricken economies, including interest rates, share prices, national income, employment and inflation rates, it was Asian exchange rates that fell fastest and furthest. For this reason, the Asian crisis was essentially a currency crisis that caused serious macroeconomic problems.

The currency turmoil East Asia experienced in 1997/98 began after foreign investors suddenly divested Asian financial assets, including deposits in and loans to Asian banks, on reassessing their risk exposure in the region. What contributed to transforming a correction of asset prices and net worth positions into a collapse of crisis proportions was the reinforcing panic behaviour of resident Asian investors who also sold off local financial assets liquidated bank deposits and reinvested their funds abroad. The outflow of foreign capital, in conjunction with the flight abroad of domestic funds sparked the massive exchange rate depreciations, especially against the US dollar, of the Indonesian rupiah, Thai baht, Malaysian ringgit, Philippines peso and South Korean won. It also led to extraordinary asset price falls in the greater East Asian region, including in Hong Kong and Singapore.

The collapse of Asian exchange rates was all the more surprising at the time, given that East Asian exchange rates had hitherto been either fixed or strongly managed over a lengthy period. The rationale for managing exchange rates this way was to provide exchange rate certainty for exporters and importers. Yet, perceived exchange rate stability also meant foreign investors in Asian financial assets focussed mainly on high relative yields and neglected exchange rate risk.

This chapter firstly identifies the characteristics of the Asian crisis of the late 1990s before analysing the main underlying causes of the huge reversal of international investment to East Asia and the associated currency crisis. It then proposes a straightforward analytical framework for interpreting how the international capital reversal depressed exchange rates and asset prices in the region. In conclusion, the chapter contends that the Asian financial crisis implies a need to sustain reform of national financial systems rather than re-regulate or tax international capital flows.

## 2. CHARACTERISING THE EAST ASIAN CURRENCY CRISIS

The greater Asian region attracted tens of billions of capital inflow a year in the 1990s, reaching a peak of $US 106 billion in 1996. This inflow contributed to remarkably strong economic growth rates, referred to as the 'Asian miracle'[1]. For example, courtesy of capital inflow, Hong Kong, Singapore, Taiwan, Indonesia, Malaysia, Thailand and South Korea all recorded economic growth rates over 7 per cent from the early 1990s, although growth in the Philippines was lower.

Simultaneously, foreign investors were attracted to Asian financial assets by strong macroeconomic fundamentals including impressive saving rates and ostensibly sound fiscal positions and apparent minimal exchange rate risk.

**Table 1: Real GDP Growth in East Asian Economies (%)**

|              | 1975-82 | 1983-89 | 1990 | 1991 | 1992 | 1993 | 1994 | 1995 | 1996 | 1997 | 1998 |
|--------------|---------|---------|------|------|------|------|------|------|------|------|------|
| China        | 6.0     | 10.7    | 3.8  | 9.2  | 14.2 | 13.5 | 12.6 | 10.5 | 9.6  | 8.8  | -7.8 |
| Hong Kong    | 9.3     | 7.2     | 3.4  | 5.1  | 6.3  | 6.1  | 5.4  | 3.9  | 4.9  | 5.3  | -5.1 |
| Indonesia*   | 6.2     | 5.5     | 9.0  | 8.9  | 7.2  | 7.3  | 7.5  | 8.2  | 8.0  | 5.0  | -13.7 |
| South Korea* | 7.0     | 9.6     | 9.5  | 9.1  | 5.1  | 5.8  | 8.6  | 8.9  | 7.1  | 6.0  | -5.5 |
| Malaysia*    | 7.1     | 5.4     | 9.6  | 8.6  | 7.8  | 8.3  | 9.2  | 9.5  | 8.6  | 7.7  | -6.8 |
| Philippines* | 5.6     | 1.1     | 3.0  | -0.6 | 0.3  | 2.1  | 4.4  | 4.8  | 5.7  | 4.3  | -0.5 |
| Singapore    | 8.0     | 6.9     | 9.0  | 7.3  | 6.2  | 10.4 | 10.5 | 8.8  | 7.5  | 8.0  | 1.5  |
| Taiwan       | 8.5     | 9.2     | 5.4  | 7.6  | 6.8  | 6.3  | 6.5  | 6.0  | 5.7  | 6.7  | 4.9  |
| Thailand*    | 7.0     | 8.1     | 11.6 | 8.1  | 8.2  | 8.5  | 8.9  | 8.7  | 6.4  | 0.6  | -8.0 |

* the 'Asian 5'

**Source:** IMF (1999) *World Economic Outlook*, May.

Historically large external deficits measuring the excess of investment spending over domestic saving were reflected in the rise in global capital inflows to the region. In general, current account deficits should not be a concern, per se, and indeed can be perceived as integral to the process of economic growth and development.[2]

Private capital inflows tend to raise current account deficits, reduce domestic interest rates, and raise aggregate investment rates in host economies. To the extent that the higher current account deficits that match increased capital inflows reflect an excess of domestic investment over domestic saving, the external deficits themselves should not be considered problematic, in and of themselves. Indeed, external imbalances can simply be interpreted as manifestations of increased international trade in saving which can contribute to higher world development.

---

[1] See World Bank (1993, 1998) for related discussion.
[2] See for instance Frenkel and Razin (1987) and Makin (2000).

## Table 2: Net Capital Flows to Emerging Asian Economies

| | 1991 | 1992 | 1993 | 1994 | 1995 | 1996 | 1997 | 1998 | 1999 | 2000 |
|---|---|---|---|---|---|---|---|---|---|---|
| **Asia** | | | | | | | | | | |
| **Crisis countries** | | | | | | | | | | |
| Net private capital flows | 24.8 | 29.0 | 31.8 | 36.1 | 60.6 | 62.9 | −22.1 | −29.6 | −18.1 | −8.2 |
|   Net direct investment | 6.2 | 7.3 | 7.6 | 8.8 | 7.5 | 8.4 | 10.3 | 9.7 | 9.4 | 8.4 |
|   Net portfolio investment | 3.2 | 6.4 | 17.2 | 9.9 | 17.4 | 20.3 | 12.9 | −7.3 | 4.5 | 5.6 |
|   Other net investment | 15.4 | 15.3 | 7.0 | 17.4 | 35.7 | 34.2 | −45.3 | −32.0 | −32.0 | −22.2 |
| Net official flows | 4.4 | 2.0 | 0.6 | 0.3 | 0.7 | −4.6 | 30.4 | 20.2 | −4.5 | −0.6 |
| Change in reserves | −8.3 | −18.1 | −20.6 | −6.1 | −18.3 | −5.4 | 30.5 | −52.1 | −39.9 | −29.9 |
| | | | | | | | | | | |
| *Memorandum* | | | | | | | | | | |
| Current account | −25.2 | −16.1 | −13.5 | −23.2 | −40.5 | −53.4 | −24.3 | 68.8 | 49.3 | 29.4 |
| | | | | | | | | | | |
| **Other Asian emerging markets** | | | | | | | | | | |
| Net private capital flows | 7.4 | −9.4 | 24.6 | 27.7 | 30.2 | 39.3 | 25.4 | −14.7 | −11.5 | 4.9 |
|   Net direct investment | 8.3 | 8.4 | 26.3 | 38.8 | 41.1 | 45.8 | 50.9 | 46.9 | 32.2 | 34.7 |
|   Net portfolio investment | −2.0 | 2.6 | 4.5 | 1.1 | −6.1 | −8.3 | −11.8 | −12.3 | −12.8 | −8.5 |
|   Other net investment | 1.2 | −20.4 | −6.2 | −12.2 | −1.7 | 1.8 | −13.8 | −49.2 | −30.8 | −21.3 |
| Net official flows | 6.5 | 8.3 | 7.9 | 10.2 | 6.0 | 4.1 | −0.4 | 7.3 | 4.1 | 2.9 |
| Change in reserves | −31.5 | −7.8 | −17.9 | −18.3 | −26.9 | −43.6 | −46.5 | −17.6 | −2.3 | −17.4 |
| | | | | | | | | | | |
| *Memorandum* | | | | | | | | | | |
| Current Account | 23.7 | 14.0 | −8.2 | 16.8 | 16.2 | 17.8 | 43.9 | 43.2 | 26.2 | 26.4 |

**Source:** International Monetary Fund, *World Economic Outlook*, October 1999

Host economies benefit because their capital stocks expand through extra investment that enables more production, whereas foreign investors gain to the extent that they can earn higher returns than in their home markets. Moreover, through international portfolio diversification, institutional investors, such as pension, superannuation funds and mutual funds are in principle able to reduce overall volatility of portfolio returns to the extent that movements in national share market prices are unsynchronised. Table 3 provides details of the nature and extent of foreign investment in Asian financial instruments before and after the crisis.

## Table 3: Gross Private Financing to Emerging Asian Economies
(billions of $US dollars)

| | 1996 | 1997 | 1998 |
|---|---|---|---|
| Bond issues | 43.1 | 45.5 | 11.5 |
| Other debt issues | 9.4 | 5.8 | 0.5 |
| Loan commitments | 56.2 | 58.9 | 17.7 |
| Equity issues | 9.8 | 13.2 | 4.4 |
| Total | 118.5 | 127.5 | 34.1 |

**Source:** International Monetary Fund, *World Economic Outlook,* October 1999.

Yet, as happened in East Asia, large capital inflows can also at times fund over-investment and contribute to asset price bubbles, especially in local property and equity markets. At the same time however, international investment in financial assets is especially sensitive to changes in investors' expectations, including expected exchange rate changes that can spark massive capital inflows or outflows. Indeed, during currency crises, changes in investors' exchange rate expectations become self- fulfilling. Investors expecting a future currency collapse will rush to sell financial instruments denominated in that currency to avoid capital losses. Accordingly, the severe contraction in demand for the currency can put official exchange rates under great pressure, depleting foreign exchange reserves of central banks and also pushing up short term interest rates in the process. An important external influences that had put pressure on the pegged East Asian currencies leading up to the crisis was an appreciation of the United States dollar against which the East Asian currencies were pegged. This worsened export competitiveness in international markets, particularly for electronics.

### Table 4: Exchange Rate Movements[1]

|  | Against $US | Against Yen | Nominal Effective | Real Effective |
|---|---|---|---|---|
| Korea | -39.0 | -31.0 | -35.3 | -30.3 |
| Indonesia | -73.9 | -70.6 | -71.4 | -63.2 |
| Malaysia | -32.3 | -23.5 | -24.8 | -23.6 |
| Philippines | -31.0 | -22.1 | -24.8 | -21.8 |
| Thailand | -37.5 | -29.4 | -31.8 | -27.1 |

[1] per cent change from June 97 to March 98, monthly average date
**Source:** International Monetary Fund, *International Financial Statistics*, various.

The sudden divestment of Asian assets by foreign financial institutions quickly reversed the huge foreign funds inflow of the early 1990s once international investors became aware that their risk exposure and expected fall in returns in Asian markets was much greater than previously assessed. In the most severely affected economies, the prices of currencies, bonds and equities plummeted and this severely affected their financial systems with consequences for real economic activity.

### Table 5: Stock Market Indices[1]

| Indonesia | -37 |
|---|---|
| Korea | -34 |
| Malaysia | -56 |
| Philippines | -45 |
| Thailand | -52 |

[1] per cent change between July and November 1997
**Source:** International Monetary Fund, *International Financial Statistics*, various.

The impact of the financial crisis on the real sectors of those Asian economies worst affected is evident from Table 1 which shows the extent of the recessions which began in the crisis affected Asian economies in 1998 after foreign funds quit these countries. These recessions in turn sharply raised unemployment levels in those economies.

Creditworthiness, as gauged by the major international credit rating agencies Moody's and Standard and Poor's also fell sharply as part of the process of raising risk premia demanded on Asian financial assets. In the wake of the crisis, credit ratings for each of the worst affected Asian economies were several grades below those awarded in the mid 1990s, pre-crisis, and upgrades became a necessary condition for lowering interest risk premia.

**Table 6: Sovereign Credit Ratings of Asian 5, June, October 1998**

|                | October |
|----------------|---------|
| Indonesia      | CCC+    |
| Korea          | BB+     |
| Malaysia       | BBB–    |
| Philippines    | BB+     |
| Thailand       | BBB–    |

**Source:** Standard and Poors, International Monetary Fund, *World Economic Outlook*, December, 1998.

In short, once international investors judge that expected returns on foreign assets are likely to fall, then the large external deficits matching the inflow of investment funds become unsustainable. At such a point, external account adjustment involving reserve rundowns, high interest rates or large depreciations is required. The following analysis explains how exchange rates can go into free-fall under these circumstances.

## 3. EXPLAINING THE EXCHANGE RATE COLLAPSES

The Asian currency crisis itself can be modelled in a very straightforward way with reference to Figure 1 below. This figure in exchange rate-foreign exchange space reveals why Asian exchange rates depreciated by so much in response to the switch out of Asian financial assets by foreigners and by resident Asian investors themselves. In the figure, the supply of foreign exchange to Asian markets, $S^{fx}$ is drawn positively related to Asian exchange rates, e, collectively defined as Asian currency per unit of foreign currency; a rise in e therefore denotes Asian currency depreciation. Total foreign exchange supplied to Asian economies is the sum of Asian export earnings (X), recorded in Asian current accounts and foreign investment inflows ($K^I$), recorded in their capital accounts.

## Figure 1: Capital Flow Reversal and East Asian Exchange Rates

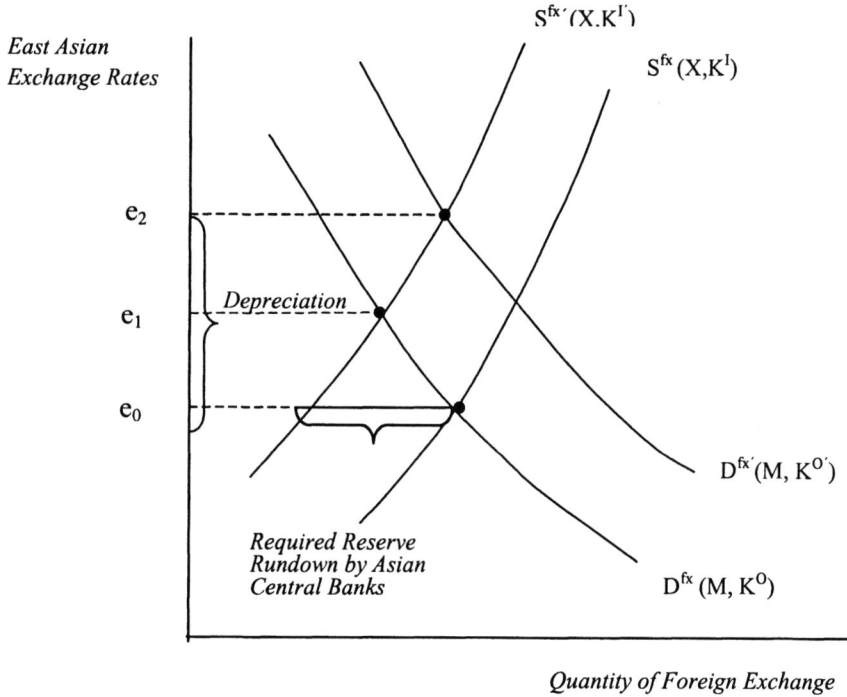

*Quantity of Foreign Exchange*

The weaker are East Asian exchange rates, the more competitive are their economies' export sectors and hence the greater is the amount of foreign exchange earned. Foreign capital inflows to East Asia on the other hand respond to differentials between East Asian interest rates, $i^A$, interest rates in the rest of the world, $i^*$, and foreign investors' perceptions of the riskiness of investing in East Asian financial markets, $R_f^A$. Hence, the

supply of foreign exchange may be represented as $s^{fx} = X(\overset{+}{e}) + K^I(\overset{+}{i}, i^*, \bar{R}_f^A)$.

On the demand side, East Asian demand for foreign exchange, $D^{fx}$, is made up of demand for foreign exchange to pay for imports of goods and services and East Asian investors' demand for foreign exchange to enable purchase of non-Asian assets, $K^0$. The weaker are Asian exchange rates, the more expensive imports become for Asian residents and firms and hence the less foreign exchange is required. At the same time, Asian investors would increase demand for financial assets in the rest of the world if financial returns abroad were relatively higher, or if they perceived a rise in the riskiness of

holding their own assets, $R_a^A$. Hence, $D^{fx} = M(\bar{e}) + K^0(\overset{+}{i}, \overset{+}{i^*}, \overset{A}{R_a})$.

Figure 1 illustrates how East Asian exchange rates came under severe pressure as foreign investors quit East Asian financial markets upon realising that risk exposure in these markets was much higher than previously thought. The $S^{fx}$ schedule shifted upwards to $S^{fx'}$ as foreign investment fell from $K^I$ to $K^{I'}$. East Asian central banks initially tried to hold exchange rate steady, but were unwilling to completely exhaust foreign currency reserves for this purpose. Accordingly, East Asian exchange rates depreciated from $e_0$ to $e_1$. This exchange rate correction turned into a crisis however, when Asian investors themselves switched funds out of Asian currency denominated assets to foreign currency assets. This caused East Asian demand for foreign currencies to increase from $D^{fx}$ to $D^{fx'}$ which caused substantial further depreciation, from $e_1$ to $e_2$ in the figure.

## 4. FINANCIAL SECTOR FRAGILITY

A sudden reappraisal by foreign investors of risk exposure midway through 1997 was the trigger for the capital flow reversal from East Asia that immediately depressed financial asset values in the region, including bond prices, equities and exchange rates. The main reasons for this reappraisal were related to misplaced presumptions about exchange rate risk, the earning capacity of real investment projects and the strength of Asian financial institutions. The exchange rate management policies of Asian central banks were critical to the asset price collapse that occurred in the region.

Foreign funds were mainly channelled through relatively fragile financial systems in many East Asian economies.[3] Moreover, funds that were intermediated through Asian banks were often officially directed to unproductive investment activities that, in turn, had been encouraged by public subsidies and regulations. Unproductive real investment of course increases GDP when undertaken and would have bolstered recorded output figures in the lead-up to the crisis itself. Many Asian banks were also government owned which lead foreign lenders to understate the risk of loan default on the presumption of implicit government guarantees, thus creating the "moral hazard" problem of too much borrowing and lending. Another factor which could have lowered perceived default risk and encouraged too much imprudent foreign lending to East Asia in the first instance was the past behaviour of the IMF in rescuing other crisis ridden economies.[4] In other words, banks lent funds on the understanding that financial support would be forthcoming if borrowers defaulted. Likewise, foreign investors provided funds on the understanding that Asian governments or IMF-arranged rescue packages would cover defaults if local institutions were unable to pay.

Prudential supervision of financial institutions in the worst affected Asian economies was generally weak. For instance, new banks were allowed to operate with insufficient capitalisation. Bank credit grew rapidly in the lead up to the crisis and high levels of foreign debt remained unhedged. There was also limited provision of economic information on the nature of government-business relations, the actual size of external debt exposure and non-performing loans, all of which may be classified as a lack of transparency in financial dealings. This lack of transparency distorted foreign investors'

---

[3] For further discussion, see Goldstein (1998), International Monetary Fund (1997b), Radelet and Sachs (1998), Mishkin (1999), Makin (1999a, 1999b) and Rogoff (1999).

[4] Calomiris (1998), Collier and Gunning (1999), Feldstein (1997), Fischer (1999), and Sachs (1998) critically evaluate the role of the IMF and the nature of its policy responses to financial crises.

awareness of the extent of the underlying structural problems in the East Asian economies.

However, once foreign investors realised the extent of these deficiencies, Asian equities and debt instruments were quickly liquidated in favour of relatively more attractive, less risky investment opportunities elsewhere around the globe. In this way, the crisis was analogous to a bank run. Bank runs have occurred in many places over past centuries whenever bank depositors suddenly fear that their bank of choice may not be able to refund deposits, with immediate withdrawals validating such fears. The evaporation of investor confidence about the security of funds therefore brought about a crisis that became self-fulfilling, even though foreign investors were acting quite rationally in seeking to preserve the value of their investments. The result however was the sharp mark-down of currencies and other asset values that seriously affected the net worth position of East Asian households, firms and financial institutions.

Indonesia, Korea and Thailand had liberalised their capital accounts in different ways between the mid 1980s and the late 1990's crisis. For instance, the Indonesian authorities allowed relatively free outflows of funds, but more slowly agreed to freer capital inflows. Korea was more cautious generally in opening up its capital markets, first permitting capital outflows and allowing only select foreign inflows into its security markets from the mid 1990s onwards. Restrictions were gradually removed on exchanges of foreign funds in Korean futures, currency options and bond markets. In contrast, Thailand pursued a more assertive strategy of promoting capital inflows through tax incentives for foreign investors, though restrictions controlling capital outflows were removed less quickly. Meanwhile, all crisis countries especially Malaysia encouraged capital inflow in the form of foreign direct investment.

Post crisis, there has been considerable financial sector restructuring in Indonesia, Korea, Malaysia and Thailand. For instance, in Indonesia many large private banks, many of which were merged, have been recapitalised, though the recovery of state-owned banks has been slower. In Korea, financial sector restructuring has gone further with many banks closed and others merged. Apart from banks, the investment trusts that have been major funders of the chaebols, have also had their balance sheets strengthened. The Malaysian financial sector was initially less adversely affected than financial sectors in the other crisis economies. Yet, considerable financial restructuring and bank merger activity also followed the ringgit crisis.

## 5. INTERNATIONAL ECONOMIC REPERCUSSIONS

The slump in the demand of foreign investors and investment funds operating on their behalf for Asian financial instruments was not the only cause of the currency and asset price collapse, however. The panic decisions of resident East Asian investors to suddenly liquidate investments in Asian assets turned what could have been a sharp, yet orderly, correction of asset prices and exchange rates into a full blown financial crisis.[5] In other words, the withdrawal of foreign investment from Asian economies was compounded by a withdrawal of funds by Asian investors from their own financial markets and institutions.

Although the Asian financial turmoil began when foreign investors adjusted their portfolios by switching out of Asian financial assets into other more attractive alternatives, the foreign capital that quit Asia was then reinvested in, for instance, Australasia, North America and Western Europe. This kept interest rates low and asset values high in the advanced economies which sustained extra economic activity and created additional trade opportunities in those regions. At the same time, the Latin American economies, notably Argentina and Chile, also continued to benefit from substantial foreign investment throughout the 1990s, as did economies in Eastern Europe, such as the Czech Republic and Hungary.

The lower interest rates in the rest of the world that resulted from the portfolio adjustment helped bouy capital spending and production preventing a serious global recession. The international capital that was switched from Asian markets to other locations also helped generate alternative world trade opportunities, providing a limited offset to reduced export opportunities in Asia. At the same time, the overshooting of Asian exchange rates and other asset values created bargains for foreign buyers and increased scope for further direct foreign investment in the region.

## 6. SUMMARY AND CONCLUSION

To sum up, the main lessons and opportunities arising from the Asian crisis are as follows. With globally integrated financial markets, foreign investors now effectively vote with their funds against economies experiencing unsustainable levels of economic activity. Sharp capital outflows provide the requisite signal that financial practices and domestic economic policies have to be changed if economies are to recover quickly. At the same time, extremely low financial and real asset prices in Asian economies improved the scope for increasing portfolio and direct investment in the financial sectors of the 'Asian 5' economies and for providing consultancy services to those countries as they rebuilt their financial systems.

The Asian currency crisis has prompted many calls for financial reforms aimed at avoiding future such crises, with an emphasis on discouraging excessive capital mobility.

---

[5] See Kindleberger (1996) for an historical treatment of financial crises.

Such proposals include prohibitions on short term capital flows and levying special taxes on international capital movements, for instance as proposed by Tobin (1978). However, measures that limit capital flows into emerging economies may also limit the future economic growth prospects of these economies to the extent that they prevent global saving from being channelled to its most productive use.

The East Asian capital flow reversal demonstrated how quickly domestic and international investors will respond to new economic information that raises perceived risk levels or lowers expected relative rates of return. The main reason for the crisis was an underestimation of default and exchange rate risk, combined with fragile financial systems in which both foreign and domestic investors lost confidence. Accordingly, the best option for minimising future financial crises is to allow continued exchange rate flexibility and strengthen the institutional banking and finance framework for channelling funds to and through the Asian economies, not to again restrict or tax short term international capital flows.

## REFERENCES

Calomiris, C. (1998) "The IMF's Imprudent Role as Lender of Last Resort", *The Cato Journal*, Winter.

Collier, P. and Gunning, J. (1999) "The IMF's Role in Structural Adjustment" *The Economic Journal*, 109, 634-651.

Feldstein, M. (1998) "Refocussing the IMF", *Foreign Affairs*, 77(2), March/April.

Fischer, S. (1999) "Reforming the International Financial System" *The Economic Journal*, 109, 557-576.

Frenkel, J. and Razin, A. (1987) *Fiscal Policies and the World Economy*, MIT Press, Cambridge, Massachusetts.

Goldstein, M. (1998) *Crisis: Causes, Cures and Systemic Implications*, Institute for International Economics, No. 55, Washington, DC.

International Monetary Fund, *International Financial Statistics* (various).

International Monetary Fund (1997a) *International Capital Markets: Developments, Prospects and Key Policy Issues*, International Monetary Fund, November, Washington, DC.

International Monetary Fund (1999) *World Economic Outlook*, International Monetary Fund, May, Washington, DC.

International Monetary Fund (1997b) *World Economic Outlook: Interim Assessment*, International Monetary Fund, December, Washington, DC.

Kindleberger, C. (1996) *Manias, Panics and Crashes: A History of Financial Crises*, 3rd ed., Wiley, New York.

Makin, A (2000) *Global Finance and the Macroeconomy*, Macmillan and St Martins Press, London and New York.

Makin, A. (1999a) "Preventing Financial Crises in East Asia" *Asian Survey*, 39(4), 668-678.

Makin, A. (1999b) "The Great East Asian Capital Flow Reversal: Reasons, Responses and Ramifications" *The World Economy*

Mishkin, F. (1999) "Global Financial Instability: Framework, Events, Issues" *Journal of Economic Perspectives*, 13(4), 3-20.

Rogoff, K. (1999) "International Institutions for Reducing Global Financial Instability" *Journal of Economic Perspectives*, 13(4), 21-42.

Sachs, J. (1998) "The IMF and the Asian Flu", *The American Prospect*, 20(10), 16-21.

Tobin, J. (1978) "A Proposal for International Monetary Reform" *Eastern Economic Journal*, 4, July/October.

World Bank (1998) *Private Capital Flows to Developing Countries: The Road to Financial Integration*, World Bank Policy Research Report.

World Bank (1993) *The East Asian Miracle - Economic Growth and Public Policy*, Oxford University Press, Oxford.

# Chapter 4

# A CONTINENT IN CRISIS. ASIA´S GROWING POLITICAL AND CONTINUING ECONOMIC INSECURITIES

*Heinrich Kreft[1]*
Foreign Office
Policy Planning Staff
Berlin

At the beginning of the new millennium new trends are shaping the face of Asia.

The vision of an incipient Asian century generated by the exemplary economic development of the last three decades has given way to growing insecurities in Asia. Since mid-1997 three events or developments in particular have substantially altered the political and strategic situation in Asia:

- the so-called Asia crisis,
- the end of the authoritarian Suharto regime in Indonesia, and
- open nuclearization in South Asia and the development of boosters in India, Pakistan and North Korea.

These events have made it clear that numerous conflicts in the past were not resolved by the East-West conflict and the economic boom, but merely hidden by them. The fact that Asia - owing to its high degree of (geographical, cultural, economic, ideological and political) heterogeneity - has not been able to establish viable multilateral security structures is now proving a disadvantage. In many countries latent nationalism has been intensified by the crisis.

---

[1] The author expresses solely his personal opinions.

The already considerable potential for conflict in Asia has increased markedly over the last three years. The dangers for Asia's stability basically derive from the following conflicts and developments:

- The difficult process of transformation in Indonesia, which in 1997 has led to an escalation of the long-simmering East Timor conflict that is jeopardizing the country's cohesion, will endanger for some time to come the stability of a region of importance for the world economy.
- On the Korean peninsula the historic summit meeting between South Korean President Kim Dae Jung and North Korea's leader Kim Jong Il has nourished fresh hopes for an easing of tensions. Despite intense efforts by the South Koreans and the US, supported by Japan and China, virtually no progress had been made for years. In the light of the continued calculated provocation by Pyongyang, which was however incalculable for the West, the US policy on North Korea scarcely progressed beyond crisis management.
- The open nuclearization and the continuing confrontation between India and Pakistan, particularly over Kashmir, has increased the danger of an arms race in South Asia and provided a setback for the international disarmament and non-proliferation endeavours. On the other hand, India's importance as a factor for stability is increasing in view of Pakistan's weakness, which was revealed not least by the military coup in October 1999, and the growing danger of "Talebanization" in South and Central Asia.
- China's self-confident striving for a role in regional politics, and increasingly also on the world stage, is leading to a confrontation with the United States, with the Taiwan issue of great (domestic) significance for both sides; however, since the interests of the two sides are in some cases identical, there will always be opportunities for cooperation between them.
- The general process of military armament in South, East and parts of South-East Asia has a destabilizing effect.

In this first decade of the new century, with the outbreak of conflicts which had at best been patched over in decades past, Asia could become a destabilizing factor in world politics. Given Asia's increased weight in the world economy, but also in view of its political significance and the large military arsenals that have been built up, this would have global repercussions.

## THE ASIA CRISIS CONTINUES

The geopolitical situation in Asia has changed considerably within four years. The main reason for this is the crisis in East Asia, which began in the summer of 1997 as a currency crisis in Thailand, developed into a financial and economic crisis, and then spread to virtually the whole of East Asia. The economic, domestic, foreign-policy and social repercussions are great. The crisis has left a deep mark on the region. It is both a fundamental crisis in the "Asian system" sparked off by globalization and liberalization and the consequence of serious microeconomic errors with macroeconomic repercussions. The crisis was triggered by several factors. It revealed considerable ordo-liberal shortcomings, including the lack of the rule of law, corruption and nepotism, government intervention in the markets, the distancing of politics from society, as well as increasing environmental destruction and widening prosperity divides.

Despite impressive growth rates, especially in South Korea, the crisis is far from over. The potential for a relapse is considerable. It is true that the financial markets and the national economies have recovered, but the underlying structural economic and socio-political shortcomings have not yet been corrected, even in South Korea and Thailand, two countries that are keener on reform. The social repercussions (e.g. the large number of children in Indonesia and Thailand leaving school early with no qualifications) are particularly serious, and will hamper the region's development for years to come.

Ethnic and religious tensions in Indonesia that were previously concealed by economic growth have been rekindled. And in Malaysia the institutionalized balance of interests between the Chinese minority and the Moslem Malays is in jeopardy, as the strong performance by Islamic parties in the last parliamentary elections showed.

What is needed if recovery is to be complete is reform of the financial systems (including public supervision of banking, bankruptcy law) as well as measures to radically reorganize the whole socio-political system.

The crisis has also increased the potential for inter-state conflict. While the majority of East and South-East Asian states felt forced to reduce their defence expenditure, China has (to date) been able to continue as planned with the modernization of the People's Liberation Army and will in future probably speed it up (not least as a reaction to the Kosovo conflict). Securing its raw materials supplies (including oil) and thus the sea routes will become more and more important to China as it expands industrial production and sees increased prosperity. Although there is no such indication at present, the possibility of a more aggressive approach by China in the South China Sea (and particularly around the Spratley Islands) in future cannot be excluded.

## INDONESIA'S DIFFICULT PROCESS OF TRANSFORMATION

The Asia crisis had the greatest impact in Indonesia. It very soon led to the fall of Suharto and to the start of a difficult process of political and economic transformation whose end and outcome are still open. The election of Abdurrahman Wahid as President and Mrs Megawati as Vice-President initially stabilized the volatile political environment. However, the new democratically legitimized leadership faces huge challenges. Growing poverty, unemployment and inflation may easily cause further destabilization in the country. The effect of continuing anti-Chinese violence is that a substantial proportion of the Chinese capital shifted out of the country does not return.

The referendum and the resulting independence of East Timor have given encouragement to separatist movements in other parts of the scattered island state, particularly in Aceh on the strategically important route from Malacca, but also in Papua. The - not very probable - severance of these provinces, small in relation to the overall state with its 210 million inhabitants, would nevertheless have considerable repercussions for the stability of the entire region, where there are more or less strong moves towards independence in other countries too. The fear that Indonesia could suffer the same fate as Yugoslavia with comparable consequences for its neighbours is widespread from Canberra to Bangkok, but it is in fact an improbable scenario.

Despite the substantial successes (democratic elections, decentralization, civilian control of the military, large degree of press freedom), the enormity of the challenges means that it is doubtful whether lasting democratization in the country will be achieved. The return to an authoritarian regime (perhaps wearing a more democratic mantle than Suharto) cannot be completely discounted. It is unlikely that Indonesia can regain its leading position as by far the biggest country and strongest military power in South-East Asia in the next ten years.[2]

## WEAKENING OF ASEAN - A POWER VACUUM IN SOUTH-EAST ASIA?

The Association of South-East Asian Nations (ASEAN) has been considerably weakened by the crisis. Indonesia, its heavyweight and federator, is facing an uncertain political and economic future. Viet Nam and Laos have abandoned the reform course which would have integrated them more firmly into the Association. Solidarity within ASEAN has already reached its limits, as all the world can see. The project to create a free-trade zone (AFTA) by 2002 seems at risk. The return of millions of guest workers and the flight of tens of thousands of Indonesians to Malaysia (and Singapore) have weighed down inter-state relations. And simmering territorial conflicts between ASEAN member states (e.g. Indonesia/Malaysia) could flare up again.

The fall of Indonesia, by far the strongest military power in the region, could produce a power vacuum in South-East Asia which China could use to exert increased pressure in the South China Sea (Spratley Islands) and possibly also on the South-East Asian mainland. Some countries in the region, for instance Singapore, have already opted to improve their security situation by intensifying their bilateral cooperation with neighbouring states and with the USA and India. ASEAN and the ASEAN Regional Forum (ARF) have proved incapable of reacting appropriately to the East Timor crisis. The ASEAN states had to let Australia, which is emerging as an important factor for stability, at least in South-East Asia, take the lead in the UN mission. This commitment and especially the lack of timely coordination with Jakarta have imposed a distinct strain on Australian-Indonesian relations. Another millstone for ASEAN is the membership of

---

[2] Heinrich Kreft, Indonesia, in: Internationale Politik, Transatlantic Edition, Berlin 2001.

Myanmar, a military dictatorship broadly despised by the international community for its human rights violations. The last two ASEAN summits held against the background of the organization's relative loss of importance were characterized by damage limitation exercises and attempts to give integration a new boost. The debate about shared ideas on integration and security (e.g. a Code of Conduct for the Spratley Islands) has just begun. The ARF remains the nucleus of the joint security-policy project and is to be complemented by more regular dialogues with the big powers in the region. It is notable that ASEAN's summit in Manila became the stage for the heads of government of China, Japan and South Korea, who met for joint talks for the first time since the Second World War. While international relations in the wider region remain characterized by mutual mistrust, ASEAN lacks both the instruments and the political will for further-reaching moves towards integration. As a result, the traditional influence of the big powers in South-East Asia has again become visible.

## THE USA - AN INDISPENSABLE GUARANTOR OF STABILITY FOR ASIA

In principle the USA is profiting from the growing uncertainty in Asia and from the great importance of the American market for the Asian economies.

The Asian crisis gave Washington the opportunity to extend the democratic and market-economy camp at a time when US foreign policy had more or less given up the enlargement strategy pursued by the first Clinton administration. It was replaced by dialogues with China, Indonesia and North Korea. At the Washington Summit in October 1997 Washington also offered Peking (de facto) a new strategic partnership. The US motive was primarily economic, but also regional. Following President Clinton's visit to Peking in the summer of 1998 a series of events and developments cast a renewed burden on relations between the two states:

- Peking's clampdown on the opposition,
- China's alleged military espionage in the US,
- The war in Kosovo and the bombing of the Chinese embassy in Belgrade,
- Endeavours in the USA and Japan, but also Taiwan, towards a missile defence system in East Asia.
- The US-spy-plnae incident in spring 2001.

Despite this considerable potential for a flare-up both sides are in principle keen to maintain their cooperation despite substantial conflicts of interest in many areas.

Since 1994 the United States has again been formulating its interests in the Pacific more in national than in regulatory categories. China's rise as a big power is regarded as inevitable in the medium term. At the same time the People's Republic is no longer regarded primarily as a (potential) military challenge, but as a partner in attempts to cool down regional hot spots like Korea and Taiwan.

So the US accepts that China has a regional role to play, just as it actively calls for Japan - with which it expanded its security alliance in September 1997 - to play a regional role. The bilateral alliance with Japan should, US strategists believe, be underpinned with China's integration in the medium term. Whether this will succeed depends crucially on China's development.

The basis for this change in course is the realization that the US dominance at sea in East Asia and the Pacific is not under threat from any individual player or coalition in the region. By promoting confidence-building among the countries of the region (the USA called upon China and Japan, Japan and South Korea, Russia and Japan to embark on security dialogues), Washington is hoping to neutralize the remaining risks.

## CHINA'S INCREASING IMPORTANCE IN REGIONAL POLICY

China initially went largely unscathed by the crisis in the region. By rejecting the idea of devaluation, which would have worsened the crisis still further in its neighbouring states, China assumed a major leadership role in the region, partly at the expense of Japan. There was praise for China's actions both within East Asia and also from the US, because devaluation would have further increased the country's big trade deficit with China, a matter about which there is much sensitivity within American politics. Owing to the political and economic weakness of the "medium powers" Indonesia, Thailand and South Korea, as well as Japan, China's role as the United States' most important partner and its rival in East Asia is becoming ever clearer.

Whether China can consolidate or further develop this positional gain basically depends on whether the leadership in Peking manages to resolve the huge problems in the country. In principle China suffers from the same shortcomings as the countries in crisis (for instance an overindebted, institutionally feeble financial system; loans granted in accordance with political criteria; inefficient entrepreneurial structure).

China is currently in its most difficult phase since it embarked on economic liberalization 22 years ago. The fundamental conflict between the market economy and an authoritarian political culture is becoming more and more obvious.

On the one hand, China is facing the huge challenge of having to restructure its economy ("privatization" of the often inefficient state-owned enterprises, rehabilitation of the ramshackle financial system) in order to be able to continue to achieve the necessary high growth rates. On the other, the Peking leadership is not unjustifiably afraid of the fact that the workers who would necessarily be cast aside in the process may embody considerable potential for destabilization. The official unemployment rate is already 8%, i.e. over 100 million. Protests against state authority are on the increase.

China was initially able to keep the impact of the Asia crisis within limits, but it had also a marked effect on its economic growth.

It is to be firmly hoped that the economic reforms are successful, as a crisis-hit China would have substantially more serious consequences for economic and political stability in the region and thus for the global economy and international security than had the crisis in the "tiger states".[3]

## JAPAN, THE "INSECURE" REGIONAL POWER

As a result of the Asia crisis, Japan, whose political status derives principally from its economic strength, has lost regional ground to China, still the biggest security-policy challenge to Japan.

Many national supporters of a "normal" and self-confident Japan have realized, since 1994 at the latest, that their country is not capable of taking on an independent political leadership role in the region in the long term. For this reason, the emphasis has shifted from seeking emancipation from the USA to strengthening the bilateral alliance, as reflected in the parliamentary approval for the new defence guidelines of spring 1999. These new defence guidelines allow the Japanese self-defence forces to provide (primarily logistical) support for US units.

North Korea's testing of a ballistic missile over Japanese territory on 31 August 1998 alerted Tokyo to its own vulnerability and rekindled the debate about a missile defence system (TMD), which in turn is meeting with strong opposition from Peking. If TMD has the potential to destabilize North-East Asia by unleashing an arms spiral, the threat from North Korea has at least led to moves towards stabilizing cooperation between Japan and South Korea and between China and South Korea. The trilateral cooperation with the USA and Korea is an indication of Japan's increasing willingness to enter into multilateral cooperation. Through its efforts to improve its relations with China and Russia, its active role in the ASEAN Regional Forum, the provision of substantial funding for Indonesia and other countries hit by the Asia crisis and particularly through its close economic links with the majority of states in the region, Japan is making a major contribution to stability, a contribution that would be even bigger if Tokyo could make up its mind to take further steps towards liberalization itself.

Given its position as the dominant economic power and the high degree of integration with the other economies of the region, the resolution of Japan's structural problems as the precondition for the country's own stable economic growth takes on great significance for the permanent resolution of the economic and financial crisis in East Asia. There are increasing signs in Japan that the longest and hardest economic crisis any industrial country has had to endure since the global economic crisis is slowly coming to an end.

---

[3] Heinrich Kreft, China die werdende Großmacht. Vom Akteur zum Objekt der Internationalen Politik, in: Aus Politik und Zeitgeschichte, December 2000.

## SOUTH ASIA AS A CHALLENGE TOR SECURITY POLICY

Open nuclearization by India and Pakistan has had a negative impact on the security situation in South Asia. There is the danger of a nuclear race, even if the economic scope for one is severely restricted on the Pakistan side. The Indian draft of a nuclear doctrine ("minimal" nuclear deterrent with second-strike capacity) provoked strong reactions in Pakistan, as was to be expected, although whether it can be financed is more than doubtful; this applies even more to the demand for a complete triad of land, sea and air-based nuclear weapons, which, it has to be said, the Vajpayee government has not made.

The nuclear tests by India and Pakistan and the continuation of the nuclear weapon and carrier programmes, including tests on potential boosters, run counter to global endeavours towards disarmament and non-proliferation. The attempts by the international community to incorporate the two de facto nuclear powers into the international non-proliferation regime have made but little progress so far (declaration of intent to sign the CTBT). However, India is issuing increasingly positive signals on the big matter of accession to the CTBT.

Although there is no immediate risk of a nuclear exchange between India and Pakistan, it must be realized that the traditional tensions between the two countries, with the dispute over Kashmir that so touches on their self-image, have taken on a nuclear dimension that heightens the risk. Since Independence, these tensions have led to three wars (most recently in 1971). The conflicts in Kargil (Kashmir) between May and July 1999 were the most serious clashes for 30 years and once again interrupted the process of dialogue that had just been restarted - in the face of domestic resistance - in February 1999 by Prime Minister Vajpayee and his Pakistan counterpart Sharif (who has since been removed from power by a military coup) with the Declaration of Lahore. The Indian BJP government and the Pakistan military are basically aware that there is no alternative to dialogue, but have not yet found their way back to the table. The demarcation line in Kashmir is to this day the scene for exchanges of fire and artillery exchanges which continue to claim victims.

Between India and Pakistan there is a pressing need both for the additional confidence and security-building measures agreed in Lahore and for the implementation of the many existing measures.

Pakistan, a country suffering from identity problems, feels threatened mainly by India, but is in itself facing major domestic and economic problems which led to the seizure of power by the military. While the military has largely been able to calm the political situation, it is more than doubtful whether it will succeed where several democratic governments had previously failed in pushing through the radical reforms needed to overcome the prevailing socio-economic crisis.

For India, China is the dominant challenge to security policy. India would dearly like to emulate China's big-power status (as a nuclear power with a UN right of veto).

As an established democracy with tremendous economic potential, it is also a decisive factor for stability in the region in the face of a growing risk of "Talebanization" emanating from Afghanistan which could become a grave threat not only to Pakistan but also to the countries of Central Asia - a threat that is being increasingly recognized also by the United States (Osama bin Laden/international terrorism) and Russia, as well as by China ("Schanghai Five") and Iran.[4]

## THE KOREAN PENINSULA - THE MOST DANGEROUS HOT SPOT IN ASIA

The Korean peninsula is probably still the most dangerous hot spot in Asia. Previously there were already indications that North Korea possesses chemical, biological and also nuclear weapons, and in August 1998 Pyongyang showed that it is also in a position to build and test ballistic missiles. Owing to the ideological isolation of the Kim Jong Il regime and the country's "vegetation" on the edge of economic collapse, endeavours by the South to achieve détente with President Kim Dae Jung's "sunshine policy" remained largely unsuccessful up until the spring of 2000. In June 1999 naval units from North and South fired at each other in the Yellow Sea for the first time since the Korean War (1950-53).

In recent years North Korea has concentrated on expanding its potential threat, in particular by developing and testing medium and long-range missiles. With this policy Pyongyang has repeatedly been able to attract international attention and to "extort" substantial international aid. The North Korean missiles are not only a serious threat to South Korea and also Japan, they also encapsulate a significant risk of proliferation.

The US is banking on removing North Korea from its isolation. Despite the 1994 agreement on stopping its nuclear programme (in return for the supply of oil and two light water reactors), an agreement advantageous to North Korea, Pyongyang has not given up its calculated - but for the West incalculable - provocations. However, contacts have been intensified with the US-North Korean talks in Berlin at the end of 1999 and the reduction of sanctions announced by the United States. The unexpected, historic summit between Kim Jong Il and Kim Dae Jung in Pyongyang on 12/13 June 2000 gave rise to hopes for a lasting easing of tensions. The new Bush Administration's initial reluctance to continue with the dialogue with North Korea has been given up recently. However, the North's willingness truly to ease tensions can by no means be taken for granted.

## DESTABILIZATION THROUGH MILITARY ARMAMENT

The quantitative and qualitative military stockpiling and modernization which has been seen in Asia for years undoubtedly increases the potential for conflict. The regional military balance, in which the US plays a central role, is one of the key elements for the preservation of stability and peace. During the course of the next two decades, however, the superiority in conventional military terms of the United States and its allies could be

---

[4] Heinrich Kreft, Südasien als sicherheitspolitische Herausforderung, in: Indien-Jahrbuch, Hamburg 2000.

reduced with the proliferation of weapons of mass destruction and booster technology and the development of modern military capacities by the People's Republic of China. Regional security regimes will therefore become more and more important for maintaining peace and security. Until such regimes are in place - if indeed they ever are - virtually all Asian states will continue to invest in military armaments.

Some countries, particularly in South-East Asia, however, will not be able to modernize their military as planned during the economic boom of the early 90s. On the other hand, the region's major military powers - China, Japan, South Korea, Taiwan and Singapore - will very probably continue to build up modern and increasingly efficient armed forces.

## A ROLE FOR EUROPE

The attractiveness of regional cooperation to promote economic and political stability, an attractiveness which despite spreading nationalism has been enhanced as a result of the crisis and the growing uncertainties in Asia could and should be supported by Europe within the framework of the EU's long-established relations with ASEAN, EU membership of the ASEAN Regional Forum and within ASEM. The EU should also do everything possible to support possible regional cooperation in North-East Asia (Japan-South Korea) and South Asia (SAARC).

Efforts to heighten Europe's profile in the Asia-Pacific region, which have been very successful in recent years thanks above all to ASEM, and the policy pursued by the US aim towards further economic liberalization and especially political opening with greater democracy, pluralism and the rule of law.

# Chapter 5

# SEASONALITY AND PURCHASING POWER PARITY

*Shigeyuki Hamori*
*Akira Tokihisa*
Kobe University
2-1, Rokkodai, Nada-Ku, Kobe, 657-8501,
Japan

## ABSTRACT

In this paper, the stability of the PPP was empirically analyzed employing the notion of seasonal cointegration. The major results are summarized as follows. Firstly, it was found that prices and exchange rates have only non-seasonal unit root. Furthermore, the cointegration tests revealed that cointegrating relation is rejected in every case. This fact tells us that no stable PPP existed between the United States and the other three countries (Germany, UK and Japan) during the period analyzed.

**JEL** classification number: F31
**Key Words**: PPP, seasonal integration, seasonal cointegration

## 1. INTRODUCTION

Purchasing power parity (PPP) is a concept that has existed for a long time. It was formulated by G. Cassel (1922) and has come to be commonly used. The basic idea of purchasing power parity is the law of one price: the fact that the same good will be sold at the same price, regardless of whether the price quoted is in dollars or in yen. This single price occurs since the exchange rate is known at any given time, and therefore the purchasing power of different currencies in buying the same goods must be equal. If the markets for goods in any two countries are internationally integrated, then purchasing power parity between these countries should be verifiable.

Consider two countries, a domestic country and a foreign country, where the variables of the latter are superscripted with a star. Let the market price of the foreign currency in period $t$ be $P_t^*$. In terms of the domestic currency, the price is equal to the value $P_t^*$ multiplied by the period $t$ exchange rate, $S_t$. In short, according to the law of one price, the domestic price at time $t$ ($P_t^*$) should have the following relationship:

(1.) $P_t = P_t^* S_t$,

or

(2.) $p_t = p_t^* + s_t$

where $p_t = \log(P_t)$, $p_t^* = \log(P_t^*)$ and $s_t = \log(S_t)$.

Many studies have been conducted in an attempt to analyze this relation empirically. The equation (1) (or (2)) has been treated as a long-run equilibrium relationship. Using time series analysis, many attempts have been made to verify this relationship by applying the idea of cointegration. Purchasing power parity is verified if there is a cointegrating relationship between the domestic price, the foreign price, and the exchange rate [e.g., Corbae and Ouliaris (1988), Enders (1988), Enders and Hurn (1994)].

Economic time series data, however, have some inherent problems of their own, one of which is seasonality[1]. When a unit root or cointegration is tested on data containing seasonality, care is required in how we handle the data. Each root must be tested separately, as Hylleberg et al. (1990) pointed out, because data containing seasonality may have unit roots with different cycles. Beaulieu and Miron (1993) carried out seasonal integration tests on aggregate data from the United States. Engle et al. (1993) estimated the Japanese consumption function by applying the idea of seasonal cointegration to Japanese consumption data. Tokihisa and Hamori (2001) proposed a framework to analyze the daily data and applied this idea to the trading volume of stock market. However, although many empirical analyses of PPP have been carried out, we have been unable to find any study of PPP that explicitly considers seasonality. This paper therefore analyses PPP utilizing the idea of seasonal cointegration.

---

[1] It is pointed out that it is not always desirable to make an adjustment for seasonality when analyzing economic data containing seasonality. In particular, if a unit root test is carried out using seasonally adjusted data, variables tend to be incorrectly regarded as random walks [Ghysels and Perron (1993), Davidson and MacKinnon (1993)]. Therefore, when a unit root or cointegration is tested using quarterly or monthly data, it is desirable to use seasonally unadjusted data.

# 2. DATA

The data used is quarterly data from March 1973 to February 1997. The PPP is tested for the following:

(i)   Germany and the United States,
(ii)  The United Kingdom and the United States,
(iii) Japan and the United States.

Exchange rates for the three countries (Germany, the United Kingdom, and Japan) are relative to the U.S. dollar. Prices were in terms of the consumer price index. All data are obtained from the OECD Main Economic Indicators database. Natural logs of raw data were taken and multiplied by 100, and the initial value for March 1973 is then subtracted as follows:

$$(3.) \quad x_t = 100[\log(X_t) - \log(X_{March,1973})],$$

where $X_t$ refers to the raw data at time $t$, which corresponds to prices and exchange rates. The purpose of subtracting the constant, $\log(X_{March,1973})$, from each observation is to normalize each series to zero for March 1973. Multiplying the log by 100 means that $x_t$ is approximately the percentage difference between $X_t$ and its starting value, $X_{March,1973}$.[2]

# 3. SEASONAL INTEGRATION TESTS

## 3.1 Empirical Techniques

Beaulieu and Miron (1993), and Franses and Hobijn (1997) extended the seasonal integration test developed by Hylleberg et al. (1990) to monthly data. The following transformations are defined for any given variable, $\{x_t\}$ $t = 1,2,...,T$,

$$(4.) \quad y_{1,t} = (1+B)(1+B^2)(1+B^4+B^8)x_t,$$

$$(5.) \quad y_{2,t} = -(1-B)(1+B^2)(1+B^4+B^8)x_t,$$

---

[2] See Hamilton (1994).

(6.) $y_{3,t} = -(1 - B^2)(1 + B^4 + B^8)x_t,$

(7.) $y_{4,t} = -(1 - B^4)(1 - \sqrt{3}B + B^2)(1 + B^2 + B^4)x_t,$

(8.) $y_{5,t} = -(1 - B^4)(1 + \sqrt{3}B + B^2)(1 + B^2 + B^4)x_t,$

(9.) $y_{6,t} = -(1 - B^4)(1 - B^2 + B^4)(1 - B + B^2)x_t,$

(10.) $y_{7,t} = -(1 - B^4)(1 - B^2 + B^4)(1 + B + B^2)x_t,$

and

(11.) $y_{8,t} = (1 - B^{12})x_t.$

Applying OLS to the following equation:

(12.)
$$y_{8,t} = \sum_{s=1}^{12} \delta_s D_{s,t} + \beta t + \pi_1 y_{1,t-1} + \pi_2 y_{2,t-1} + \pi_3 y_{3,t-1} + \pi_4 y_{3,t-2} + \pi_5 y_{4,t-1}$$
$$+ \pi_6 y_{4,t-2} + \pi_7 y_{5,t-1} + \pi_8 y_{5,t-2} + \pi_9 y_{6,t-1} + \pi_{10} y_{6,t-2}$$
$$+ \pi_{11} y_{7,t-1} + \pi_{12} y_{7,t-2} + \sum_{i=1}^{p} \phi_i y_{8,t-i} + u_t$$

an estimate of each coefficient is obtained, and it becomes possible to test for seasonal integration by testing the significance of the parameters, $\pi_i$ $(i = 1,2,...,12)$, where $B$ is the lag operator, $t$ is the deterministic time trend, $D_{s,t}$ is the seasonal dummy variable, which takes a value of 1 in season s and 0 otherwise, and $u_t$ is the i.i.d. error term.

In equation (12), $y_{1t}$ is a transformation that removes season^al unit roots and preserves the long run or zero frequency unit root. The remaining transformations include $y_{2t}$, which preserves the frequency $\pi$ corresponding to a six month period; $y_{3t}$ which retains the frequency $(1/2)\pi$ $[(3/2)\pi]$ corresponding to a three month period; $y_{4t}$ which retains the frequency $(5/6)\pi$ $[(7/6)\pi]$; and $y_{5t}$, $y_{6t}$, and $y_{7t}$ which retain the frequencies $(1/6)\pi [(11/6)\pi]$, $(2/3)\pi [(4/3)\pi]$ and $(1/3)\pi [(5/3)\pi]$ respectively. The tests for long run unit roots and seasonal frequencies are then based on the $t$-values and $F$-values as described in Table 1. [See Hylleberg et. al. (1993) and Franses and Hobijn (1997) for details.]

## 3.2 Empirical Results

Seasonal integration tests were conducted based on equation (12). For the deterministic part of equation (12), two lines of analyses were used to examine the robustness of the result. In the first case, both the seasonal dummy and the time trend were taken into account, whereas in the second case only the seasonal dummy was taken into account. The lag degree $(q)$ in equation (12) was selected by SBIC (Schwarz Bayesian Information Criterion; Schwarz (1978)). To determine the value for $(q)$, the values from 0 to 12 were tried and that giving the lowest SBIC was selected. Consequently, $q = 0$ was selected for all variables except for the Japanese price level.

**Table 1. Tests of Seasonal Unit Root in Monthly Data**

| Unit Root at Frequency | Transformation | Hypothesis Testing | | Test Statistics |
|---|---|---|---|---|
| | | Null Hypothesis | Alternative Hypothesis | |
| $0$ | $y_{1t}$ | $\pi_1 = 0$ | $\pi_1 < 0$ | $t(\pi_1)$ |
| $\pi$ | $y_{2t}$ | $\pi_2 = 0$ | $\pi_1 < 0$ | $t(\pi_2)$ |
| $\frac{1}{2}\pi, \frac{3}{2}\pi$ | $y_{3t}$ | $\pi_3 \cap \pi_4 = 0$ | $\pi_3 \cup \pi_4 \neq 0$ | $F(\pi_3, \pi_4)$ |
| $\frac{5}{6}\pi, \frac{7}{6}\pi$ | $y_{4t}$ | $\pi_5 \cap \pi_6 = 0$ | $\pi_5 \cup \pi_6 \neq 0$ | $F(\pi_5, \pi_6)$ |
| $\frac{1}{6}\pi, \frac{11}{6}\pi$ | $y_{5t}$ | $\pi_7 \cap \pi_8 = 0$ | $\pi_7 \cup \pi_8 \neq 0$ | $F(\pi_7, \pi_8)$ |
| $\frac{2}{3}\pi, \frac{4}{3}\pi$ | $y_{6t}$ | $\pi_9 \cap \pi_{10} = 0$ | $\pi_9 \cup \pi_{10} \neq 0$ | $F(\pi_9, \pi_{10})$ |
| $\frac{1}{3}\pi, \frac{5}{3}\pi$ | $y_{7t}$ | $\pi_{11} \cap \pi_{12} = 0$ | $\pi_{11} \cup \pi_{12} \neq 0$ | $F(\pi_{11}, \pi_{12})$ |

Tables 2 through 8 show the empirical results for each of the four countries studied. These tables raise some interesting points. Firstly, they make it clear that the non-seasonal unit root cannot be rejected for most variables. In the case of the US price level, for instance, as Table 2 shows, $t(\pi_1)$ is -1.972 when the seasonal dummy and the time trend are used as deterministic terms, and $t(\pi_1)$ is -2.498 when the time trend is excluded. Therefore, in neither case is it possible to reject the existence of non-seasonal unit roots. Furthermore, this result is common to all variables except for the Japanese price level, as is clearly shown in Tables 3 through 8. Secondly, the tables also show that the existence of seasonal unit roots should be rejected. For the US price level shown in Table 2, for example, the null hypothesis is rejected in all test statistics, from $t(\pi_2)$ to $F(\pi_{11}, \pi_{12})$. Similar results are obtained in Tables 3 through 8: no variable has seasonal unit roots and the $(1-B)$ filter is found to be effective.

## Table 2. Seasonal Integration Test
## USA
## Price

| Deterministic Term | Test Statistic | |
|---|---|---|
| | Seasonal Dummy and Trend | Seasonal Dummy |
| $q$ | 0 | 0 |
| $t(\pi_1)$ | -1.972 | -2.498 |
| $t(\pi_2)$ | -5.761* | -5.751* |
| $F(\pi_3, \pi_4)$ | 24.093* | 24.186* |
| $F(\pi_5, \pi_6)$ | 28.507* | 28.400* |
| $F(\pi_7, \pi_8)$ | 18.461* | 18.887* |
| $F(\pi_9, \pi_{10})$ | 27.647* | 27.610* |
| $F(\pi_{11}, \pi_{12})$ | 25.941* | 26.372* |

(*) shows that the null hypothesis is rejected at the 5% significance level.

## Table 3. Seasonal Integration Test
## UK
## Price

| Deterministic Term | Test Statistic | |
|---|---|---|
| | Seasonal Dummy and Trend | Seasonal Dummy |
| $q$ | 0 | 0 |
| $t(\pi_1)$ | -3.035 | -4.111* |
| $t(\pi_2)$ | -5.083* | -5.077* |
| $F(\pi_3, \pi_4)$ | 27.615* | 27.624* |
| $F(\pi_5, \pi_6)$ | 43.272* | 43.377* |
| $F(\pi_7, \pi_8)$ | 28.584* | 29.384* |
| $F(\pi_9, \pi_{10})$ | 13.165* | 13.166* |
| $F(\pi_{11}, \pi_{12})$ | 17.729* | 17.821* |

(*) shows that the null hypothesis is rejected at the 5% significance level.

### Table 4. Seasonal Integration Test
### UK
### Exchange Rate

| Deterministic Term | Test Statistic | |
|:---:|:---:|:---:|
| | Seasonal Dummy and Trend | Seasonal Dummy |
| $q$ | 0 | 0 |
| $t(\pi_1)$ | -2.450 | -2.274 |
| $t(\pi_2)$ | -5.007* | -5.009* |
| $F(\pi_3, \pi_4)$ | 19.914* | 20.092* |
| $F(\pi_5, \pi_6)$ | 37.612* | 37.668* |
| $F(\pi_7, \pi_8)$ | 18.781* | 18.969* |
| $F(\pi_9, \pi_{10})$ | 21.128* | 21.306* |
| $F(\pi_{11}, \pi_{12})$ | 22.449* | 22.657* |

(*) shows that the null hypothesis is rejected at the 5% significance level.

### Table 5. Seasonal Integration Test
### Germany
### Price

| Deterministic Term | Test Statistic | |
|:---:|:---:|:---:|
| | Seasonal Dummy and Trend | Seasonal Dummy |
| $q$ | 0 | 0 |
| $t(\pi_1)$ | -1.773 | -1.185 |
| $t(\pi_2)$ | -5.487* | -5.486* |
| $F(\pi_3, \pi_4)$ | 28.278* | 28.516* |
| $F(\pi_5, \pi_6)$ | 26.632* | 26.741* |
| $F(\pi_7, \pi_8)$ | 20.555* | 20.733* |
| $F(\pi_9, \pi_{10})$ | 28.820* | 28.961* |
| $F(\pi_{11}, \pi_{12})$ | 32.066* | 32.458* |

(*) shows that the null hypothesis is rejected at the 5% significance level.

**Table 6. Seasonal Integration Test**
**Germany**
**Exchange Rate**

| Deterministic Term | Test Statistic | |
|:---:|:---:|:---:|
| | **Seasonal Dummy and Trend** | **Seasonal Dummy** |
| $q$ | 0 | 0 |
| $t(\pi_1)$ | -2.413 | -1.898 |
| $t(\pi_2)$ | -4.529* | -4.539* |
| $F(\pi_3,\pi_4)$ | 26.338* | 26.692* |
| $F(\pi_5,\pi_6)$ | 27.864* | 28.013* |
| $F(\pi_7,\pi_8)$ | 28.310* | 28.969* |
| $F(\pi_9,\pi_{10})$ | 29.702* | 29.944* |
| $F(\pi_{11},\pi_{12})$ | 32.700* | 33.169* |

(*) shows that the null hypothesis is rejected at the 5% significance level.


**Table 7. Seasonal Integration Test**
**Japan**
**Price**

| Deterministic Term | Test Statistic | |
|:---:|:---:|:---:|
| | **Seasonal Dummy and Trend** | **Seasonal Dummy** |
| $q$ | 2 | 2 |
| $t(\pi_1)$ | -2.626 | -3.477* |
| $t(\pi_2)$ | -3.001* | -3.023* |
| $F(\pi_3,\pi_4)$ | 15.642* | 15.807* |
| $F(\pi_5,\pi_6)$ | 13.587* | 13.775* |
| $F(\pi_7,\pi_8)$ | 37.654* | 38.005* |
| $F(\pi_9,\pi_{10})$ | 11.984* | 12.068* |
| $F(\pi_{11},\pi_{12})$ | 27.080* | 27.373* |

(*) shows that the null hypothesis is rejected at the 5% significance level.

**Table 8. Seasonal Integration Test**
**Japan**
**Exchange Rate**

| Deterministic Term | Test Statistic | |
|:---:|:---:|:---:|
| | Seasonal Dummy and Trend | Seasonal Dummy |
| $q$ | 0 | 0 |
| $t(\pi_1)$ | -2.974 | -1.262 |
| $t(\pi_2)$ | -5.961* | -5.948* |
| $F(\pi_3,\pi_4)$ | 13.722* | 14.329* |
| $F(\pi_5,\pi_6)$ | 35.249* | 35.244* |
| $F(\pi_7,\pi_8)$ | 16.147* | 17.208* |
| $F(\pi_9,\pi_{10})$ | 26.379* | 26.469* |
| $F(\pi_{11},\pi_{12})$ | 24.323* | 25.261* |

(*) shows that the null hypothesis is rejected at the 5% significance level.

# 4. SEASONAL COINTEGRATION TEST

Next, cointegration tests were carried out. Following Hylleberg et al. (1990), we first assumed the cointegrating vector of [1, -1, -1] for $[p_t, s_t, p_t^*]$ and applied the residual-based-method. Differences between our analyses and Hylleberg's analyses should be noticed. The analyses of Hylleberg et al. (1990) were carried out based on the condition that every variable had different unit roots. However, in our analysis, as Tables 2 through 8 show, all variables have only the non-seasonal unit root. Thus, we have only to test for cointegration at the zero frequency. Thus, let us consider the following cointegrating relationship:

$$(13.) \quad p_t - s_t - p_t^* = u_t,$$

where $u_t$ is a stationary process. To analyze a cointegrating relationship, consider the following regression model for this residual.

$$(14.) \quad \Delta u_t = \rho u_{t-1} + \sum_{i=1}^{q} b_i \Delta u_{t-i} + e_t$$

where $e_t$ is the residual from the regression. This cointegration test is conducted by testing the significance of this regression coefficient, $\rho$, by using the distribution table of Dickey and Fuller (1979,1981).

The results obtained are shown in Tables 9. The null hypothesis of the test is that the cointegrating vector does not exist, while the alternative hypothesis is that the cointegrating vector does exist. As Table 9 clearly shows, cointegration is rejected in every case. For example, the table shows that the value of the test statistic is -1.575 for Germany, and hence, the null hypothesis cannot be rejected. Similar results can be found for the UK and Japan. Therefore, no stable PPP existed during the period studied.

**Table 9. Seasonal Cointegration Test at Frequency 0**

| Country | $q$ | Test Statistics |
|---|---|---|
| USA and Germany | 1 | -1.575 |
| USA and UK | 1 | -0.312 |
| USA and Japan | 1 | -1.412 |

(*) shows that the null hypothesis is rejected at the 5% significance level.

## 5. CONCLUSIONS

In this paper, the stability of the PPP was empirically analyzed employing the notion of seasonal cointegration. The major results are summarized as follows. Firstly, it was found that prices and exchange rates have only non-seasonal unit roots. Furthermore, the cointegration tests revealed that cointegrating relation is rejected in every case. This fact tells us that no stable PPP existed between the United States and the other three countries (Germany, UK and Japan) during the period analyzed.

## REFERENCES

Beaulieu J. J., and J. A. Miron, (1993), "Seasonal Unit Root in Aggregate U.S. Data," *Journal of Econometrics*, Vol.55, pp. 305-328.

Cassel G., (1922), *Money and Foreign Exchange after 1914*, Constable and Co.,

Corbae D. and S. Ouliaris, (1988), "Cointegration and Tests of Purchasing Power Parity," *Review of Economics and Statistics*, Vol. 70, pp. 508-512.

Davidson R., and J. G. MacKinnon, (1993), *Estimation and Inference in Econometrics*, Oxford University Press.

Dickey D. A. and W. A. Fuller (1979), "Distribution of the Estimators for Autoregressive Time Series With a Unit Root," *Journal of the American Statistical Association,* Vol. 74, pp. 427-431.

Dickey D. A. and W. A. Fuller (1981), "Likelihood Ratio Statistics for Autoregressive Time Series with a Unit Root," *Econometrica*, Vol. 49, pp. 1057-1072.

Enders W., (1988), "ARIMA and Cointegrating Tests of Purchasing Power Parity," *Review of Economics and Statistics*, Vol. 70, pp. 504-508.

Enders W. and S. Hurn, (1994), "The Theory of Generalized Purchasing Power Parity: Tests in the Pacific Rim," *Review of International Economics*, Vol. 2, pp. 179-190.

Engle R. F., C. W. J. Granger, S. Hylleberg, and H. S. Lee, (1993), "Seasonal Cointegration: The Japanese Consumption Function," *Journal of Econometrics*, Vol. 55, pp. 275-298.

Franses P. H., and B. Hobijn, (1997), "Critical Values for Unit Root Tests in Seasonal Time Series," *Journal of Applied Statistics*, Vol. 24, pp. 25-47.

Ghysels E., and P. Perron, (1993), "The Effects of Seasonal Adjustment Filters on Tests for a Unit Root," *Journal of Econometrics,* Vol. 55, pp. 57-98.

Hamilton J. D., (1994), *Time Series Analysis*, Princeton University Press.

Hylleberg S., R. F. Engle, C.W. J. Granger, and B. S. Yoo, (1990), "Seasonal Integration and Cointegration," *Journal of Econometrics,* Vol. 44, pp. 215-238.

Hylleberg S., C. Jorgensen, and N. K. Sorensen, (1993), "Seasonality in Macro-economic Time Series," *Empirical Economics*, Vol. 18, pp. 321-335.

Schwarz G., (1978), "Estimating the Dimension of a Model," *The Annals of Statistics*, Vol. 6, pp. 461-464.

Tokihisa A. and S. Hamori, (2001), "Seasonal Integration for Daily Data," *Econometric Reviews,* Vol. 20, pp. 187-200.

# Chapter 6

# ANALYZING AND BUILDING NATIONAL POLITICITY IN A MULTILATERAL SETTING: REGIONAL SECURITY FOR THE PACIFIC CENTURY

*Laure Paquette*[*]

Rutgers University

I have proposed elsewhere a method and a model for explaining and predicting policy-making by governments, based on how values influenced policy. That earlier book also produced a model that explained why some governments would work well together and why some do not. The present chapter presents the end result of a series of case studies that show this second hypothesis about values influencing strategy or policy to be again valid, a special sub-application of that theory. This time, however, it is about the congruence of those policies which influence the interactions between governments, sometimes to the extent of having a regional influence. The last case, strategy used by international organizations with member and non-member states, is the subject of later investigation. This chapter also presents the three main applications of the theories.

As case studies I chose a group of countries whose relations are full of contradictions and a region but also favored with phenomenal recent economic potential yet plagued by flashpoints: North East Asia, where the major actors are Japan, China and North and South Korea plus US and Russia traditionally known as the 2 + 4.

To the 2 + 4 I add Taiwan -- and the US's Asia policy during the first Clinton administration from as early as 1992 until about 1995. The Russian Republic has been due to its early decisions although the domestic problems there are such that East Asia is no longer the priority it was in the early years of the Republic. Some countries share

---

[*] Visiting Research Professor at Centre for American Women and Politics, Rutgers University, and Associate Professor Of Political Science, Lakehead University, Thunder Bay, Canada. www.laure.paquette.com; laure.paquette@lakeheadu.ca.

some cultural foundations, like Confucianism, but manage to look totally different: the People's Republic of China, whose austerity until the Deng reforms was legendary, and Japan, with its startlingly superficial Westernization, all bright neon and loud noises. At times, as much as 1000 years of history comes into play -- Japan, Korea and China have all colonized each other. And yet, there are some strange bedfellows: the last Stalinist regime on earth, North Korea, and the US, the leader of the free world. All of these contradictions provide ample opportunity to prove any model wrong. But it also has one significant advantage: research about Asia is no longer about getting more information... it is about understanding better what we already know.[1]

The method and model used to analyze these countries dictates the structure of this book. Each country study included a determination of the independent and dependent variables, values and policy respectively. As the country studies accumulate, it becomes possible to examine how the policies interact and to predict how the bilateral relations will develop. This provides a backdrop against which it then becomes possible to propose a new national policy on security, for three situations: one set of bilateral relations, in this case inter-Korean relations; a policy on security for one country, in this case for Japan; and some recommendations for the region as a whole, suitable for consideration by the outsiders, the US and Russia.

Since the relationship between values and strategy has already been established, the various case studies focus only on the independent and dependent variables. The identification of the various policies proved to be the most challenging tasks, requiring primary interviews as well as content analysis of documents. The method is the same in each case: the analysis of government decision-making using a combination of document analysis and interviews. Documents are from official sources (research bureaus within the ministries of defense, of foreign affairs, of national defense colleges and any government research institutes), political sources (partisan thinkers or researchers, political parties' policy wing, politicians), and academic sources. Interviewees are influential decision- and policy-makers: in the past they have included public officials, members of the national legislature, aides to Cabinet ministers, military, and academic experts. Documents analyzed also include communiqués, media releases, treaties, memoranda of understanding, minutes of debates on related issues. (Japan, South Korea and Taiwan provide extensive translations into English. Interviews were conducted through interpreters where necessary.) This multilateral analysis looks not only at the decision-making about national security, but also at the core values of each country, which has a profound influence on its future. The obstacle to direct quotations is the ticklishness of discussing security matters with influential people. Every single interviewee refused to be quoted by name, 95% refused to be quoted anonymously, and 40% declined to be thanked by name in the general acknowledgment section! These numbers are not unusual for this area, but it certainly explains why scholars has quoted individuals so seldom, and relied on official printed sources only. The next section explains how each country was analyzed.

---

[1] Among the studies linking social characteristics and foreign policy are Tadashi Aruga, "Foreign Policy and Social Change: Japan and the United States," *Tocqueville Review* 16:2 (1995), 79-97.

# THE FRAMEWORK

At the heart of the framework is the relationship between each country's culture and its action. The relationship between culture and society is one of the oldest problems in social science, and "[c]ritics of international security studies have often suggested that [such] questions are neglected by the field."[2] Specifically, this framework looks at the values of the various states involved and relates it to the overall posture that country takes in the region or the world. Once that relationship is established, then the interactions of that state with its own population, other organizations like the UN and other states can be better understood. The distinction between international political economy and security studies now being more academic than practical, those interactions are examined in terms of the most salient political, economic and military events within a given time frame.[3] The framework is comprehensive enough to provide guidance for all of us who "Now that walls of our [Cold War] prison have suddenly collapsed ...emerge, bewildered, into a new and unfamiliar world."[4] It was developed for the purpose of determining the overall posture, known more technically as the national strategy, of a state in conditions of high uncertainty, such as the end of the Cold War.

The new general theory of strategy on which this study is based is tested by studying the strategic decisions of states. The theory focuses on the formal and informal aspects of state policy- and decision-making, which are not well understood. It takes political and cultural factors (or national values), as the independent variable which is linked to the posture of states in the international system (policy or national strategy). These two variables are linked by three processes: cognition, appreciation and evaluation. Through **cognition**, states gather raw information. The state then uses standards inspired by national values as well as experience to judge whether any particular bit of information is accurate at all, whether it is relevant to a particular situation, and how urgent it is. As information available grows and tasks become more complicated, cognitive standards become more and more important. National values also shape the institutions that a state creates to achieve its goals and carry out its functions. **Appreciation** is the process which attempts to capture the non-rational factors in decision-making. A preference is a state's inclination or bias when it comes to a particular decision, or decisions in a particular area. If the process of decision-making respects a state's preferences and tastes, nothing happens. If it does not, then the state may find it difficult to implement the decision. A preference is a state's inclination or bias when it comes to a particular decision, or

---

[2] Joseph Nye and Sean Lynn-Jones, "International Security Studies:  A Report of a Conference on the State of the Field," *International Security* 12:4 (Spring 1988), 5-27, 17; Robert E. Osgood,  *Ideals and Self-Interest in America's Foreign Relations? The Great Transformation of the Twentieth Century* (Chicago: University of Chicago Press, 1953), i; the other reference is to:  Kenichi Ohmae, *The Mind of the Strategist* (New York:  Penguin, 1982); Kenneth J. Arrow, "Values and Collective Decision-Making," chapter in *Philosophy and Economic Theory*, Frank Hahn and Martin Hollis, eds.  (Oxford:  Oxford University Press, 1979), 110-1.

[3] Jonathan Krishner, 'Political Economy in Security Studies After the Cold War," *Review of International Political Economy* 5:1 (Spring 1998), 64-91.

[4] Sir Michael Howard, "The Remaking of Europe", *Survival* XXXII: 2, 95-106, 99.

decisions in a particular area. By making repeated observations of state decisions, it is possible for an analyst to identify the set of priorities from which the decision-makers are working. Evaluation is the process by which the state sets objectives. Sub-decisions in the process of considering options, such as the winnowing down of possible options and the selection of options to be considered in more detail, are made on the basis of appreciative standards. It is significant that experience is a factor in the drawing of conclusions, which is an operation carried out by **evaluation**. Experience plays more or less the same role in evaluation as perceptions do in cognition. The state then either stores the information, modifies its own grid or takes the decision to move on to the next step. Learning is a modification of a behavioral tendency by experience. But there are also obstacles to learning. A number of them have been identified, including a complex and constantly changing international environment, and the limitations of human beings as processors of information. The theory proposed here suggests that learning contributes endogenous information to the decision-making process. This information is internally consistent only to the extent that the state's population is itself consistent. It contributes to the creation of taste in the same way that processing information contributed to learning, i.e. incrementally. Learning also builds reflex responses. The conclusions drawn from various individual experiences accumulate.

The process of analysis can be broken into six steps. The first involves identifying a sea-change in policy, is a reliable indication of the last time a new strategy was introduced. Strategies change relatively rarely, and such a major shift is often accompanied by major social upheavals. Russia's, for instance, was easy to identify following the disintegration of the former USSR and the birth of the new Russian federation. This takes into account that security is a policy objective 'like no other.'[5]

The second step involves identifying new tactics, values and national strategy. Tactics are the most obvious manifestations of a new strategy. Tactics are the means at a state's disposal. This stage of the analysis looks for changes in the economic, military, diplomatic, and political sectors, and they also usually provide the material for identifying the values.

Values are a key factor in determining the long-term compatibility of strategies, since my own previous research shows that they underpin the entire national strategy. The identification of values also helps narrow the range of possibilities that must be considered. For the purposes of this analysis, national values are defined as the accepted standards of historical or ideological origin as well as the national heritage cherished by the population as a whole. This analysis is best served by a classification adapted from Talcott Parsons' typology of social values: (1) self-orientation versus collectivity-orientation; and (2) materialism versus non-materialism.[6]

National strategy is defined as the comprehensive direction of all the elements of national power to attain national objectives, and to support and pursue the general goals

---

[5] David Baldwin, "the Concept of Security," *Review of International Studies* 23:1 (January 1997), 5-26, 5.

[6] Talcott Parsons' classification in R.F. Bales, Edward Shils and Talcott Parsons, Working Papers in the Theory of Action (Glencoe: Free Press, 1953), passim; Michael Sullivan, Measuring Global Values (New York: Greenwood, s.d.), passim.

provided by a nation's leaders. It can be identified by answering three questions. (1) Is a Particular State Using Strategy? The trick here is to tell a strategy apart from a plan, policy or program. Plans, policies and programs organize means to an end as much as a strategy does. But strategy is both an idea and an action, while plans, policies and programs are not. A state using strategy is going to use a core idea to orchestrate its actions in a variety of fields. The core idea can be hard to identify, unless the state is suing something obvious, like slogans or strong images used for the public. A state using plans, policies and programs does not rely on slogans or strong images. (2) Is the State Using a National Strategy? A strategy is national when it uses a broad spectrum of the means available to the state, and tries to achieve objectives important to the whole rather than to parts.[7] In other words, the strategy must cut across several areas of state behavior: economic, political, cultural, military, etc. (3) What Strategy Is the State Using? It is not easy to pick out the exact strategy a state is using from so many possibilities. The best way to proceed is to start by reducing the number of possibilities one has to consider, i.e. by identifying the type of strategy.

André Beaufre's typology of strategy classifies them according to their nature: direct strategy of action, direct strategy of persuasion, indirect strategy of action, indirect strategy of persuasion. The difference between strategy of action and strategy of persuasion is straightforward: the first involves physical engagement of the state's material resources, while the second involves threats, discourse, posturing -- all means and actions that require non-material resources. The difference between a direct strategy and an indirect one is not quite so obvious: a direct strategy is one that changes the opponent's direction or momentum itself; an indirect strategy changes the opponent's direction using an intermediary. Once the type of strategy is identified, then only those possibilities need be considered. The next step is to identify the components of strategy, each by its own preferred source of information: (1) goal, by analysis of official statements;[8] (2) means or tactics, by direct observation; (3) style, by secondary analysis; and (4) core idea, by analysis of official statements, where possible.[9]

The review of the declaratory policy or political rhetoric (official documents, speeches, debates in the legislatures, etc.) in order to identify the goals of the national strategy. Possibly it is explicit in the declaratory policy of the state. If not the strategy can be identified by its characteristics. Typically, a national strategy covers several sectors. It is also true that the best strategies are not made public or even explicit in sources available to the scholar. Also, some states like Canada or South Korea in the 1990s, have no particular strategy. They simply drift, rely on incremental policy- or decision-making, or manage crises as they arise.

---

[7] Ray S. Cline, World Power Trends and U.S. Foreign Policy for the 1980s (Boulder: Westview Press, 1980), 2.

[8] Although he calls it aims; F.B. Ali, "The Principles of War", Journal of the Royal United Services Institution for Defense Studies 108 (May 1963), 159-165.

[9] "The entirety of traditional practices and habits of thinking which, in a society, governs the organization and the use of the military forces in the pursuit of political objectives." Author's translation, as quoted by Bruno Colson, "La culture stratégique américaine", Stratégique 8 (1988), 15-82, 33.

Values interact, strategies interact, and components of strategy interact. Those interactions can be neutral, identical, synergistic, cooperative, complementary, competitive or antithetical (see Table 1.1, Possibilities of Strategic Interactions). Those interactions can also occur in varying degrees of intensity.

Compatibility exists when the two strategies are either identical, neutral, cooperative, complementary or synergistic at the global and the component level. Some components' interactions are more important than others, just as compatibility of certain components is essential to the compatible interactions of strategies. For instance, if the style is not compatible, it is harder for strategies to be synergistic because it is harder for them to communicate with each other. Misunderstandings occur more easily, but still it is possible for the strategic goals to be attained since each strategy is implemented by a different population. If the values are incompatible, however, then relations between states are quite likely to be conflictual. It will also be more difficult to mobilize the population, in the case of liberal democracies at least, to accomplish the strategy.

Any of the components of strategy (goals, tactics, styles, core ideas) can interact, and any of these interactions can range among the possibilities outlined above. It is easy to imagine complementary interactions if one country's goals are direct and the other indirect, if one country's tactics are material and the other non-material, etc. For other components, like the core idea, the components are so central or so basic to the nature of the strategy that any significant positive interaction necessitates the strategies being mutually known and mutually understood. Problems arise when they are not. The type of interaction may change if the strategy of one state changes. The type of interaction may also change if any of the components of the strategy change.

Certain components change less frequently than others: values do not change frequently, for instance, but tactics can and do. The duration of various types of interactions, therefore, depends on the durability of the strategic components (see Table 1.2, Compatibility in the Short and Long-Term). Long-term compatibility means that there will be a lasting foundation for good relations.

The case studies are each limited over time, as is obviously necessary with an undertaking of this extent. The most significant event that occurred that is not examined in detail is the Asian currency crisis. As most experts since have agreed, the countries have by the time of this writing largely recovered, and the security relations in East Asia have been largely unchanged.[10]

---

[10] K. Y. Park and W. H. Lee, "The Financial Crisis of 1997-1998 and its Impact on Security Relations in East Asia," *Asian Perspective* 23:3 (1999), 129-151. See also on the conservative effect of the Asian flu, Graeme Cheeseman, "Asian-Pacific Security Discourse in the Wake of the Asian Economic Crisis," *Pacific Review* 12:3 (1999), 333-356.

## Table 1: Possibilities for Strategic Interactions

| Possibility | Description | Example |
|---|---|---|
| neutrality | strategies do not affect each other | two countries completely isolated from each other |
| identity | 2 strategies are identical | bloc or alliance strategy |
| synergy | when one national strategy reinforces the other | Franco-German proposal for joint brigade as nucleus for new EC armed forces |
| cooperation | deliberate, conscious common strategy addressing mutual concern | Canada-US joint surveillance of Far North |
| complementarity | s address different concerns but in with each other | Japan and US position on DPRK nuclear issue |
| antithesis | two strategies in conflict | PRC and Taiwan |

## Table 2: Compatibility in the Short and Long-Term

| Component | Duration of Incompatibility |
|---|---|
| strategy | long |
| values | long |
| core idea | medium |
| goals | short |

## MULTIPLE USES OF THE FRAMEWORK

The framework of analysis proposed allows us to perform three types of tasks over and above the analysis (explanation and prediction) itself. It proposes what a particular country's strategy could be. It proposes how to increase the compatibility between two states. And it proposes how to deal with potential conflict at a regional level. This next section provides examples of each of those possibilities: it proposes a strategy for Japan; it proposes how to increase stability on the Korean Peninsula; and it proposes how to defuse potential conflict in the region. Finally, it presents a summary of national strategies and strategic interactions in East Asia.

flu, Graeme Cheeseman, "Asian-Pacific Security Discourse in the Wake of the Asian Economic Crisis," *Pacific Review* 12:3 (1999), 333-356.

## Proposal for Japan

Japan has not fundamentally altered its position in the international society of states since the end of the Cold War. It is now the only major player in the Northeast Pacific not to have done so. The task is increasingly urgent because of the nature and the number of challenges facing Japan both domestically and internationally.

Japan should carefully cast itself in the role of key interlocutor in East Asia, i.e. play the part of the honest broker, the altruistic facilitator and, should it ever become necessary, the mediator of the region.[11] Such a role has practical implications in several areas: Japan's quest for a more normal status; the concentration of its diplomatic efforts on certain key issues; its relationship with its principal ally, the US; and its relations with other countries.

There has been a considerable amount of discussion in recent years about Japan acquiring a more normal status in international affairs. Most agree that a more normal status means a greater role for Japan on the international stage, commensurate with its actual importance. Most include some change in the role for the JSDF as well. This greater role for the military is thought necessary for Japan to share the burden of its own defense, but also the risk to the lives of its people. Usually those risks are taken by military personnel in combat positions, and that is a problem for Japan. However, risks are increasingly taken by humanitarian workers and support staff. It is possible Japan could in future play a role more commensurate with its international importance, without substantially altering the role of its armed forces. By not taking a leading role, Japan can avoid worrying other states in the region who have been attacked, occupied or colonized by it in the past. Rather, it could opt for quiet diplomacy on matters of security, development or arms control. Becoming the key interlocutor means investing in initiatives which will not necessarily produce immediate results or great returns for Japan. It means being altruistic, displaying the same generosity the victors showed the vanquished after World War II, rather than exacting reparations after World War I. In hindsight, the US' motives are not as altruistic as they may have seemed, but generosity might still be a better option than self-interest. A Japan working in favor of arms control, disarmament, multilateral dialogues, putting the interests of peace in the region above its own would be a position commensurate with its espoused convictions. A permanent seat on the Security Council of the United Nations, with Japan systematically voting against aggression, would be symbolically significant. In its altruism, Japan should stay realistic, and not take on commitments that exceed its willingness or its ability to pay.

Adopting a new strategy will mean a re-focusing of the tactics Japan has adopted. It would mean concentrating efforts on issues of critical importance. The engagement of China, for instance, is critical to the future stability and order of the region. Although the death of Deng may not result in any major change in the PRC's economic reforms, the

---

[11] Japan hosted the South Pacific Forum on October 1, 1997, despite not being a member of the SPF, reportedly in order to increase its supporters for a permanent seat in the United Nations Security Council. "South Pacific Forum (SPF) to be Held in Tokyo For First Time," *Yomiuri Shimbun* evening edition, March 3, 1997, 1.

new government might mishandle any number of issues: Hong Kong, the ROC, the income gap between cities and villages, and the minorities. This could in turn affect the international community.[12] Becoming the key interlocutor would also mean setting aside other issues, where the chances of success are not great enough. The problem with seeking a permanent seat on the Security Council, for instance, is that the chances of reform of that revered institution are actually quite low. Becoming the key interlocutor would also mean regularizing and routinizing contacts with many other nations, not just the US.

Becoming key interlocutor will also mean re-examining the place of each bilateral relationship in the constellation of Japan's foreign policy. Japan knows the dangers of having too strong a single political leader emerge, and has guarded against it. Japan is aware of the dangers of having too strong an armed force, under weak civilian control, and it has guarded against it. Is Japan aware of the dangers of too dominant an ally in its foreign policy? Of being too closely identified with another country's positions? Of having too dependent a foreign policy, an intelligence capability? Of having a divergence of interest? Japan is an overtly pacifist country closely allied to the greatest military power in the world. Perhaps the time has come to broaden the scope of its relations with the rest of the world.

However, it is important not to overstate the case. The US-Japan Treaty should not be abrogated, nor the alliance set aside. That would be throwing out the baby with the bath water. No country can fight and win a war alone. No country should ignore the US when it shapes its foreign policy. But the adoption of a new role for Japan might mean broadening the focus of its international relations. It means examining whether it needs to develop a greater independent capacity for analysis. It might look to the European Union, it might look to Canada.[13]

There two sets of reasons why Japan should play this role. The first reasons have to do with Japan's international environment – there are Japan's international imperative. The second set of reasons have to do with Japan's domestic situation. Even from a brief discussion of these broad issues, Japan emerges as the only nation which can play the interlocutor's role.

The theory outlined above predicts that China will act out its international role in very specific ways. Following Deng's death in 1997, President Jiang Zemin actively consolidated his power by courting the army. Because he was not as powerful as Deng was, and Deng was not as powerful as Mao, an oligarchy will emerge, with Jiang ruling in close contact with Premier Li Peng and economic czar Zhu Rongji. If an oligarchy does not emerge, neither hardliners nor reformers would dominate until the gerontocracy passed out of power. Policies would come from compromise, which means patchwork decisions, especially in economics.

The theory also predicts that China will play a greater role in international affairs. It will assert itself, although not enough to incur international opprobrium. It will not settle

---

[12] "How Should We Deal with Post-Deng China," *Yomiuri Shimbun* (Tokyo), February 21, 1997, 3.

[13] Dong-Ik Shin and Gerald Segal, "Getting Serious About Asia-Europe Security Cooperation," *Survival* 39:1 (Spring 1997), 138-155, 153.

any territorial questions *per se*, but it will reach pragmatic working understandings about issues like hijacking or fishing rights. It will turn a conveniently deaf ear to US criticism about human rights. It will reduce but modernize its armed forces, both in high technology and in training.

The outlook for political reform is not good in the near-term: hamburgers will not mean freedom.[14] By Western standards, the leadership will be heavy-handed in dealing with: (i) increasing ethnic conflict, as the harsh crackdown in Western China (Yining) in late February 1997 shows; (ii) requests for freedom of expression, which will continue to be made and ignored; and (iii) 'economic crimes' i.e. fraud and corruption, and increasing social disparities.[15] These social disparities will be the main consequence of the government's difficulties in managing the economy and its own provinces and local governments. The economy will slow down when the legal, social and physical infrastructure for larger businesses proves inadequate. Policies designed to regulate or guide the economy will be hit-and-miss in both implementation and effect.

Taiwan is a nation of very real consequence but almost without diplomatic recognition. It cannot engage China alone. It will continue its so-called quest for independence. It will no longer pretend either that it really represents the entire Chinese people, or that it plans to re-conquer the mainland. As Hong Kong is integrated into China, Taiwan and Macao are now the only unrecovered territories. Taiwan's foreign policy will continue to be dollar diplomacy. Economics might be its saving grace, but its unique position as interlocutor and interpreter of mainland China will be its greatest asset.

Implicated in the Hanbo Steel loan scandal, Kim Young Sam became a lame-duck president. Barred by law from seeking a second term, he left the presidency in 1997. He was unable to play king-maker as he had hoped. Kim Dae Jung came to command enough support at the time of this writing to win the next presidential election. Korea's economy will continue to be uncomfortably sandwiched between the fully industrialized West and the newly industrialized Southeast. South Korea's policy of engaging North Korea has been slightly too aggressive to be effective. It has no other choice but to rely on the mediating presence of the US. Eventually, US-DPRK relations will decline, so the ROK should focus on the development of a more appropriate policy.

North Korea will have neither a soft nor a hard landing. Its period of transition will be lengthy. In the next two or three years, the generational split in the leadership will intensify, as Kim Jong Il struggles with the gerontocracy. Shortages of food and fuel near the disaster mark, with the population at risk of disturbingly common malnutrition. With the slow pace of economic reforms, it is possible that the government will slide into the habit of aid.

The time required for the US to deploy troops in a crisis will continue to rise slowly. Force levels in Asia-Pacific and defense spending in general are under constant scrutiny, so the US is less effective as a psychological deterrent. As Japan's economy matures,

---

[14] Stefano Cingolani, "Commentary," *Corriere della Sera* (Rome), February 21, 1997, 2.

[15] Patrick E. Tyler, "Terrorist Bombs Strike China's West," *International Herald Tribune* (Tokyo), February 27, 1997, 1 and 6.

demographics shift, and the domestic market shrinks, it may also become less important to the US.

Boris Yeltsin was fond of saying that Russia is as Asian as it is European, but he was never convincing.[16] Plainly, even under Putin, Russia's attentions are elsewhere. East Asia will rise again on Russia's foreign policy agenda at some point, once Russians realize how interdependent the international economy is, and how important international trade is to economic expansion. This can only happen once the government has ironed out ethnic conflict in the republics, and that may take as much as a decade, if not longer.

Japan does not enjoy the unmixed trust of other nations in the region. Its most recent history as a liberal democratic nation constitutionally incapable of engaging in war has not been enough to entirely reassure its neighbors. But Asian countries have pragmatism in common. They will fear a new threat more than an old enemy. The alliance with the US guarantees not just Japan's security, it also guarantees Japan's restraint.

The only alternative to Japan being the key interlocutor regionally is to become the key interlocutor extra-regionally. There are two problems with this alternative. First, Japan has been heavily involved in aid and humanitarian pursuits extra-regionally since world War II. If that has failed to restore its neighbors' trust, will more of the same make any difference? Second, becoming interlocutor is more difficult outside the region than in East Asia. Japan is limited by the great consideration it shows for the US positions on various issues. It hesitated to advocate differing positions in the past, and advocating humanitarian, altruistic positions will be no easier. Finally, Japan is not as experienced or knowledgeable about extra-regional conflicts like the Middle East, parts of Africa or Latin America. Those conflicts are particularly difficult to resolve. Japan ought to act where it has some common history, however unhappy.

The proposed role of Japan as key interlocutor is also suited to Japan's demographics and economic circumstances. The peak of the population is in sight. That means a shrinking tax base for the government, at a time when it will be facing greater demands on the welfare state, the health care system and the social infrastructure. It may also mean a greater conservatism, as politicians respond to an ageing and more conservative voting base. Willingness to commit to long-term objectives in foreign policy may decrease. It will also mean shifts in the structure of the domestic market, away from consumer goods and towards services.

At the same time, Japan's economy is maturing. A mature economy usually means some upheavals, as society questions its goals and aspirations.[17] Much of Japan's human capital has been invested in the pursuit of affluence. Social tensions will arise from groups whose sacrifices have not necessarily been rewarded: women and young people.

---

[16] In March 1997, the Russian First Vice Premier excused himself from attending the second session of the bilateral intergovernmental committee on trade, economic, scientific and technological cooperation in Tokyo. He told the head of the Japanese delegation, Japan's Foreign Minister, that he could not leave Russia due to grave problems in the social sphere. He then flew to Lausanne to lobby for St Petersburg's bid to host the Olympics. (Sergey Agafonov, "A Diplomatic Rudeness," *Izvestia* (Moscow), March 7, 1997, p. 1)

[17] Research Institute on Peace and Security, *Asian Security 1996-97* (London: Brassey's, 1997), 104.

In a nutshell, then, China is the problem and no one but Japan can engage it properly. Taiwan cannot engage it, Russia will not, South Korea is busy with North Korea, North Korea is busy with its own problems, and the US-PRC relationship is not good.

**Table 3: A Proposed Strategy for Japan**

| Goal | have Japan play a role commensurate with its importance as a nation, consonant with the aspirations of its population |
|---|---|
| Strategy | become the interlocutor of East Asia |
| Core Idea | Japan as Key Interlocutor |
| Tactics | quest for normal status; broadening of bilateral relations beyond the US; focusing on issues of strategic importance; quiet diplomacy |
| Style | discrete, behind-the-scenes |

## A Proposal for the Korean Peninsula

Good inter-Korean relations is one of the goals of the ROK. There are three suggestions relevant to that goal.

First, the ROK should look carefully at which major powers can help move its relations forward. Direct inter-Korean negotiations are fraught, although improving. Given the ROK's strategic disadvantage, working indirectly through other countries' good relations will be more productive. The ROK has a choice between the US and China. The US has recently negotiated successfully with the DPRK, and it has pursued a strategy of engagement throughout the mid-1990s. The long-term prospects for the relationship are not good since neither strategies and nor values are compatible. China is the long-standing ally of North Korea. Hardliners in Beijing value relations with Pyongyang. Relations have been strained by China's opening of relations with South Korea, but not to the breaking point. China's trade with North Korea has fallen off sharply, since Beijing no longer extends credit to Pyongyang, but again relations were not strained to the breaking point. It even survived the crisis brought about by the 1997 defection of a high-level party member.[18]

Second, the ROK should await for economic reforms in North Korea to change its values. The effects of the market system on values and political systems are well-known. Eventually, economic reforms lead to political reforms. It is not in South Korea's interest to absorb North Korea too quickly.The ROC on Taiwan and the DPRK do not figure prominently on each other's foreign policy agenda, but the ROC might be an unexpected source of help. Both the ROC and the DPRK have plenty of experience at being international pariahs. The ROC needs substantive relations with other countries, and it is

---

[18] The defection of Hwang Jang-yop in February 1997, widely reported, including in the *International Herald Tribune* of February 14, 1997, p. 1 and 12 ("Defector Has China Torn Between Two Koreas").

prepared to invest to get them. The DPRK needs investment, and it is untroubled by controversy DPRK-China relations are resilient, so further rapprochement between the two may pay some unexpected dividends.

Finally, the ROK should give the North a rest from engagement. The ROK has its own crowded political agenda. It has recently democratized. Its economy is sandwiched between the fully industrialized and mature economies of Japan and the West, and the tigers of Southeast Asia. The South Korean leadership has to contend with widespread domestic corruption. The public is concerned about safety after a series of deadly disasters throughout the 1990s, including the spectacular collapse of a department store in 1995. Moreover, the South is hardly disinterested in its dealings with the North. Pyongyang sees South Korea's efforts at engagement as rough wooing. Unfortunately, there is considerable domestic pressure against laissez-faire in South Korea. Reports of recent hardship in the North is difficult for relatives, but the strong focus on North Korea has been constant through decades of authoritarianism. Domestic concerns have manifested themselves in South Korean elections. Ironically, the recent democratization has actually reduced the leadership's room to manoeuver. In any event, inter-Korean relations will not improve overnight -- public opinion may yet evolve in a direction more favorable to some sort of change.

## Table 4: Verified Hypotheses

| Prediction | Evidence |
|---|---|
| US military presence necessary until reunification | diminishes mutual perception of threat |
| DPRK tactics are of very gradual economic reform, no political reform | analysts advocate the Chinese model of reform as being appropriate |
| Japan dominated by bureaucratic politics | direct observations of their power, confirmed by numerous other observers |
| PRC must control dissident closely | recent human rights issue record, US retreat on human rights issue |
| PRC-DPRK compatible | close allies, PRC serving as model for DPRK |
| distance to be bridged greater since democratic reforms in ROK | commented on by a number of ROK scholars; recent deterioration of ROK-DPRK relations after liberal democratic reforms took greater hold in ROK |
| DPRK will best US in negotiating | Geneva framework agreement and Light Water Reactor (LWR) agreement<br>ROK's criticism of US weakness |
| DPRK-ROK will have trouble negotiating | negotiations over rice, LWR, Red Cross have been rocky |
| DPRK can mobilize population easily | reaction to Kim Il Sung's death, social quiescence despite food shortages |
| engagement threatening | DPRK reaction likely, so caution indicated |
| strategic environment less favorable to ROK | increased security burden, nuclear development on DPRK |
| prospects for reunification are not good in either the near or the medium term | consensus among majority of analysts |
| reunification if clearly not on the cards | opinion of moderate and left-leaning scholars |
| Nordpolitik will make DPRK react | caused strong, i.e. nuclearist, reaction in DPRK |

## Proposal for a Regional Strategy

The national strategies of the 2+4 are summarized in Table 9.4, A Strategy for East Asia. From the foregoing analysis, it is clear that China must be engaged as it struggles with its domestic problems and emerges form isolation to play a more important regional role. It is also clear that pragmatism is what all the East Asian nations share, strategically.

### Table 5: A Strategy for East Asia

| Goal | engage China |
|---|---|
| Strategy | develop a web of relations on various levels between China and its neighbors |
| Core Idea | creating a counterweight to China |
| Tactics | use US presence as a damper, quiet diplomacy, pursuit of affluence, mutual reassurance, US as stopgap pacifier, protection of strategically sensitive points; nation-specific tactics |
| Style | pragmatism |

There are three potential flash points: Korea, the Taiwan Straights and the South China Sea. Deliberate conflict is still a slight possibility in Korea. North Korea might in desperation launch a military attack against the south. Because North Korea would quickly exhaust its slender reserves of fuel and food, there is no potential for a long, drawn-out war. The conflict would probably end before the US had time to mobilize its extra-territorial troops fully. The obvious solution meanwhile is for North Korea to receive economic aid, to stave off that desperation. The second flash point is the Straits of Taiwan. Shows of force by the PRC, Taiwan or the US periodically occur for political reasons, and there is always a chance of an accidental escalation into actual conflict. Although in most cases cooler tempers would prevail, it is possible to imagine scenarios the PRC and Taiwan would exchange fire, and the US would come to Taiwan's aid, making the situation much more serious. A third flash point would be another accidental escalation in the South China Sea. Overall the region is safe, although it is worth watching trends and strategic pressure points. Defense spending rose throughout the 1990s. Arms procurement trends also indicate the overall state of affairs. Some countries may make a bid for regional leadership.

Power among the major players in East Asia is sure to equalize in the next decade. China will lurch along, its economy slightly beyond the control of its leadership. Russia's relative disinterest in the region will eventually end. The psychological effectiveness of the US's deterring presence will continue to decline slowly, even though it is sure to come through in a pinch. In the first State of the Union address of his second Administration, Clinton stated clearly how high a priority Asia had on his foreign policy agenda. Every time the U.S. reviews its commitments abroad, its presence in the Pacific will come under scrutiny. If China, Russia and the U.S. do not compete for influence in the region within a decade or so, then China will simply assert itself more and more. Any nation wishing to gain influence in the region will therefore quickly focus on its most sensitive points.

This is a region of large islands and small seas. The sea-lanes of communication are the lifeblood of both Northeast and Southeast Asia. The SLOCs are not only strategic for commerce. When the Cabinet Security Office reviewed Japan's policy on emergency measures it became concerned about the security of the sea lanes when it came to the protection of citizens overseas, contingencies for a mass of refugees, and the patrol of important off-shore facilities.

The first move of any country faced with these prospects is going to be to increase its own naval capabilities if possible. Maritime power rose throughout the 1990s, and there are limits to how much spending can be attributed to modernization. Only Japan's slight decrease on the number of ships stands outside the regional trend. One option is to let the competition take place, hoping that the strain and expense of competition will weaken the countries involved. This type of attrition presents too many risks to be desirable. Attrition take time, and throughout flash points remain. Allowing not-unfettered competition in the region is not in anyone's best interest, especially if Russia, China and the US were relatively equal in resources committed to the area.

This prospect is therefore rather somber. But as in any evolving situation, there are also real opportunities.

The goal of the proposed strategy is to engage China, by involving it in a web of relations on various levels and in various areas. The core idea is to balance out China's growing importance, rather than creating bargaining chips, as the US did in the 1990s. Among the tactics to be considered are: using the US presence as a damper in situations of rising tensions; using quiet diplomacy on a variety of issues; pursuing affluence among all nations; promoting measures which result in mutual reassurance; and protecting the strategically sensitive points. Each nation would pursue its own national interests as well, using tactics that would be nation-specific. The overall style proposed would be pragmatism.

For such a strategy to be put in place, each nation would pursue its own interests but approach relations with other states in the region to balance out the preponderance of China and every opportunity to engage it as well. Overtly the various national leadership would continue to look to the US as the sole remaining superpower. Behind the scenes, extensive diplomacy would be conducted, leading without seeming to lead, being strong without seeming to be strong, involving without seeming to imprison r limit. It would require resolve and finesse.

In the late 1990s, it was still true that China was neither a threat nor a problem: it is a worry because, uninvolved, it has the potential to create many problems. China, like other nations, is modernizing its armed forces and shifting away from counterinsurgency to the defense of national sovereignty. To keep its ambitions and its assertiveness in check, China must be treated both with respect and generosity. The strategy proposed here has the added advantage of paving the way for East Asia to deal with other blocks of nations, the European Union and members of the North American Free Trade Agreement.

**Table 6: National Strategies of the 2+4**

| Component | ROK | DPRK | US | PRC | ROC on Taiwan | Russia | Japan |
|---|---|---|---|---|---|---|---|
| Values | materialism, individualism | non-materialism, collectivism | materialism, individualism | materialism, collectivism | materialism, individualism | materialism, individualism | materialism, collectivism |
| Strategy | -- (drift) | high-stakes gambling | enlargement of democracy and market system | pragmatism | pragmatic diplomacy | step in the USSR's shoes and exploit the position | regain self-respect via economic performance |
| Core Idea | -- | -- | from containment to enlargement | "it doesn't matter if it is a black cat or a white cat, so long as the cat gets the mouse" | pragmatism, vision, flexibility | -- | beating the US at its own game |
| Goals | continued economic growth, more domestic reform, eventual integration with DPRK | regime survival | reducing costs of being world leader | regime survival | develop substantive relations with other countries | improved economy | become an economic power |
| Tactics | economic opening to international competition; deterrence, Nordpolitik and engagement of DPRK; alliance with US | Juche; extremely gradual economic reform; no political reform; nuclearization as bargaining chip | shifting responsibility for international security; using political clout to improve economic position | gradual economic reform; maintain domestic political status quo | diplomacy based on economics, strong ties to the US, strategic investment in Southwest of PRC | domestic reforms; foreign relations based on actual or potential economic contributions | priority to economy; weak political leadership; emasculated military |
| Style | new liberal democratic | unpredictability; piecemeal decision-making | weak, indecisive | personalized politics | focused, systematic, relentless | rhetoric | restrained rhetoric, conservative |

# Chapter 7

# Chinese State–Owned Enterprises: A Case of Government Failure?

## *A.S. Bhalla*
Sidney Sussex College, University of Cambridge

In this paper we argue that the Chinese state-owned enterprises (SOEs) represent a case of government failure at reform and restructuring. This is not to deny that these enterprises have improved performance over the years in response to government efforts but the fact remains that despite successive proclamations to reduce losses of these enterprises through an increase in productivity and economic efficiency, the results have not been very encouraging. The jury is still out on the relative merits of government and market failures. Although failures occur in both too much emphasis is placed on one or the other in isolation. We argue elsewhere (Bhalla, 2001) that it is neither market nor government failure as such but the failure to implement and enforce that is the relevant issue.

In China there were lapses in the enforcement of declared policies regarding SOEs. Are these failures inherent in the nature of public management of production which is often motivated by multiple and noneconomic objectives? Are they due to asymmetric information and principal-agency problems? Or are they due to failure to *implement* policies for various non-economic, political and humanitarian reasons? We attempt to answer some of these questions by examining the economic performance of state enterprises in China in the light of two main interrelated criteria, namely, the soft-budget constraint and excess labour or overstaffing.

After a brief discussion of general issues concerning the soft-budget constraint and overstaffing in the first two sections, the third section briefly reviews the reform policies for Chinese SOEs. The subsequent section then analyses the soft-budget constraint facing these enterprises. In this context, evidence is presented of the economic performance of these enterprises including state subsidies and bank loans to them. Another section discusses excess labour, wages and bonuses in SOEs. The concluding section makes some general remarks regarding the hardening of the budget constraint and its relevance to Chinese SOEs.

# THE SOFT-BUDGET CONSTRAINT

The concept of the soft-budget constraint developed by Kornai (1980, 1986, 1993, 1998) to explain poor economic performance of state enterprises in socialist countries is closely linked to issues of principal and agent, asymmetric information and rent-seeking. Managers of state enterprises can be considered as agents of the principal (the government) who, because of asymmetric information, may have interests divergent from those of the principal. In the absence of perfect information (difficulties of monitoring and coordination complicate information problems) the principal (government or state banks) may finance uneconomic projects, and may not offer timely delivery of inputs. The principal is less informed than the agent (the firm manager) about the requirements of the enterprise. Thus the principal rather than the agent may be responsible for wrong decisions for which a compensation to the agent may be necessary in the form of additional credits and subsidies (see Dewatripont and Maskin, 1995; Li and Liang, 1998). As we note below, problems faced by Chinese SOEs is one of the principal, and not the agent.

Kornai refers to the politicians' influence on the behaviour of enterprises as an element of the soft-budget constraint. For example, the principal may be interested more in noneconomic objectives than economic ones, and may try to gain political strength by raising output and employment of firms beyond what is dictated by profit-making principle which the agent may prefer to pursue (see Shleifer and Vishny, 1994). As we discuss below, this factor partly explains low productivity and profit-making in Chinese SOEs.

A soft-budget constraint can arise when the agent exploits his better information and knowledge about the enterprise to seek rent from the principal. The agent will actively seek to maximize his rent (in the form of direct and indirect subsidies) rather than passively waiting for government assistance (Raiser, 1997a). Active rent seeking is likely to be the act of bargaining between the principal and the agent for mutual benefits rather than a one-way support from the principal to the agent. Thus the principal may receive bribes and political support in exchange for grant of rent (subsidy) as seems to be the case in China particularly at tle local level of government (Reiser, 1997c). In China the soft-budget constraint faces state enterprises at both central and local levels.[1]

The soft-budget constraint may arise due to insider control or managers' control right (Li and Liang, 1998). Managers who hold key control of the firm being the main decision makers may be able to borrow from large creditors even if they are not entitled to full rights over the firm's assets. In the face of losses, managers would oppose firm's

---

[1] In actual practice, there is considerable overlap of administrative control among central, provincial and local authorities. Local enterprises (provincial and county level) under the administrative level of local government may also be subject to some central government control (Huang, 1996).

liquidation because they enjoy significant benefits associated with their control of the firm. Thus, many bankrupt state enterprises may continue to survive because insiders successfully prevent their liquidation.

Some authors have argued that regional decentralization in China increases competition among provincial and local governments for investment funds which may raise the opportunity cost of subsidizing inefficient firms, thus hardening the budget constraint. But the soft-budget constraint may still operate as long as local governments continue to enjoy easy access to credit through state banks at the local level. Such easy access is a consequence of decentralization of monetary and banking institutions (Qian and Roland, 1994). The budget constraint becomes 'soft' when the excessive expenditure and subsequent losses of state enterprises are covered by an external agency, the state or government-owned banks.

It follows from the above discussion that the soft-budget constraint refers to both *financial* (and economic) and *political* factors. At the political level it is state's paternalistic and protective support to state-owned and private firms which may explain their continued existence despite their poor economic and financial performance. The soft-budget constraint can operate in several ways. It may take the form of subsidies by central and local governments to firms with excess expenditure over earnings, 'soft taxation', subsidized credit (lower than market interest rates), increase in loans and borrowing, lower repayment of loans, government-controlled prices and so on (Kornai, 1986; Hay *et al.*, 1994). All funding of enterprises need not, however, be subject to a soft-budget constraint. A distinction needs to be made between government payments in the form of subsidies to cover losses of enterprises and those as equity investments into profitable state enterprises (Hay *et al.*, 1994). Our concern is mainly with government subsidies for 'bail outs'.

While the concept was originally confined to firms' *ex post* financial situation, it has many non-financial ramifications based on the *ex ante* expectations of firms, probability of obtaining support, and confidence that the support would be forthcoming. Thus, the behaviour of firms and government or bureaucrats (or decision makers) forms an important element of the soft-budget constraint. For example, confidence in obtaining government support may cause 'X-inefficiency' and failure to cut losses and introduce innovations. It may also encourage overspending and over-investment thus causing a shortage economy in the context of which Kornai originally developed the concept.

The problem of measuring the extent of the soft-budget constraint are formidable. Most attempts at quantification use such indirect indicators as low profitability, government subsidies, below-market rate bank credit, and so on. Kornai (1998) mentions an alternative way of measuring the soft-budget constraint, namely, that of examining its primary and secondary effects in the form of declining efficiency and insensitivity of prices and costs. The difficulty with such an approach is that there are factors other than the soft-budget constraint which also affect efficiency. Below we will discuss the above-mentioned indicators for the Chinese SOEs to assess the existence of the soft-budget constraint.

## EXCESS LABOUR OR OVERSTAFFING

The high costs of production and resulting enterprise losses may be symptomatic of failure to adjust to relative factor and product prices, employment of excess labour as an important factor accounting for losses. However, the concept of excess labour (or overstaffing) in industry has not been carefully defined and it is not obvious what it means. The literature on labour surplus economy (Lewis, 1954; Fei and Ranis, 1964) refers to excess supplies of rural labour which can be productively reabsorbed in industry in the urban areas. This literature postulates redeployment of labour from low-productivity agricultural/rural occupations to high-productivity industrial/urban ones. In such a model innovation and accumulation is a necessary condition for rapid labour absorption. Excess labour in industry and 'overstaffing' are not foreseen. However, the latter situation can arise in the absence of accumulation by private enterprises and state-owned enterprises which may assume social welfare responsibilities (beside direct productive activity) including education and health and payment of pensions. Thus in this case excess labour or overstaffing may just be a form of unemployment insurance.

Under a hard-budget constraint a firm would be forced to downsize or shed labour in order to cut down costs of production, but not so in a soft-budget situation where financing of losses by the government may perpetuate overstaffing and low labour productivity.

For the study of SOEs, our concern is to define excess labour in industrial enterprises.Consistent with the early literature on surplus labour in developing economies, overstaffing can be equated with zero marginal product of at least some workers whose removal would not adversely affect output but would favourably affect cost of production. As agricultural activity differs from industrial activity in terms of seasonality, capacity utilization, profit maximization and so on, zero marginal product of labour concept alone may not be helpful in defining excess labour in industrial enterprises. Furthermore, as Harberger (1971) notes this notion is restricted and oversimplified. A more appropriate measure of the opportunity cost of labour would be the product foregone in other sectors which may be well above zero.

It is necessary to make some assumptions about firms' objectives before one can define or measure overstaffing or surplus labour. In principle, a firm may aim at one of the following: (i) profit maximization; (ii) output maximization, and (iii) maximization of labour productivity. It would be interested in eliminating surplus labour to improve economic efficiency so that either output is maximized with given productive capacity and technology, or labour productivity is maximized with a given level of output. Profit would be maximized when cost per unit of output is reduced to the minimum. Potential labour surplus is likely to be different under each of these options. Knight and Song (1995, p. 101), while recognizing the difficulty of estimating urban surplus labour in Chinese enterprises, suggest that 'surplus labour is ... any employment in excess of the profit-maximization benchmark'. How appropriate is it to assume profit maximization as a realistic goal for state-owned enterprises in China? Apart from failing to satisfy the neoclassical competitive condition, these enterprises are in the public sector precisely because they have multiple goals other than profit maximization. Jefferson (1998, p. 428) argues that the Chinese state-owned enterprise 'is a kind of impure public good with clear externality and public-policy implications'.

The concept of overstaffing in industry needs to be distinguished from that of labour hoarding, which is a sort of surplus labour at any given point in time. The above discussion relates to a *static* view of labour surplus at a point of time which does not allow for any 'labour hoarding'which may be necessary for long-term capacity expansion and output maximization. The motivation to hoard labour may vary from firm to firm depending on market conditions and growth in output. Under a hard-budget constraint, a firm may hoard labour in conditions of recesssion hoping that the cost of hoarding would be much less than that of firing and rehiring of labour when boom conditions return. Thus in a dynamic context it may be perfectly rational for a firm to hoard labour for future expansion in productive capacity in response to increase in demand. Therefore, a distinction needs to be made between labour hoarding of this kind and straightforward labour redundancy.

Firms may hoard labour for several reasons. Firstly, there may be legal constraints on firing workers. In China, labour legislation until recently prohibited any worker dismissal from SOEs. Thus in these conditions redundant labour may be the sum of excess labour (whatever way defined) and hoarded labour due to stringent labour laws. Secondly, as we noted above it may be costly to lay off workers and rehire them when demand conditions are more favourable (Bowers *et al.*, 1982 reject this explanation of labour retention during a slump in the context of British industry). Thus labour hoarding or a temporary labour surplus will be consistent with long-run profit maximization. Thirdly, firms may have invested in skilled workers and may be reluctant to forego return on that investment. Fourthly, technical inflexibility of production may militate against firing of redundant labour.

The above discussion pertains to firms facing competition and enjoying freedom to hoard or shed labour. Under rigid labour-market conditions (as in China), firms may not be interested in labour hoarding as a voluntary strategy.

## THE REFORM OF CHINESE STATE-OWNED ENTERPRISES

The scope and interpretation of Chinese state-owned enterprises (SOEs) is less straightforward than one may believe. Therefore, it is appropriate to begin with what constitutes these enterprises at the central and provincial levels. There are both large and small SOEs; generally large SOEs are controlled by the central government whereas the smaller ones are controlled by provincial and local governments.[2]

---

[2] Granick (1990) argues that Chinese SOEs operating at the provincial level face hard budget constraints as they must remit taxes to the central authorities, whereas SOEs controlled by the central government face soft-budget constraint. We show, as did Hay *et al.* (1994) for China, that soft-budget constraint operates at both levels.

SOEs have accounted for a significant proportion of total number of enterprises since the revolution in 1949. At the end of 1998, SOEs accounted for over 71 per cent of the urban labour force, or over 12 per cent of the total labour force; 28 per cent of total gross industrial output, and 54 per cent of total fixed investment (see Table 1). Although SOE employment has declined as a proportion of the urban labour force it has remained remarkably high and stable between 1985 and 1998. Even as a proportion of the total labour force, during the 1980s and 1990s it varied between 15 to 18 per cent, which is quite significant.

China introduced state-sector reforms as an important component of its overall economic reforms. In principle, it had three options: (a) sale of state enterprises (or privatization), (b) leasing, and (c) use of private management contracts. Initially China did not adopt option (a); it did not envisage privatization as a central policy until 1997 when the 15th Central Congress of the Communist party accepted this option for the first time. Instead, until 1997-98 emphasis was placed on raising the efficiency of state enterprises without changing their ownership status. This was to be achieved by exposing SOEs to greater competition from collective and private enterprises, mergers of SOEs with non-state firms, establishment of joint stock companies, and commercialization of banks (Bhalla, 1995a, 1995b; World Bank, 1996a). SOE reforms consisted of: restriction of central planning and gradual introduction of market and price system, profit-sharing schemes, and greater autonomy of state enterprises in decision making regarding production and wage fixing (Xu, 1997). These measures were intended to raise productivity and economic efficiency without changing their ownership pattern. First, a profit retention scheme was introduced under which enterprises could retain a certain proportion of total profits for innovation and investment (Raiser, 1997a). Gradually bargaining over plan targets gave way to that over profit retention (Naughton, 1985). In the 1980s, the emphasis was more on enterprises paying taxes. The reforms placed emphasis mainly on improved efficiency, managerial autonomy and accountability. As a result of competition from collective and private enterprises the number of SOEs has been steadily declining relative to collective and private enterprises.

In China the difference between non-state enterprises (collective urban enterprises and town and village enterprises) is not so much in terms of ownership (as in India and other developing countries) as different levels of government ownership and supervision (central, provincial, district, local). While supervision of SOEs is the responsibility of central and provincial bureaus, that of collective enterprises is the responsibility of the local or township governments.[3] State enterprises obtain most inputs and sell outputs through a combination of plan and market activity whereas collective enterprises are

---

[3] State enterprises in China are often distinguished from 'collectives' and town and village enterprises (TVEs) which are run by the local county governments rather than the central government. Although they are sometimes labelled as 'non-state' sector in the literature, strictly speaking they are also local state enterprises since they rely on the local governments for raw materials and other inputs. Rural (township and village) enterprises are different from urban collectives in that they have to compete for inputs and product markets. Their ownership pattern is difficult to define as either public or private. On the one hand, they are supervised by local township governments and are thus state entities; on the other, they are most market oriented (Hussain and Zhuang, 1997).

largely outside the purview of planning and thus are more market oriented. Thus it is generally believed that most collective enterprises face a hard-budget constraint whereas SOEs face a soft-budget constraint (see Peroti *et al.*, 1998).

## Table 1: Main Features of Chinese SOEs (1985-98)

| Year | Staff & workers (000) | % of urban labour force | % of total labour force | Total fixed investment (billion yuan) | (%) | Gross industrial output (billion yuan) | (%) |
|------|------|------|------|------|------|------|------|
| 1985 | 89,900 | 72.7 | 18.0 | 168 | 66.0 | 630 | 64.9 |
| 1986 | 93,330 | 72.9 | 18.2 | 208 | 66.6 | 697 | 62.3 |
| 1987 | 96,540 | 73.0 | 18.3 | 245 | 64.6 | 825 | 59.7 |
| 1988 | 99,840 | 73.4 | 18.4 | 302 | 63.5 | 1,035 | 56.8 |
| 1989 | 101,080 | 73.5 | 18.0 | 281 | 63.7 | 1,234 | 56.1 |
| 1990 | 103,460 | 73.6 | 16.2 | 299 | 66.1 | 1,306 | 54.6 |
| 1991 | 106,640 | 73.5 | 16.4 | 371 | 66.4 | 1,495 | 56.2 |
| 1992 | 108,890 | 73.6 | 16.6 | 550 | 68.0 | 1,782 | 51.5 |
| 1993 | 109,200 | 73.5 | 16.4 | 793 | 60.6 | 2,772 | 57.3 |
| 1994 | 108,900 | 73.3 | 16.2 | 961 | 56.4 | 2,620 | 37.3 |
| 1995 | 109,550 | 73.5 | 16.1 | 1,090 | 54.4 | 3,122 | 34.0 |
| 1996 | 109,490 | 73.7 | 15.9 | 1,201 | 52.4 | 3,617 | 36.3 |
| 1997 | 107,660 | 73.4 | 15.5 | 1,309 | 52.5 | 3,599 | 31.6 |
| 1998 | 88,090 | 71.4 | 12.6 | 1,537 | 54.1 | 3,362 | 28.2 |

**Source:** Based on data from *Comprehensive Statistical Data and Materials on 50 Years of New China* (Beijing:China Statistical Press) (1999).
**Notes:** Since 1996, the definition of 'urban' was changed, the employment ratios for the earlier period may not be comparable.

Another component of SOE reform is the private management contracts between SOEs and private enterprises. These relationships may take the form of ownership by SOEs of COEs as their subsidiaries, or joint ventures with foreign firms. There is a growing contracting out of production to non-state enterprises suggesting a business relationship similar to that between large and small businesses in Japan and elsewhere in market economies (Hussain and Zhuang, 1997).

The latest phase of SOE reform involves the conversion of several SOEs into joint stock shareholding companies. Some equity of these companies is traded on the Shanghai and Shenzhen, and Hong Kong and New York markets. This reform, heralded as one of the most ambitious since 1978 (Broadman, 1995), is being undertaken within the framework of the Company and Enterprise Laws which allow the establishment of corporations as legal entities separate from owners (shareholders) with modern Western-style Boards of directors and management structure.

The Chinese SOE reforms are based on the premise that a change in ownership, and separation of ownership from management and control are not necessarily the only and most important preconditions for efficiency improvements and profitability. Some scholars (e.g. Jian, 1996) (comparing privatization in China and Taiwan to that in Russia) argue that the share of SOEs in China is relatively lower than in Russia (with a sizeable non-state sector) and the loss of employment resulting from privatization more acute.

However, since 1995, China has gradually privatized small SOEs at the county level while retaining state ownership in large SOEs although the official policy towards privatization was adopted only in 1997. By the end of 1996 a substantial number of such enterprises were privatized. China's high savings rate and the relatively low net worth (due to large debt-asset ratio) and thus sale price may have facilitated this process (Cao *et al.*,1999). Despite privatization however, the State continues to hold control on privatized enterprises as they are joint-stock holding companies with employees and government owning shares. There are also restrictions in share transfers.

Despite various efforts at SOE reform, however, operational autonomy to SOE management and corporatization (that is, introducing modern Western methods of corporate board management) remained limited (McNally & Lee, 1998). Lardy (1998, p.22) concludes that 'reforms to date have failed in large portions of the state-owned sector....' In the absence of an effective implementation of such reforms as profit retention, price reforms and interest payments by SOEs, greater managerial autonomy (even if achieved) would not have raised their allocative efficiency in the use of resources.

Zhang (1998, p.17) argues that 'changes in the financial structure of SOEs and bankruptcy have failed to play a role in disciplining managers'. This is partly because, despite the management contract (or leasing) system the managers have little stakes in their firms. In fact, managerial autonomy resulting from management contracts have had adverse effects in the form of such phenomena as profit diversion and asset stripping (see below).

## THE SOFT BUDGET CONSTRAINT IN CHINESE SOES

SOEs are a burden on the Chinese economy in several ways. First, subsidies, which cover SOE losses raise fiscal deficits and cause macroeconomic instability. Secondly, absence of SOE reforms blocks banking and financial reforms. State banks, which are obliged to lend to loss-making SOEs under political presssures, accumulate mounting bad debts. Thirdly, slow pace of SOE reforms hinders the process of social welfare reforms. Finally, SOEs suffer from undertutilization of human resources in the form of redundant labour or 'disguised unemployment'.

Why have the Chinese SOEs continued to survive without going bankrupt, with few recent exceptions? Answer to this question may lie in the soft-budget constraint under which the government allows these firms to survive. Lin *et al.* (1998, 1999) argue that SOEs suffer from 'policy burdens' imposed by the government: social welfare costs, redundant labour and distorted prices, which account for their large losses and failure to compete with non-state enterprises. Strictly speaking, the government should be responsible only for the losses incurred due to these policy burdens. But under asymmetric information the government is unable to distinguish between policy-induced losses, for which the government should be responsible and those that are operational losses due to the managerial or worker slack, for example, for which SOEs should be responsible.The government ends up being responsible for all the losses of SOEs introducing the soft-budget constraint and worsening moral hazard and associated agency problems discussed above. The soft-budget constraint will persist as long as policy burdens are imposed on SOEs.

SOEs continue to be responsible for their profits but not their losses, a situation labelled as 'privatization of assets and socialization of liabilities' (Broadman and Xiao, 1997). In 1995, 'about 40 per cent of state enterprises made losses..subsidies to these loss-making enterprises increased by more than 50 per cent between 1986 and 1994' (Huang and Duncan, 1997, p. 69). The share of loss-making state enterprises has actually been steadily rising; according to World Bank (1996b) their share rose from 26.4 per cent in 1992 to 44 per cent in 1995. The State Economic and Trade Commission of China reported that 49 per cent of large and medium-sized state enterprises made losses in 1998. Of the 512 large state companies about one-third are reported to have suffered losses in the first half of 1998 (see World Bank, 1999, p. 21). These enterprises suffer from severe underutilization of productive capacity and growing indebtedness. Their debt-asset ratios are noted to be as high as 85 per cent (see *Singapore Monetary Authority*, 1997). A survey of 124, 000 SOEs noted the asset-liability ratio to range between 71.5 per cent and 83.3 per cent (see *South China Morning Post*, 30 August, 1997). It is, therefore, clear that SOEs are a major burden on the state budget. The increasing losses of SOEs (see Table 2) has led to a decline in the government tax revenue from SOEs, much more than that from the collective enterprises (COEs) (see Figure 1).

Disaggregated data are needed on profit-making and loss-making SOEs to determine whether and how these enterprises face different types of the soft-budget constraint. Two empirical studies based on detailed field surveys of SOEs have attempted to test the soft-budget constraint (Hay *et al.* 1994; Li and Liang, 1998). Using data on large SOEs for 1984-87, Hay *et al.* undertake a flow-of-funds analysis of (a) long-term loss makers, (b) short-term loss makers and (c) profitable firms. These firms have three main sources of funds: government subsidies, bank loans and firm's own resources. Their findings show that: subsidies for long-term loss makers are much higher (15 per cent) than those for short-term loss makers (4.1 per cent) and profitable firms (0.9 per cent); bank loans was an insignificant source for both long-term and short-term losers; and firm's own resources was an important source for long-term losers. Using data from two large surveys of SOEs in Jiangsu, Jilin, Shanxi and Sichuan covering 1980-89 and 1990-94 Li and Liang (1998) conclude that SOE financial losses were due to political interference, creditors' lack of information, and insiders' control. Excess supply of labour (largely non-production workers), excessive bonus payments to workers and bad investments were among the symptoms of the soft-budget constraint.

**Fig. 1 China: Government Tax Revenue from SOEs and COEs**

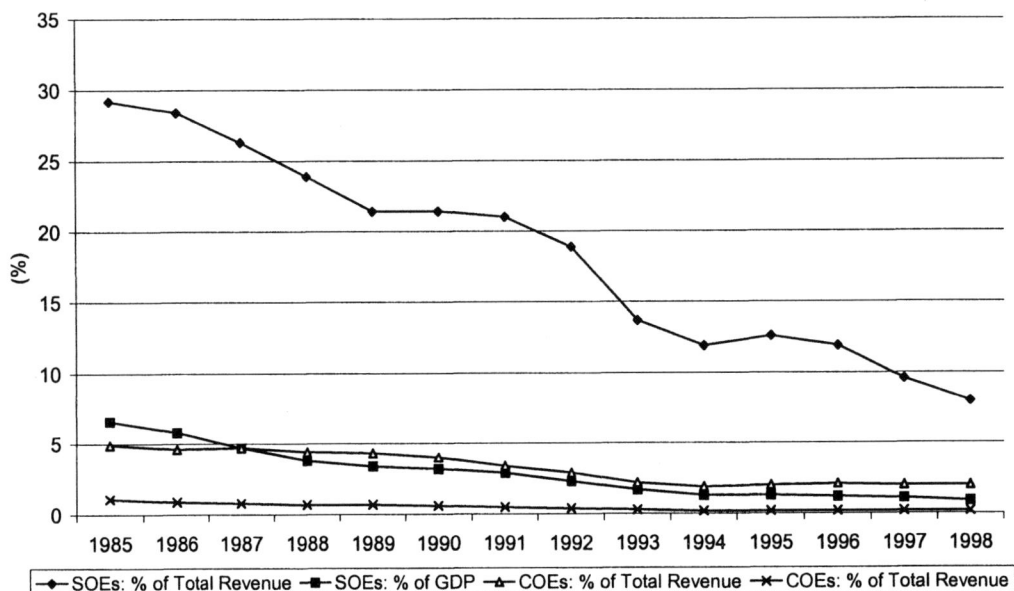

Source: Based on data from the *China Statistical Yearbook* (1999).

Of course, SOEs may face hard-budget constraints in respect of some variables and soft-budget constraints in respect of others. On the basis of regression analysis using survey data of 300 SOEs in six Chinese cities, Kueh *et al.* (1999) show: (a) enterprise retained profit bearing a weak relationship to the payment of workers' bonuses in the early phase of the reforms which became somewhat stronger later on, (b) correlation of growth in enterprise capacity with past profitability to have declined between 1985 and 1988 suggesting a softening of the budget constraint, and (c) enterprise demand for such inputs as materials being price elastic (contrary to the soft-budget constraint hypothesis) whereas that for bank loans is inelastic (supporting the soft-budget hypothesis).

We now examine in detail below SOEs profitability over time, subsidies, bank loans, social burdens, and excess labour, factors some of which are beyond the control of these enterprises.


## Economic Performance of SOEs

The financial performance of SOEs is generally measured by their profits or excess of revenues over costs because such data are easily available in their balance sheets. In Chinese SOEs profitability has been declining over time. World Bank (1996c) notes that profits of industrial SOEs fell from over 6 per cent of GDP in 1987 to about 2 per cent in 1994. Jefferson *et al.* (1994) show (on the basis of World Bank firm-level data) that profit rates have been declining over time in SOEs, urban collectives and TVEs, but export-oriented enterprises were more profitable than the non-exporting enterprises. A survey of SOEs, collective enterprises and TVEs during 1990-94 in Jilin, Shaanxi and Sichuan interior provinces, compared to an earlier survey of similar enterprises in coastal provinces (namely, Guangzhou, Shenzhen, Xiamen, and Shanghai), shows that average net rate of return (gross profits less net of all taxes paid over the net value of fixed assets) was 13 per cent in TVEs compared with 7 per cent in SOEs and collective enterprises (Raiser, 1997b; Table 4).

Several reasons account for the declining SOE profitability: growing competition in product markets as a result of entry of non-state enterprises reducing SOEs market share (Fan *et al.*, 1998; Mcmillan and Naughton, 1993), loosening of government control on wages resulting from greater enterprise autonomy which raises non-wage costs (Fan and Woo, 1996), social burdens of SOEs in the form of expenditure on workers' education, health and pensions which are not incurred by non-state enterprises, and underreporting of profits. The social burdens noted above also involve employment of extra workers to administer these schemes which are unnecessary for production, which partly explains large magnitudes of surplus labour in SOEs (see below). Substantial increase in SOE losses (see Table 2) has also accounted for a declining rate of return on SOE investments. Lardy (1998, p. 34) notes that 'in the first quarter of 1996 the state-owned sector as a whole, for the first time ever, was in the red...' Price controls under which SOEs were required to sell bulk of their output at below- market prices may also explain SOEs losses (see Lin *et al.*, 1999). However, this explanation may be more relevant to the early 1980s than in the later period when price liberalization on most products was effective. Greater autonomy of local governments and SOEs is also known to have resulted in asset stripping: TVEs are reported to have bought SOE assets at below market prices. Lack of managerial ownership and asset holding in SOEs (lack of adequate property rights) seems to have encouraged these buy-out transactions (see Xiang, 1998). Another example of asset stripping is the leasing out of enterprise assets to workers. Short of asset stripping SOEs may borrow loans from state banks at low interest rates and relend them to collective enterprises at much higher interest rates. This drain of state assets has been estimated at 230 billion yuan between 1987 and 1992 (or an annual sum of 33 billion yuan) and 300 billion yuan between 1990 and 1995 (or an annual sum of over 50 billion yuan (see Lardy, 1998, pp. 51-52). Depletion of state assets represents an interesting example of divergent interests of the principal and the agent discussed above.

An evaluation of profitability of SOEs is a mammoth task under distorted price structure and incomplete and imperfect markets. Under monopolistic or imperfect market conditions enterprises could enjoy profits without any increase in economic efficiency; thus profitability and rates of return would be a poor index of efficiency. Therefore, one needs to be careful in deriving any definite conclusions about SOEs'economic performance. It may be better to examine growth of total factor productivity (TFP) (although its estimation also suffers from various methodological problems) or partial productivity.

## Table 2: Losses in State-Owned Industrial Enterprises
### 'As Independent Accounting Units' (1978-94)

| Year | Amount of losses (billion yuan) | Total SOE profits (billion yuan) | Losses as % of profits | Total profit before tax (billion yuan) | Losses as % of total profit before tax |
|------|------|------|------|------|------|
| 1978 | 4.2 | 50.9 | 8.3 | 79.1 | 5.3 |
| 1979 | 3.6 | 56.3 | 6.5 | 86.4 | 4.2 |
| 1980 | 3.4 | 58.5 | 5.9 | 90.7 | 3.8 |
| 1981 | 4.6 | 58.0 | 7.9 | 92.3 | 5.0 |
| 1982 | 4.7 | 59.8 | 8.0 | 97.2 | 4.9 |
| 1983 | 3.2 | 64.1 | 5.0 | 103.3 | 3.1 |
| 1984 | 2.7 | 70.6 | 3.8 | 115.3 | 2.3 |
| 1985 | 3.2 | 73.8 | 4.4 | 133.4 | 2.4 |
| 1986 | 5.4 | 69.0 | 7.9 | 134.1 | 4.1 |
| 1987 | 6.1 | 78.7 | 7.8 | 151.4 | 4.0 |
| 1988 | 8.2 | 89.2 | 9.2 | 177.5 | 4.6 |
| 1989 | 18.1 | 74.3 | 24.2 | 177.3 | 10.2 |
| 1990 | 34.9 | 38.8 | 89.9 | 150.3 | 23.2 |
| 1991 | 36.7 | 40.2 | 91.2 | 166.1 | 22.1 |
| 1992 | 36.9 | 53.5 | 69.0 | 194.4 | 19.0 |
| 1993 | 45.3 | 81.7 | 55.4 | 245.5 | 18.4 |
| 1994 | 48.2 | 82.9 | 58.2 | 287.6 | 16.8 |

Source: Xiang (1998).

Several studies on TFP in SOEs show rather conflicting results. Actual estimates are sensitive to the price deflators used for input and output. K. Chen *et al.* (1988) estimated that total factor productivity (TFP) in SOEs increased by 4-5 per cent per annum between 1978 and 1985 while it stagnated between 1957 and 1978 (that is, during the pre-reform period). A comparison between state and collective enterprises shows that productivity increased in both but it grew faster in collective enterprises. Woo *et al.* (1994) show that during the 1980s growth of TFP was zero or negative for SOEs whereas it was positive for TVEs.

It is generally believed that TFP has been rising in SOEs although not as fast as that in COEs. If productivity has been rising, why have profits been falling? This paradoxical situation may be explained by the soft-budget constraint under which corruption by enterprise managers (for example, deliberate underpricing of products in exchange for kickbacks) persists under uncertain property rights in the form of managerial shareholding. The perception of managers makes them confident that the state will bail them out (see Xiang, 1995, 1998).

## State Subsidies

Discussion of subsidies and their magnitude is of interest for two main reasons. First, subsidies create budgetary deficits which in turn cause macroeconomic instability.

Secondly, subsidies, if granted over a long period, can create a disincentive for efficiency improvements. In China state enterprises very rarely go bankrupt despite laws having been promulgated to that effect. Their losses are covered either by state subsidies out of the government budget or by loans from the state banks offered under government directives. In recent years the government has been cutting down subsidies; the losses of SOEs are increasingly covered by bank loans.

Apart from direct subsidies, indirect subsidies may include not only subsidized loans at below-market rates, but also subsidized raw materials and other inputs, and relaxation of government taxes on SOE profits from the use of state-owned fixed assests (Perkins and Raiser, 1994). In making a total estimate of SOE subsidies, Sachs and Woo (1994) assume that 'half of the new bank credits not financing the central budget deficit are used for financing of state-owned enterprises'. Thus estimated the Sachs-Woo estimate of indirect subsidies is much higher than the estimates (World Bank,1996a) which we use in Fig. 2. The World Bank report does not give the methodology underlying their estimate so that it is difficult to explain the discrepancy between the two estimates.

Sachs and Woo (1994) erroneously include price subsidies in estimating total subsidies to SOEs which are shown to be 8 per cent of GDP in 1991, a figure more than twice as high as the official estimates of direct subsidies. Although price subsidies may exercise an indirect effect on SOEs (in the sense that they can enable managers to offer lower wages to workers) they are not targeted directly at SOEs; instead, they are subsidies intended for the benefit of urban consumers and are thus likely to move in step with inflation.

Declining share of state subsidies to SOEs does not necessarily mean that SOE losses have gone down or loss-making SOEs have been closed down. The decline in subsidy may have been made up by an increase in state bank loans to SOEs under political pressure by the central and local governments. As Table 3 shows, the losses of SOEs have been going up since the reforms began in 1978. The ratio of subsidies to losses of SOEs, though declining is still quite high. In 1991, subsidies to industrial SOEs were equivalent to 70 per cent of the losses of these enterprises (see Lo, 1997). Furthermore, subsidies continued to be a substantial proportion of total government expenditure (24.5 per cent in 1990 and about 11 per cent in 1994) (World Bank, 1996a, Table 22).

A decline in central government subsidies may have been matched by an increase in indirect financial support through banks at the local level. Local governments in China own and control the bulk of SOEs. Under regional decentralization, their much greater autonomy implies that they can thwart the central government plans.

## Bank Loans

The industrial SOEs rely heavily on banks for loans for bailing them out. Most of the non-performing loans go into covering losses of these enterprises. In conditions of low interest rates, these bank credits are an indirect form of subsidy to the enterprises. Since the reform of the early 1980s, bank financing of SOEs replaced fiscal transfers (subsidies) by the State. The sources of SOE finance include (i) government subsidy, (ii) bank loans and (iii) self-financing out of SOEs profits. While the opportunity cost of direct government subsidy is zero, the cost to SOEs of self-financing will depend on market rate of interest. If it is higher than the state bank loans, there will be incentive to rely on 'soft' loans. Hussain and Stern (1991) show that the government allocation of funds and tax policy make loans more attractive than self-financing. Both the interest on loans and repayment of principal sum by SOEs is tax deductible which encourages borrowing and narrows the tax base. Secondly, soft-budget constraint is indicated by the very low nominal interest rates, and low or even negative real interest rates on which loans are advanced by the banks.

We assume that state bank annual loans to SOEs consist of loans to industrial and commercial enterprises (loans to construction companies are quite small and are excluded) almost all of which are SOEs. These annual loans to SOEs are much higher than the magnitude of enterprise loss subsidies. However, it is not appropriate to assume that all loans to SOEs reflect a soft-budget constraint. We need information on policy loans to SOEs at below-market interest rates, which is not available. However, there is some indication that policy loans (those advanced at central and local levels under instructions from the government) have been increasing in the 1990s. At the end of 1995 outstanding state bank loans to SOEs amounted to 3.36 trillion yuan, or 83 per cent of all outstanding bank loans. Bank lending for fixed investments (also concentrated on SOEs) by the Industrial and Commercial Bank of China accounted for more than 90 per cent of the total (Lardy, 1998, p. 83). There is also evidence to suggest that local governments collude with local branches of banks to obtain 'soft' loans for SOEs under their control.

Fig. 2 shows changes over time in (a) enterprise loss subsidies, (b) financial sector subsidies (indirect subsidies in the form of low-interest loans to SOEs and unpaid principal and interest), and (c) state bank loans as a proportion of GDP. While (a) has been steadily going down since 1985, there is no clear trend in (b) which shows a trough between 1989 and 1991 before rising again in the early 1990s. Loans by the state banks to SOEs as a proportion of GDP have been rising between 1988 and 1991; although they declined somewhat in the 1990s, they have generally been rising while the state subsidies as a proportion of GDP have been falling. Loans to urban collectives and rural credit cooperatives have been rising less rapidly, and those to rural credit cooperatives and to individual businesses remained stagnant. Xu (1998, p.160) notes that more than 70 per cent of the specialized banks' assets are tied up in loans to loss-making state enteprises.

**Fig. 2 China: State Subsidies and Loans to SOEs**

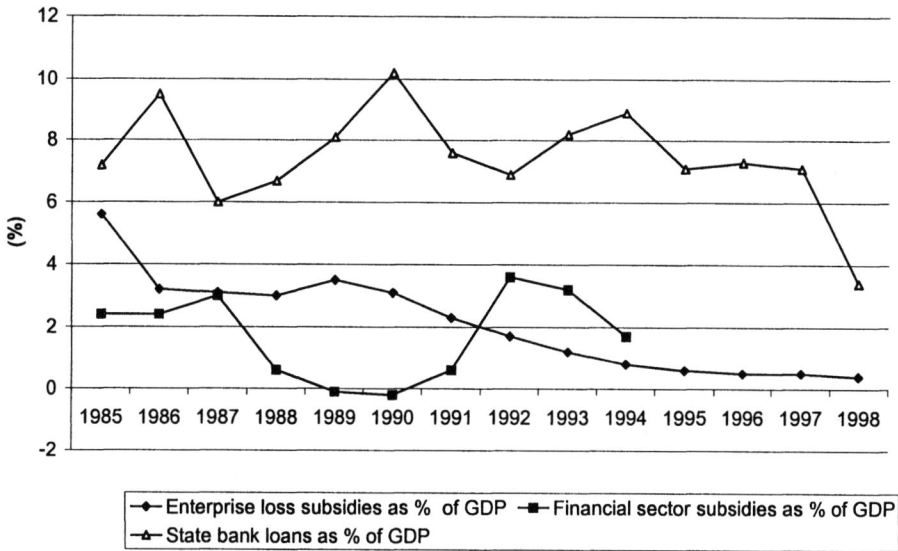

**Sources:** China Statistical Yearbook;Comprehensive Statistical Data and Materials on 50 Years of New China (1999).
**Notes:** (1) Loans of SOEs= industrial plus commercial loans; construction loans are not included as separate data are not available. However,construction forms only a small proportion of total loans. (2) Data on loans refer to annual loans.

A large proportion (estimates vary from 20-30 per cent) of total loans to state enterprises remain unpaid. Since the banks are still state-owned, they are under constant pressure to lend to SOEs on the basis of political rather than commercial considerations. This is particularly so at the local government level. Xu (1998, p. 157) notes that 'bank credit, which was lent out as policy loans, was in effect like fiscal grants the use of which was beyond the banks' control'. The banks' lending behaviour may continue to be based on the perception that lending to SOEs would continue to be implicitly guaranteed by the government on moral and social grounds.

## EXCESS LABOUR, WAGES AND BONUSES IN CHINESE SOEs

### Excess Labour

Estimates vary on the size of redundant labour in the Chinese SOEs. This is all the more so because of a lack of agreement on the methodology of estimation. The Chinese managers in SOEs are generally asked whether they could produce the same output with less labour, and if so, by how much. Enterprise surveys are a common method for estimating surplus labour in SOEs (Fan *et al.*, 1998). In the literature, it is taken for granted that there is abundant surplus labour in Chinese SOEs. Knight and Song (1995, p. 97) note that China is 'a labour surplus economy *par excellence* and the institutions of the labour market have to be viewed in that light'. Li and Liang (1998, p.106) assume that non-production workers in SOEs are potentially redundant whose removal would on an average reduce SOE financial losses by about 38 per cent. We noted earlier that estimation of labour surplus in industry is fraught with major problems even in industrial countries where far more emphasis has been placed on studying the underutlization of capital than of labour. Without an appropriate conceptual and measurement framework, the estimates of surplus labour in Chinese SOEs are no more than rough orders of magnitude. True picture of the extent of labour surplus in Chinese industry as a whole is currently not available.

Various official and unofficial estimates of labour surplus in Chinese SOEs are presented in Table 3. Two notable features of these estimates are (a) a very wide range and (b) their partial and micro nature. The estimates vary depending on the assumptions and the perceptions of enterprise managers since most of them are made on the basis of interview surveys. Lim *et al.* (1996, p.31) estimate labour surplus in Chinese industrial SOEs and other forms of ownership on the basis of an ILO field survey undertaken in February-March 1995. 'In job' labour surplus was estimated by asking enterprise managers whether the same level of output could be achieved with fewer workers, and if so by what percentage. The responding enterprises that noted that labour could be cut by 17 per cent of their current total workforce. Amongst all the ownership categories, the highest level of labour surplus was reported in joint stock companies (18.9 per cent) followed by labour service enterprises (16.4 per cent) and state-owned enterprises (15.6 per cent).

In addition to the 'in job' labour surplus, a phenomenon peculiar to China is that of 'on leave' surplus labour (*xiagang* or lay-offs) which represents a phased labour redundancy in SOEs. Although these workers vacate their posts they continue to be paid a partial salary or allowances during a specified period during which they are encouraged to look for alternative jobs. There were about 5.6 million such workers in 1995 whose number increased to 16 million in 1998 (see Yang and Tam, 1999). This dramatic increase in 'on leave' workers may be explained by increase in the number of SOEs bankruptcies. This slow retrenchment no doubt softens the blow and social hardship, but in terms of the budget constraint, it continues to remain a financial burden on SOEs at least temporarily. Apart from receiving a partial salary *Xiagang* workers continue to receive subsidies and social insurance fees from their employing SOEs. In contrast fully redundant workers do not benefit from such assistance although they may receive some unemployment benefits from the local labour bureaus.

## Table 3: Estimates of Excess Labour in Chinese SOEs

| Source | Estimate | Comments |
| --- | --- | --- |
| Lim *et al.* (ILO) (1996)* | 18.4 % of urban workforce | Based on current output |
| World Bank I (1993) | 11% | Based on 100% capacity utilization |
| Broadman (1995) | 30-40% of SOE employees | |
| World Bank II (1999) | 30% of SOE employees | Resident Mission in China |
| China I | 10-12% of urban SOE employees | Ministry of Labour; based on 15,000 enterprises in 11 provinces |
| China II | 25% of SOE employees | Officials in charge of planning and systems reform |
| China III | 15-20% of urban SOEs | State Economic & Trade Commission |
| China IV | 20-25% | |
| China V | Over 33 % of workforce | Estimates of research institutes |
| China VI | 20 % of employees | Survey of 45 reforming SOEs in Shanghai |

**Sources:** World Bank (1993, 1999); Broadman (1995); Lim *et al.* (1996); Knight and Song (1999).
* includes 'on leave' and 'in job' surpluses.

Excess employment by level of ownership has also been estimated (see Table 4). Results show that it is not the highest among the SOEs (14 per cent) but instead among COEs (18 per cent); it is the lowest among TVEs (11 per cent). The estimate of net profit to fixed capital suggests that it is very close for both SOEs and COEs. This implies that higher excess employment in COEs has no adverse influence on their profitability. Furthermore, if one were to believe the data one could not agree with those who claim that COEs increasingly face hard-budget constraint (see above) under which they should record much lower excess employment. As we noted above, distinction between SOEs and COEs is fuzzy as both are strictly state-owned. Therefore, it is unlikely that the behaviour of COEs would be very different from that of SOEs.

Excess labour by industrial sectors shows that it is the highest in food (24 per cent) followed by textiles (21 per cent) (Raiser, 1997b). The sectoral variations correspond roughly to profitability and may be due also to differences in product demand and the nature of industry. A large number of textiles and garment factories are closing down in Shanghai suggesting a decline in demand.

**Table 4: Excess Employment, Taxation and Profitability by Ownership Levels
(1990-94 Averages)**

|                                          | SOEs | COEs | TVEs |
|------------------------------------------|------|------|------|
| Net profit to net fixed capital (%)      | 7.4  | 7.6  | 13.0 |
| Total tax to net value added (%)         | 16.6 | 15.5 | 20.5 |
| Optimal employment to current employment | 0.86 | 0.82 | 0.89 |

**Source:** Raiser (1997b).

**Notes:** 1. Excess employment is subjectively estimated by managers in responses to qualitative questionnaire. 2. SOEs- state enterprises; COEs-collective enterprises and TVEs- town and village enterprises.

One needs to be careful in interpreting the above data based on managers' responses. We do not question the existence of surplus labour but the feasibility of removing it at least in the short run in a labour surplus economy. One needs to distinguish between labour surplus economy (a macroeconomic issue) where excess labour is disguised for lack of any formal or informal unemployment insurance mechanism, and surplus labour in enterprises (a microeconomic issue) with which most of the Chinese literature is concerned.

Whether shedding of labour surplus in Chinese SOEs will harden the budget constraint and improve economic efficiency will depend *inter alia*, on the reasons for labour surplus in the first place. In the pre-reform period, to ensure full employment the Chinese government used SOEs as an employment-generating mechanism and expected enterprises not only to take on workers who were not necessary for production but also to provide jobs to the children of their workers. Although in theory, the Chinese government now allows SOEs to lay off workers, in practice labour market flexibility (hiring and firing) is not common due in part to the failure of a comprehensive social security system and availability of resources at the level of local governments to take responsibility for their social welfare. Labour mobility is restricted by the fact that workers forego social welfare benefits of housing, education and health services (and even pensions) once they leave SOEs. These benefits are not available to workers employed under other forms of ownership, for example, joint ventures, and collective and private enterprises.

Under hard-budget constraint, surplus labour may arise from slack in demand, technological modernization, or reorganization of production. In the ILO survey reported in Lim *et al.* the enterprise respondents noted the following reasons for the existence of labour surplus:

-   developments in the product market (26 per cent of the respondents);
-   technological and organizational changes (22 per cent);
-   poor labour quality (15 per cent).

There is evidence that the Chinese government, faced with the problem of massive lay offs and resulting social instability, has often discouraged SOEs from shedding surplus labour (see Lim *et al.*, 1996).

## Wages and Bonuses

Payment of wages and bonuses under hard-budget constraint would be linked to economic performance and would reflect reward for above-average worker productivity. However, in China even loss-making SOEs are known to have raised wages and disbursed bonuses. The relatively constant share of wage bill of industrial SOEs between 1981 and 1995 despite falling employment and profitability suggest payment of high wages and bonuses (Perkins, 1999). Between 1985 and 1996, the average real wage of SOE workers increased by 50 per cent, which was double that of workers in collective enterprises (Huang *et al.,* 1999). There is ample evidence on the payment of excessive bonuses (see Fan and Woo, 1996; Huang *et al.*, 1999; Perkins, 1999).[4] Li and Liang (1998) estimate that 39 per cent of the SOE losses were due to excessive bonus payments, and that about 81 per cent of SOEs in their sample distributed excessive bonuses. Sachs and Woo (1994, p. 119) note incentives for managers (under the soft-budget constraint) to 'strip the state enterprise income and assets to their personal benefit... by distributing profits in the form of higher compensation.... (since) nobody is in place to defend the interests of the enterprise capital'.

Under the Chinese enterprise reforms, bonuses (not exceeding 25 per cent of the basic wage bill) were allowed in order to induce increase in labour productivity. There are indications that wages bonuses and allowances for increase in cost of living paid by many SOEs were well in excess of this ceiling even when they are making losses. This is likely to be due to the soft-budget constraint. Wage increases have also exceeded labour productivity increases by a wide margin particularly in loss-making SOEs (World Bank, 1996a). Such increases would not be possible without the tacit support of the government or the financial sector.

Wage shares in Chinese SOEs show a steady increase since 1978, rising from 23 per cent in 1978 to nearly 53 per cent in 1995(see Hussain and Zhuang, 1998, p. 48). In non-SOEs the wage share was higher than in SOEs in 1978 but it was much lower in 1995. Such factors as decentralization of wage determination, scope of increased wage bargaining in the absence of threat of bankruptcy or lay-offs are responsible for a rapid increase in the wage share in Chinese SOEs.

The enterprise reforms and resulting SOE autonomy seem to have had the opposite effect to what was intended by the Chinese reformers. Instead of raising profits they have led to overconsumption due to the soft-budget constraint. This is particularly so at the local (county) level where wage bill including bonuses, subsidies and allowances increased more than at the higher levels between 1995 and 1997 (see Table 5). Fan *et al.* (1998, p.37) note that in '1993 the bonus payment accounted for more than 22 per cent of the total wage bill in coal mining and oil extraction even though the two sectors have suffered consistent losses'. If losses are attributed to such exogenous factors as price and

---

[4] Empirical evidence is not conclusive, however. For example, Jefferson and Rawski (1995) argue that from 1980 to 1990 total labour compensation (both cash and in-kind) as a share of gross output of SOEs did not exceed labour's output elasticity.

foreign exchange controls, SOEs (the agent) can successfully negotiate with the principal (their supervisory government bodies) hidden or open financial support.

**Table 5: Wage and Bonus Increases in SOEs by Level of Control (1995-97)**

| Control/administrative level | 1995 (billion yuan) | 1997 (billion yuan) | Increase over 1995 (billion yuan) | % increase |
|---|---|---|---|---|
| SOEs under central government | 173 | 214 | 41 | 23.7 |
| SOEs under provincial government | 114 | 135 | 21 | 18.4 |
| SOEs under prefectural government | 151 | 173 | 22 | 14.6 |
| SOEs under county government | 169 | 216 | 47 | 27.8 |
| National Total | 608 | 735 | 127 | 20.9 |

**Source:** *China Labour Statistical Yearbook* (1997, 1998).

## CONCLUDING REMARKS

In this paper we have explained government failures in terms of soft-budget constraints in state enterprises in China. Direct and indirect subsidies (direct financial support from the central budget, tax concessions, subsidized loans and so on) propped the enterprises, which acted as a disincentive for managers to improve their economic performance. Failure of the government to let these enterprises go bankrupt despite China having promulgated bankruptcy laws has meant loss of government credibility. Kornai (1993) notes that introduction of a hard-budget constraint as a stop-gap arrangement is unlikely to change the behaviour of enterprise managers from passiveness to active pursuit of economic goals. He notes that a shift from soft-budget constraints to a hard-budget constraint calls for credibility and commitment on the part of the government both of which may be thwarted by political constraints. This is precisely what happened in China. After having declared that the state would no longer bail out SOEs either directly or through soft loans by the state banks, China did precisely that in 1998 for political and humanitarian reasons. When threat of massive unemployment and resulting social unrest became imminent) the government urged the banks to grant additional policy loans to these enterprises. The problems of SOEs will mount even further after China's accession to the WTO(see Bhalla and Qiu, 2001). The threat of unemployment will loom even larger in the future.

# REFERENCES

Bhalla, A.S. (1995a), *Uneven Development in the Third World* (London:Macmillan).

Bhalla, A.S. (1995b) 'Recent Economic Reforms in China and India', *Asian Survey,* June.

Bhalla, A.S. (2001) *Government or Market Failures? An Asian Perspective* (London: Palgrave).

Bhalla, A.S. and S. Qiu (2001) *'China's WTO Accession-Its Impact on Chinese Employment-* paper prepared for the UNCTAD Division on Globalization and Development Strategies, Geneva. (October).

Bowers, J., D. Deaton and J. Turk (1982) *Labour Hoarding in British Industry* (Oxford: Basil Blackwell).

Broadman, Harry G. (1995) 'Meeting the Challenge of Enterprise Reform', *World Bank Discussion Paper* no.283.

Broadman, Harry G. and Geng Xiao (1997) 'The Coincidence of Material Incentives and Moral Hazards in Chinese Enterprises', *HIID Development Discussion Paper* no. 606 (October).

Cao, Y., Y. Qian and B.R. Weingast (1999) 'From Federalism, Chinese Style to Privatization, Chinese Style', *Economics of Transition*, vol. 7, no.1.

Chen, K., G.H. Jefferson, H.Wang, T.G. Rawski, and Y. Zheng (1988) 'New Estimates of Fixed Investment and Capital Stock for Chinese State Industry', *China Quarterly*, June.

Dewatripont, M. and E. Maskin (1995) 'Credit and Efficiency in Centralized and Decentralized Economies', *Review of Economic Studies*, October.

Fan, G. and W.T. Woo (1996) 'State Enterprise Reform as a Source of Macroeconomic Instability:The Case of China', *Asian Economic Journal*, vol. 10, no.3.

Fan, Gang, Maria Rosa Lunati and David O'Connor (1998) 'Labour Market Aspects of State Enterprise Reform in China', *OECD Development Centre Technical Paper* no.141 (October).

Fei, J. C.H. and G. Ranis (1964) *The Theory of the Labour Surplus Economy* (Irwin: Homewood, Ill.).

Government of China (1997, 1998) *China Labour Statistical Yearbook* (Beijing: China Statistical Publishing House).

Government of China (1999) *Comprehensive Statistical Data and Materials on 50 Years of New China* (Beijing: China Statistical Press).

Government of China (1999) *Statistical Yearbook of China* (Beijing: China Statistical Press).

Granick, D. (1990) *Chinese State Enterprises: A Regional Property Rights Analysis* (Chicago: Chicago University Press).

Harberger, A.C. (1971) 'On Measuring the Social Opportunity Cost of Labour', *International Labour Review*, vol.103, no.6 (June).

Hay, D.A., D.J. Morris, G.Liu and S. Yao (1994) *Economic Reform and State-owned Enterprises in China 1979-1987* (Oxford: Clarendon Press).

Huang, Y. (1996) *Inflation and Investment Controls in China* (Cambridge: Cambridge University Press).

Huang, Y. and R. Duncan (1997) 'How Successful Were China's State Sector Reforms?', *Journal of Comparative Economics*, February.

Huang, Y., W.T.Woo and R. Duncan (1999) 'Understanding the Decline of China's State Sector', *MOCT-MOST: Economic Policy in Transitional Economies*, vol. 9.

Hussain, Athar and Nicholas Stern (1991) 'Effective Demand, Enterprise Reforms and Public Finance', *STICERD Paper CP no.10* (March) (STICERD:London School of Economics) (November).

Hussain, Athar and Juzhong Zhuang (1997) 'Chinese State Enterprises and their Reform', *Asia Pacific Business Review*, vol. 3, no. 3 (Spring).

Hussain, Athar and Juzhong Zhuang (1998) 'Enterprise Taxation and Transition to a Market Economy', in Donald J.S. Brean (ed.) *Taxation in Modern China* (London: Routledge).

Jefferson, Gary H. (1998) 'China's State Enterprises: Public Goods, Externalities, and Coase', *American Economic Review-Papers and Proceedings*, May.

Jefferson, G., T. Rawski and Y. Zheng (1994) 'Productivity Change in Chinese Industry: A Comment', *China Economic Review*, vol. 5, no.2.

Jefferson, G. and T. Rawski (1995) 'How Industrial Reform Worked in China: The Role of Innovation, Competition and Property Rights', *Proceedings of the World Bank Annual Conference on Development Economics 1994*.

Jian, T. (1996) 'Priority of Privatization in Economic Reforms: China and Taiwan Compared with Russia', *HIID Development Discussion Paper* no. 566, December.

Knight, J. and L. Song (1995) 'Towards a Labour Market in China', *Oxford Review of Economic Policy*, vo. 11, no.4.

Knight, J. and L. Song (1999) 'Employment Constraints and Sub-optimality in Chinese Enterprises', *Oxford Economic Papers*, vol. 51, no.2 (April).

Kornai, J. (1980) *The Economics of Shortage* (Amsterdam: North-Holland).

Kornai, J. (1986) 'The Soft Budget Constraint', *Kyklos*, vol.39,no.1.

Kornai, J. (1993) 'The Evolution of Financial Discipline under the Postsocialist System', *Kyklos*, vol. 46, no.3.

Kornai, J. (1998) 'Legal Obligation, Non-compliance and Soft Budget Constraint', in R. Newman (ed.) *The New Palgrave Dictionary of Economics and the Law* (London:Macmillan).

Kueh, Y.Y., J.C.H. Chai, and G. Fan (1999) *Industrial Reform and Macroeconomic Instability in China* (Oxford: Clarendon Press).

Lardy, N.R. (1998) *China's Unfinished Economic Revolution* (Washington DC:Brookings Institution).

Lewis, W.A. (1954) 'Economic Development with Unlimited Supplies of Labour', *Manchester School*, May.

Li, David D. and Minsong Liang (1998) 'Causes of the Soft Budget Constraint :Evidence on Three Explanations', *Journal of Comparative Economics*, March.

Lim, L.L., G. Sziraczki and X. Zhang (1996) 'Economic performance, Labour Surplus and Enterprise Responses:Results from the Chinese Enterprise Survey', *ILO Labour Market Papers* no.13, Employment Department (Geneva:ILO).

Lin, Justin Yifu, Fang Cai and Zhou Li (1998) 'Competition, Policy Burdens, and State-Owned Enterprise Reform', *American Economic Review-Papers and Proceedings*, May.

Lin, Justin Yifu and Guofu Tan (1999) 'Policy Burdens, Accountability, and the Soft Budget Constraint', *American Economic Review-Papers and Proceedings*, May. Fan et al. (1998)

Lo, D. (1997) 'Reappraising China's Stateowned Industrial Enterprises', *School of Oriental and African Studies (SOAS) Department of Economics Working Paper Series* no.67 (London: SOAS).

McMillan, J. and B. Naughton (1993) 'How to Reform a Planned Economy: Lessons from China', *Oxford Review of Economic Policy*, vol.8, no.1.

McNally, C.A. and P.N. Lee (1998) 'Is Big Beautiful?-Restructuring China's State Sector Under the *Zhuada* Policy', Issues and Studies , vol.34, no.9 (September).

Naughton, B. (1985) *Growing Out of the Plan: Chinese Economic Reform 1978-93* (Cambridge: Cambridge University Press).

Perkins, F. (1999) 'The Cost of China's State-owned Enterprises', *MOCT-MOST:Economic Policy in Transitional Economies*, vol.9.

Perkins, F.C. and M. Raiser (1994) 'Enterprise Reform and Macroeconomic Stability in Transition Economies', *Kiel Working Papers no. 665* (Kiel:Institute for the World Economy).

Peroti, E.C., L. Sun and L. Zou (1998) 'State-owned versus Township and Village Enterprises in China', *UNU/WIDER Working Papers no. 150* (September).

Qian, Y. and G. Roland (1994) 'Regional Decentralization and the Soft Budget Constraint:The Case of China', *Centre for Economic Policy Research (CEPR) Discussion Paper* no.1013 (September) (London:CEPR).

Raiser, M. (1997a) 'Evaluating Chinese Industrial Reforms: SOEs Between Output Growth and Profit Decline', *Asian Economic Journal*, vol. 11, no.3 (September).

Raiser, Martin (1997b) 'How are China's State-owned Enterprises Doing in the 1990s? Evidence from Three Interior Provinces', *China Economic Review*, vol. 8, no.2.

Raiser, Martin (1997c) *Soft Budget Constraints and the Fate of Economic Reforms in Transition Economies and Developing Countries*, Kiel Studies 281 (Tubingen: J.C.B. Mohr).

Sachs, Jeffrey and Wing Thye Woo (1994) 'Reform in China and Russia', *Economic Policy*, no.18 (April).

Shleifer, A. and R.W. Vishny (1994) 'Politicians and Firms', *Quarterly Journal of Economics*, November.

Singapore Monetary Authority (1997) *Recent Developments in China's Stateowned Enterprises Reform  and Financial Reform: Study Trip Report,* 28-31 July, External Economic Division.

Woo, W.T., W. Hai, Y. Jing and G. Fan (1994) 'How Successful Has Chinese Enterprises Reform Been? Pitfalls in Opposite Biases and Focu', *Journal of Comparative Economics*, June.

World Bank (1993) *China: New Skills for Economic Development- The Employment and Training Implications of Enterprise Reforms* (Washington DC: World Bank).

World Bank (1996a) *The Chinese Economy-Fighting Inflation, Deepening Reforms* (Washington DC:World Bank).

World Bank (1996b) *World Development Report* (Washington DC: World Bank).

World Bank (1996c) *China: Reform of State-owned Enterprises*, China and Mongolia Department, East Asia and Pacific region (Report no. 14924-CHA), 21 June.

World Bank (1999) *China:Weathering the Storm and Learning the Lessons* (Washington DC:POverty Reduction and Economic Management Unit, East Asia and Pacific Region) (Report no. 18768 CHA) (25 May).

Xiang, Bin (1995) 'Managerial Corruption, Managerial Ownership and Corporate Governance', *Working Paper*, Hong Kong University of Science and Technology, September.

Xiang, Bin (1998) 'The Reform of China's Large State-owned Enterprises:The Indispensable Role of Stock Markets', in Joseph Y.S. Cheng (ed.) *China in the Post-Deng Era* (Hong Kong:Chinese University Press).

Xu, L.C. (1997) 'The Productivity Effects of Decentralized Reforms: An Analysis of the Chinese Industrial Reforms', *Policy Research Working Paper 1723* (Washington DC: World Bank), February.

Xu, Xiaoping (1998) *China's Financial System under Transition* (London:Macmillan).

Yang, M. and C.H. Tam (1999) 'Xiagang:The Chinese Way of Reducing Labour Redundancy and Reforming State-owned Enterprises', *East Asia Institute (EAI) Background Brief* no.38 (Singapore:EAI) (20 July).

Zhang, Weiying (1998) 'China's SOE Reform: A Corporate Governance Perspective', *Institute of Business Research Working Paper Series* no. 1998E04, Peking University.

# Chapter 8

# China's Opening to Outside World with Facing Economic Globalization

### *Linyuan Quan*

Visiting Scholar in East Asian Institute, Columbia University, from P. R. China
Permanent Mail Address:
Building 20-C-3, 83 Fu Xing Road, Beijing 100856, P. R. China
Tel: 86-10-66772847 (O), 86-10-66825635 (H)
Fax: 86-10-62875650

With the acceleration of the global economic integration process and the intensification of opening to the outside world, the potential uncertainties and risks of an open economy will increase worldwide. Especially after the Asian financial crisis that swept across the whole world, international economy is now faced with the harshest threat since the beginning of the second half of the twentieth century. People have come to a better realization of the mutual relationship, mutual infiltration, mutual influence and mutual dependence of all nations within the open economy. Economic globalization has become an unavoidable reality. With this reality, the People's Republic of China is facing many questions related to how to harmonize with the development of the world economy while taking a more conscious and more active attitude.

## I. The Asian Financial Crisis and China's Opening to the Outside World

Since the beginning of the twentieth century, very few regional economic crisis have attracted as much worldwide attention as the one that hit Asia in 1997. The Asian financial crisis appeared to be a financial problem, but was actually a result of paradoxical movement of demand and supply in real economy and production. It also resulted from readjustment in industrial structures. This financial crisis was not destructive to the Chinese domestic economy. One reason for this was that China's currency, *Renminbi* (RMB), is inconvertible in capital transaction. Another reason was that China's capital market has not been opened to foreign capital. More important than either of these reasons, however, is that China has accumulated considerable economic strength in the twenty years of reform and opening to the outside world (1980-2000). A few years ago, China began to enforce the policy of macro control in connection with unstable factors in economic operations. It is not surprising that China could stand firm against the impact from the outside. One way to see the situation is by thinking of industry as the root and finance as the leaf. To maintain the healthy development of national economy is the basis to prevent financial risks and defend national financial and economic security. Drawing on the experience and lessons from foreign countries, we believe an effective way to prevent risks is to optimize the domestic economic structure and strengthen the fundamentals of domestic economy.

The Asian financial crisis reveals that there was a serious disconnection between the international movement of capital and real economy. The stagnation of material production on the one hand and the increasing expansion of virtual capital on the other were the underlying causes of the financial fluctuation and crisis. The unprecedented intensification of economic globalization and financial integration and the accelerated development of computer science and high technology were the two bases for the short-term rapid international movement of capital. With financial globalization as the background, the lack of supervision and restriction over the thousands of billions of idle capital moving daily in the international financial market contributes to the instability of global market and world economy. Accordingly, in an open economy, the possibility of financial crisis in China increase as it opens to the outside world. A crisis is bound to break out at some vulnerable point and would create some variety of shocks to the global economy. Therefore, the key to preventing financial crisis lies in improving financial systems and strengthening financial supervision. In the case of China, the most urgent task is to centralize on dissolving bad bank loans and to strengthen reform of financial systems in connection with the in-depth of reform in state-owned enterprises.

The Asian financial crisis did have some negative impact on China in the export market. First, China boasts of more than 50 percent of the total export volume to Japan and other East Asian countries and regions. These regions fell into an economic slump as result of influence of the crisis, which constituted a considerable impact to their trade with China. In 1998, the increase rate of export in China was only 0.3 percent, a bottom low in China's twenty years of reform and opening to the outside world. Some 65 percent of the foreign capital utilized by China came from East Asia. The financial crisis has led to a large-scale reduction of this portion of capital.

Second, the financial crisis imposed heavy pressures on the exchange rate policies. China has paid a high price to keep stability of the exchange rates. What deserves special emphasis is that the Asian financial crisis broke out at a critical time when the Chinese economy was recovering from a recession. From 1998 to the end of 1999, the government was concentrated on reinvigorating the economy without achieving an ideal result. We can not say that this has nothing to do with unfavorable international environment brought about by the Asian financial crisis and the pressure it imposed on China's domestic economy.

The Asian financial crisis promoted a greater awareness of the financial risk within the government and various social circles. People began to reflect on the road that they had traversed so as to adjust their development policies. After twenty years of reform, China has now entered into the most critical stage in the reform of many areas. Unless China adheres to the market economic system, draws lessons from the Asian financial crisis, takes further steps in intensifying reform, and expands the scope of opening to promote more rapid and better development of economy, it will not be ready to enter the international market. China must actively overcome the various kinds of potential risks and crisis to accelerate the modernization process.

## II. BACKGROUND FOR THE ECONOMIC GLOBALIZATION TREND

The economic globalization process occurs at a time when the global tensions are lessening and countries are giving priority to developing their economies and actively integrating them with the international market. It is also occurring as new technologies as well as a knowledge economy develop with rapidity. Both of these provide unprecedented convenience in the economic exchange among all nations of the world. As long as the law of socialized production exists, the pace of technological innovation will not stop and the trend of economic globalization can not be held back. This is the inexorable trend of social progress as well as that of social economic development. With a foothold on the formulation of policies, China can integrate its economic development into the mainstream of world economic development.

Economic globalization is fundamentally an international industrial restructuring led by advanced nations and propelled mainly by multinational corporations. The industrial restructuring in the economic globalization has not only resulted in a complete transfer of some industries, but more importantly a transfer of some links in the production chain within the same industry. In most cases in the past, due to the limitation of various technological conditions, the division of labor in industry and adjustments in the industrial structures were conducted within the border of a single country. With the further expansion of the market and closer relations of international economic exchange, it takes more money and time to conduct industrial restructuring within one single country than doing it through the process of economic globalization. In western countries such as the United States, where investment and trade are relatively open, the economic transition is now going from the industrial economy to knowledge economy due to their fulfillment of readjustment and optimization in the whole world. They have, therefore, maintained a strong momentum of economic growth.

At present, against the background of economic globalization, structural readjustment has already become a theme of world economy. Both developing and developed countries are trying hard to find their shares of division of labor and positions in the new international economic environment so as to determine their individual competitive advantages. Generally speaking, the opportunities that are brought about for China by economic globalization are reflected in several ways.

First, economic globalization has expanded the space for the application of resources. From traditional elementary products and raw materials to appropriate applicable technology and production equipment, from high and new technology to advanced business management knowledge, from direct investment of foreign capital to loans and funds from different sources and different kinds--these are all available in the world market. Appropriate use of these resources can produce enormous profits, which can be turned toward direct productive force.

Second, globalization has also provided an applicable and expanding international market. The wide coverage and multivalent property of the international market has made it possible for China's commodities, labor, or service to get into it with comparative advantage.

Third, China itself possesses a huge economic scale and market potential, which are very attractive to other countries and regions. This, in turn, creates opportunities for China to make use of international resources. Such external economic effects offer an important opportunity to China, a country that is undergoing the process of transition.

The process of economic globalization is often accompanied by a blind market leading force and a high degree of uncertainty. "Freedom of economy and trade" is the preferred slogan of economic powers in international economic relations. China should take a cautious attitude to the further intensification of opening to the outside world.

First, economic globalization brings harsh challenges and threats apart along with the benefits and opportunities. One of the basic principles is that the globalization of world economy also means a universality of market economy in the scope of the whole world. China's opening to the outside world to participate in international cooperation also means that it must compete under the rule of market economy in the world. To a great extent, it is a competition of perfection degree of the market economic system and a competition of the international competitive power of a nation's enterprises. For a developing country like China, undergoing the transition to market economy, this is an arduous test of its ability to stand firm in the competition while simultaneously developing itself.

Second, intensifying the China's opening to the outside world in order to cater for the process of economic globalization involves paying careful attention to the establishment and improvement of risk prevention mechanisms. These are two sides of the same coin. It is also the greatest implication people have drawn from the Asian financial crisis.

Third, economic globalization is essentially about benefit. China should not blindly follow the economic mainstream led by the present economic powers. China must start from the point of its national interest in order to avoid a passive adjustment to and blind following of the trends and rules advocated by developed nations.

Fourth, national interest should be properly protected in the course of globalization and integration. Such protection does not mean going against the policy of opening to the outside world, nor does it mean unconformity with the world trends, but rather keeping in mind the requirement for China own survival and development. Any nations will tend to take a protective attitude when their fundamental interests are being threatened.

## III. PROBLEMS AND CHALLENGES FOR CHINA
## AFTER ENTERING THE WTO

The trend of economic globalization increases a mutual reliance among nations. The influence of the World Trade Organization is, therefore, also increasingly extensive and far-reaching. It casts direct influence on the economic situation of the non-member states as well as its member states and on the development of enterprises all over the world. In the first round of the General Agreement on Tariff and Trade (GATT), the total trade volume of the 23 signatory states to the agreement accounted for only one-fifth of the total world trade volume of the time. Towards the end of 1994, however, the trade volume of more than 100 signatory states accounted for over 90 percent of the total trade volume of the world. Before the founding of the WTO, over 85 percent of China's export items were accepted by GATT. Because China was not a member nation of GATT, however, it could not enjoy the preferential treatment given to GATT member nations. This explained the arbitrary restrictions imposed in international economic and trading activities on China by the western society, and undermined the unsteady development of Chinese enterprises, especially those related with foreign businesses. China's entrance into WTO is of great significance to the Chinese economy and the Chinese enterprises that are going step by step into the big international market.

The early entry of China into the WTO is of very important significance. It is beneficial to the increase of export volume when the macro economic situation for domestic enterprises is declining. The increase in the operating rate of capacity, along with the further opening of the domestic market, introduction of new competitors, acceleration of readjustment of the economic structures, product mix, investment priorities and management systems of domestic enterprises, are beneficial to China's adaptation to the international competition and development of international competitive strength in the open market environment.

According to findings of an empirical research project, China, at the macro level, will raise its efficiency greatly after entry into the WTO. It is estimated that, if China begins to carry out its commitment for accessing the WTO in 2000 and fulfils all its promises, by 2005 the country's actual GDP and the social welfare benefits will rise, respectively, by 195.5 billion and 159.5 billion RMB (according to the price standard of 1995), accounting for 1.5 percent and 1.2 percent of the GDP of the year. The main factor that promotes the increase of actual GDP is the increased of efficiency made possible by the reallocation of resources according to comparative advantages. Under such conditions, in the years from 2000 to 2010, the annual increase rate of GDP in China will be nearly one percentage point higher than it would be if it did not enter the WTO.

At the micro level, China's entry into the WTO will bring about a relatively big readjustment in the domestic economic structure. The highly protected agricultural production and the capital-intensive production such as automobiles, instruments, cotton, wheat etc. will record a considerable lower output level, while the labor-intensive production--such as textile and garment manufacturing--will be major beneficiaries. More specifically, liberalization in agricultural trade will not threaten "food security". Even if the import quotas for agricultural products are cancelled, the rate of food self-sufficiency in 2005 would still be maintained at over 92 percent. Considering the scale economy and the monopolistic nature of the auto industry, the negative influence on the auto industry and employment will be less than expected if China enters into the WTO and the declining rate in the output and employment will be around 12 percent. The competition brought about by trade liberalization would reduce the number of auto manufacturers by 27 percent, but the size of auto companies would expand, which will help increase their efficiency and competitive edge in the international market. Due to the impact of the entry into the WTO on the agricultural sector, the actual household income in rural areas, in spite of the transfer of some rural labor to non-agricultural sectors by 2005, would be 2.1 percent lower than it would be if China does not enter into the WTO. The actual household income in urban areas, however, would increase by 4.6 percent.

China's entry into the WTO will impact heavily on the export market of labor-intensive products and the import market of primary agricultural products in the world. The international market share of garment products made in China will rise by 10 percentage points, thus reducing the market shares of other countries. The increase in the import of land-intensive primary agricultural products in China can hopefully exceed that of Japan in 2010 to turn China into the largest import country of agricultural products.

China's entry into the WTO will determine the orientation of its domestic policy readjustments, as summarized below.

(1) The policy of industrial readjustment will provide support to capital and technology-intensive industries to stimulate the upgrading of the industries which, in turn, will offset the unfavorable impact brought about by the opening of trade on these industries.

(2) The policy of tax readjustment will strengthen the function of redistribution of tax revenues to slow down the expansion of possible income differences and prevent any social instability related to these differences.

(3) A policy of creating conditions for the transfer of agricultural labor force is necessary. The flow of agricultural labor force into the secondary and tertiary industries and from rural areas into urban areas is a precondition as well as the chief challenge for the realization of industrialization and modernization in China. In a relatively long period of time, this task will be more formidable than the re-employment problem now facing state-owned enterprises. China's accession to the WTO will ensure the entry of labor-intensive products into the international market.

(4) The promotion of a relatively high savings rate should secure and attract more inflow of foreign capital.

From the perspective of near future, China should start from the background of globalization to optimize the commodity structure of export and participate in international trade on all fronts. The basic direction is to occupy those technology-intensive parts of the industry with high added value as determined by China's own comprehensive advantages and transfer labor-intensive production with low added value to other countries, rather than trying to occupy the entire spectrum. Next, a long-term cooperative relationship should be established with transnational corporations in trade investment. This is the focal point for China's utilization of foreign capital to develop trade. With this as a basis, China should facilitate the development of China's transnational business. China should also participate actively in multilateral and regional cooperation in economy and trade. In particular, China should strive to participate in the formulation of the new rules and regulations for international trade and investment. In the liberalization process of trade investment initiated by the multilateral or regional economic organizations, China should safeguard the interest and benefit of the developing countries and foster a fair and rational new order of international economic trade on the basis of balanced rights and obligations.

## IV. INTERNATIONAL COMPETITIVE ADVANTAGE AND THE ROLE OF GOVERNMENT

In the next 10 to 20 years, China will be faced with the double challenge of industrialization and globalization. China's efforts to enter the WTO is a specific manifestation of such challenge. In this process, the economic functions of the government are of crucial importance.

According to the latest research, the main challenges imposed by economic globalization on the economic roles of governments in developing countries can be summarized as follows.

First, when it is a situation of globalization of the product market and massive entry of multinational corporations, the key to extending the production scope and upgrading industrial and export structures lies in how a government can help domestic enterprises enter new sectors of production and improve the competitiveness of the new products.

Second, government must strengthen the control over capital flow, maintain flexible policies on exchange rates and establish a sound domestic financial system.

Third, with the impact of external factors (such as the deterioration of trade conditions, sharp decline of external demand, unfavorable changes in foreign interest and exchange rates ), there should be an emphasis on the role of the government in income redistribution. The focal point here is for government to reduce the negative influence brought about by external factor on the low-income social stratum to prevent this social stratum from becoming a source of social instability. A government should spread benefits gained from international competition to the largest number of people by means of taxation, transfer payments and establishment of a perfect social security system.

China's economy is now undergoing a transformation from agriculture-based rural economy to industry-based urban economy and from the planned economic system to a market economic system. The government economic role is based on and determined by this transformation. Problems and difficulties arising in the course of economic transformation are undoubtedly the focus of the government's work. Only a healthy and perfected internal economic system can offer greater flexibility in response to economic globalization.

The result of economic globalization is bound to be an unprecedented intensification of international competition. China enjoys the following advantages in the international competition.

In the first place, it has a domestic market with huge potentials. This is the fundamental factor that distinguishes the economy of a big country from that of a small one. As long as the domestic market is unified and competitive, the enormous market scale will provide the necessary market condition for improving the international competitiveness of newly emerging industries.

The second advantage is China's virtually unlimited supply of cheap labor. This will ensure China's competitive advantage of labor-intensive products for a long period of time.

Third, China has a high savings rate. This will provide a foundation for huge investments needed for rapid economic development.

Fourth, and finally, overseas Chinese all over the world and international trade and financial centers such as Hong Kong will play an extremely important intermediary role in foreign economic activities. All these advantages are the objective basis upon which China has benefited from international competitions over the past twenty years, and they will also be the basis upon which China continues to benefit from international competition in the future.

## REFERENCES

(1) Zhou Jianming: *Towards a Better understanding of the Trend of Economic Globalization and a Higher Level of Opening to the Outside World*, carried in Shanghai Economic Studies, November 1997.

(2) zhang Zhuoyuan: *Review of the Twenty Years in Economic Reform and Future Prospects*, Chin Planning Press, September 1998.

(3) Di yinqing: *Strategic Thinking Concerning the Entry into the WTO*, carried in Opening Pioneering, No.2-3,1998.

(4) Wu Jinglian: *Contemporary Economic Reform in China: Strategies and Implementation,* Shanghai Far East Press, January 1999.

*Chapter 9*

# LOCI AND SCOPE OF STATE POWER: CENTRAL-PROVINCIAL TENSIONS IN CHINA

## *Linda Chelan Li*
City University of Hong Kong

## INTRODUCTION

The onset of economic reform and its twists and turns over the past two decades has coincided with an increasing concern over the escalating tension between the central and provincial governments in China. Attention focused on the nature of relationship between the central government and the provinces: to what extent it is a principal-agent relationship, or whether the relationship is more akin to a specific kind of partnership. Whilst these questions are not dissimilar to those asked to countries in quite different political systems, the answers given in the case of China have varied with changes in circumstances.[1] In the 1950s and 1960s provincial governments were seen as mere agents of the central government. This image was then replaced by that of the assertive 'partners' after economic reform took off in the late 1970s. Politics in reform China have been described as resembling a 'bargaining treadmill' with bureaucracies at various levels bargaining fiercely with one another, and the central government not necessarily calling the tune (Lampton, 1987a).

One major difficulty in the literature has been to explain change in the central-provincial relationship. Towards resolving this problem, a number of theoretical attempts

---

[1] A sample of major works on central-local relations in post-1949 China include Donnithorne (1969, 1976), Lampton (1987a, b), Lardy (1975, 1976), Goodman (1986, 1997), Segal (1994), Goodman and Segal (1994), Chung (1995b), Huang (1996), Jia and Lin (1994), Yang (1997), Li (1997, 1998), Lyons (1987), Oksenberg and Tong (1991), Tong (1989), Lieberthal and Oksenberg (1988), Lieberthal and Lampton (1992), Shirk (1990), Shue (1988), Solinger (1977, 1996), Teiwes (1966, 1971, 1974), Vogel (1989), Wang (1995), White III (1976), Whitney (1969), Wong (1991), Wu and Cheng (1995), Breslin (1996), Hendrischke and Feng (1999), and Zhao (1990).

have been made to recast critical concepts and suggest new analytical approaches (Li, 1997a, 1998b; Chung, 1995b). This essay seeks to continue this effort. Building on a non-zero-sum conception of power, it argues that, to deepen understanding, analysts need to move beyond questions on the loci, or distribution, of state power *per se*, but relate the loci questions to those on the scope of state power in society as well.[2]

This linkage is particularly important in understanding the ferocity and frequency of central-local conflicts in contemporary China. Unlike in the imperial period the cycles of adjustment between the two poles of centralization and decentralization have now taken a much shorter span to complete. Tensions at the central-local (and especially provincial) interface have accumulated much more quickly. Within merely four decades of the establishment of the People's Republic, the alarm bell was rung regarding possible disintegration threats from the peripheries, whilst the average dynastic cycle during the imperial time was 155 years.[3] The central question addressed here is thus: why have tensions ridden so high in the recent decades within so short a time, as compared with past history? Is it because the distribution of central-local power since 1949 has been substantially different from what was the case in the long imperial history, or is it because of some other reasons?

This essay argues that an answer lies beyond a narrow focus on the locale of power. There is a need to examine a separate but related dimension, the scope of state power, which has seen very substantial change since the turn of the Twentieth Century, and especially since 1949. The contention is that it is the interaction of the two dimensions, the loci and scope of state power, that has resulted in the high level of tension in the former arena.

## LOCI OF STATE POWER

There are two dimensions to the internal distribution of state power within the state structure, functional and spatial, each posing its own issues and problems. Historically, tensions between functional departments were often 'papered over' through the presiding role of the authoritarian ruler, be it the imperial emperor or the modernizing Party.[4] Tensions at the spatial faults had been less amenable to such exercises. Central-local

---

[2] Some major works on the question of the scope of state power in China are, for instance, Schram (1985, 1987), and Shue (1988).

[3] Alarm bells were heard both within and outside China. See for instance Goldstone (1995), Wang and Wu (1993), Chang (1992), Segal (1994), and Friedman (1995). The 155-year figure was arrived by taking the average of the duration of 12 imperial dynasties when China was under unified rule. If five 'short' dynasties were discounted (Qin: 15 years, Xi Jin: 51 years, Dong Jin: 104 years, Sui: 37 years, Yuan: 98 years), the average dynastic cycle becomes 223 years. Standard deviations for the two measures are, respectively, 92 years and 51 years. The longest-lasting dynasty is Tang (290 years), followed by Ming (277 years) and Qing (268 years). Author's calculations based on *Zhonghua Lidai Shixi biao* (A Chronology of Chinese Dynasties), Hong Kong: Zhonghua Bookstore, 1987.

[4] The state organs in imperial China have highly differentiated duties under an under-differentiated power of the sovereign, the emperor. See Vandermeersch (1985: 5)

relations often led to explicit conflicts, to the extent that local authorities had sometimes been accused of threatening the integrity of the country. The recurrence and ferocity of tension gave rise to the old popular folklore: 'the country will become united after being divided for a long time; but it will in time divide and fall apart again'. Apparently the political system faced a major challenge in the vast expanse of China, and in the country's wide disparity in human and physical conditions.[5] The sheer size of the country resulted in the proliferation of local authorities at various levels, and there was a paradoxical co-existence of interdependence and threat between the central and local authorities. The former has led to intermittent, and recurrent, unity; the latter, it was perceived, contributed to division and disintegration (Li, 1998a, Ge, 1994).

The prominence of the spatial dimension has been validated by developments since 1949. Guided by development strategies that favoured local initiatives, waves of decentralization in the late 1950s, the 1970s and 1980s have nurtured local power, laying the ground for explicit central-local conflicts in the 1960s and especially since the late 1980s. The level of conflict was revealed by the repeated references to the warlord period of the 1920s, and by the use of the description of 'kingship economies' to refer to local economies under the management of local governments. Such use of language suggested a country under the threat of disintegration.

The shadow of historical incidences of disintegration has resulted in a notion of zero-sum power in the conduct and perception of spatial politics.[6] The Centre and the provinces are often seen as being locked in a situation of perpetual conflicts, each scrambling for gains at the expense of the other. Another problem of the contemporary disintegration thesis lies in its suggestion that China could possibly disintegrate as a result of the economic initiatives of the local governments to implement reform. This suggestion dramatizes the political implication of central-provincial (and sub-provincial) conflicts, which are, to start with, mostly related to the management of the economy.[7]

There is no doubt that conflicts abounded at the central-provincial interface and their intensity has been increasing since reform. Tensions over economic issues could also, and do, have political spill-over effects. The problem with a zero-sum concept of power was, however, that conflicts were being emphasized to the exclusion of other important developments, and in particular, the occurrence and opportunities of co-operation. Also the political spill-overs of economic conflicts were excessively inflated to the scale of possible national dismemberment. The sole focus on conflicts reinforced the historical obsession with integration concerns and led one to look for mechanical centralization as a remedy to the tension, neglecting other possible alternatives. In this process the endless cycles of unity-division-unity, and centralization and decentralization in Chinese political history were being continuously reproduced.

---

[5] That the topographical conditions, including the size, of a country have great influence on the configurations of, and the dynamics within, the state structure has been well noted. See Bunger (1987: xvii)

[6] For a full critique of the zero-sum conception of power in the context of spatial politics in China, see Li (1997a).

[7] For a rebuttal of the disintegration thesis, see Huang (1995).

## SCOPE OF STATE POWER

The scope of state power refers to that which constitutes the state power in society that is to be distributed between the Centre and the provinces. On the question of state and society an observation of an historian is illuminating:

"One could say that in China, the state is all. History explains this. The state was not an organism which developed little by little and was obliged to make a place for itself among other powers, as was the case in the West, where the state had to impose itself on the independent powers of the Church, of feudalism and of the nobility, come to terms with the merchants and seek the support of the financiers. In China, the state was an established reality from the beginning, or in any case from the time when the formula was worked out in the state of Qin... *It was the great organizer of society and of territory.* The administrative division into districts responsible to the central authorities came into existence in China in the third century B.C., whereas in Europe no equivalent appears prior to the French Revolution.... The only problem for the Chinese state, in the course of its long history, was to *prevent* the development of powers other than its own, such as that of the merchants, the armies, the religious communities, and to prevent dangerous splits at the top." (emphasis added) (Gernet, 1985: xxxii)

Notwithstanding the dominance of the Chinese state, traditionally the intensity of state power in practice was much more circumscribed and limited (Schwartz, 1987). Underneath the political and social ideal for 'total consensus' and 'harmony', there was in fact considerable room for substantive disagreement, as the subject of what required consensus had often, during most years of the imperial period, remained vague and loosely defined. For example, the 'orthodoxy' of Confucianism during imperial history had not precluded the 'alien' influences of Buddhism and other intellectual streams such as Daoism (Schwartz, 1987, p. 4). In a similar vein, the supreme authority of the political order *vis-a-vis* the social and moral orders was characterized by the eclectic nature of the authority itself. On the one hand, the state had unlimited authority in social and economic activities. On the other hand, state intervention in society and in the economy in practice was intermittent and *ad hoc*. Most activities in society took place with minimal participation by the state.

It is worth noting that such an eclectic relationship was also found within the structure of the state, between the emperor as the source of state authority and the functional organs of state power. The early existence of the Chinese state had resulted in its early maturation in terms of structure, so that a sophisticated structure of government with specialized organs of power and a merit-based bureaucracy was already in place in China by the Eleventh Century, at the time of Sung Dynasty (Gernet, 1987: xviii). The emperor theoretically possessed supreme authority within a highly centralized state structure. In practice his authority was more of a moral and religious nature, and organisational means of control remained weak and underdeveloped. As in the case of state-society relations, there was a clear gap between theory and practice in the case of power distribution within the state structure. The scope of state power was supposedly all encompassing but in practice the state exercised only limited, if also arbitrary, intervention in the society. On the loci question, power was supposedly concentrated at the top of state structure but in practice it was more dispersed and the situation much more ambiguous and indeterminate.

One possible explanation for the gap is that the major intellectual influences in traditional China all prescribed for a limited government (Schwartz, 1987: 6). The Confucians talked about government by virtue. Good governance was to be achieved not by active substantive policies and measures by the government, but by the exemplary influences on the behaviour of the common people by the good conduct and moral integrity of the emperor and, to a less extent, of his officials. The Daoists, meanwhile, promoted the philosophy of naturalism, whereby the best governance was, simply, no government. These exerted an impact on the state power holders through long years of education so that authoritarian leaders were taught to exercise their power with restraint.

Another explanation stressed institutional and technological factors, so that the gap arose out of a lack of the capacity of control in a pre-modern time. The paradox was, according to this line of thinking, more a result of technical and institutional capability rather than intention.

This is not the place to engage in a full discussion of these possibilities. For the current purpose the important point is that the eclectic nature of the Chinese state structure has, to a large extent, survived to the contemporary period, although the scope and actual exercise of state power over other domains has changed considerably. The delineation of jurisdiction between agencies and levels of government has remained vague, leaving plenty of room for conflicts and mutual shrugging of duties. This has led to recurrent complaints of ambiguity and arbitrariness in the assignment of duties among various levels of government and state agencies, a problem partly attributable to the lack of the rule of law in the political system. On the other hand, the external political environment since mid-Nineteenth Century has, over time, transformed the governing ethos from one of maintenance to one of fostering change. Change was perceived as needed, as a matter of urgency, to save the 'Middle Kingdom' from the humiliation it suffered from unwelcome foreign guests. Gradually, the scale of change perceived as necessary moved beyond the more peripheral aspects to encompass the core of the traditional order. The crisis was 'total', and thus the remedy had to be a total one. In fact, the overthrow of the dynastical system in favour of a republic was itself part and parcel of the 'total remedy'. The reconstituted Chinese state had the unprecedented task of bringing the society to modernity, and recapturing the fame and glory that China had enjoyed for so long a time in the past.

As the state sought to achieve a wide range of specific substantive objectives, it required new institutions through which to implement the new objectives. With more to do, the question of how to distribute power and get the job done became more problematic than before when the agenda of the state was far more modest. It was thus in this context that the long-existing dilemma of centralization and decentralization had caused so much more tension within the relatively brief history of the People's Republic. The following section will outline some recent empirical trends in the dimensions of loci and scope of state power that resulted in the increased tension, and emergent trends that subsequently sought to ameliorate the tension.

# FROM NEGATIVE-SUM TO POSITIVE SUM:
# THE TRANSITION TO THE TAX-SHARING FISCAL SYSTEM

The heightened tension was partly a result of the historical perception of the loci question by the concerned parties: that power distribution between the Centre and provinces always constituted a zero-sum game. It has been said that Chinese politics was historically characterized by a 'total victory-total failure' situation, whereby the contending parties engaged in a zero-sum struggle until one side fully won and the other side was brought to total destruction (Tsou, 1994). The problem with a zero-sum conception of power is that it is static and cannot foresee change from within the system. Under this framework the Centre is bound to gain as much as the provinces lose, and vice versa. Whilst a 'total victory/total failure' situation might apply to palace politics, where contenders for the top leadership position often sought the 'elimination' of competitors to safeguard their hold on power, it was quite insufficient in the context of central-provincial relations. There a situation of mutual dependence replaces, as a rule, one of mutual elimination. All central governments require intermediaries to govern the country, and intermediaries by definition need a central government to complement their very existence. Individual provincial leaders may be dismissed by their central superiors, and individual central leaders may be ousted as a result of provincial pressure, but the structural interdependence of the Centre and the provinces, as two constitutive components of the state structure, is there to stay.

Moreover, the zero-sum conception often leads one to equate the central government with the state itself, and see the adjustment of power distribution between the Centre and its intermediaries in a mechanical, 'one loses, one gains', schema. To the extent that one party gains as much as the other party loses, this vision of power relations cannot envisage any possibility of qualitative change to the system. The winning party would have little incentive to seek change, other than furthering its own gain, whilst the losing party would have no ability to achieve change.

Even though this perception of power does have an impact on the consciousness and behaviour of the relevant parties, it does not reflect in full the conduct of politics in practice. The actual working of the central-provincial relationship, it has been argued, can be better understood in a non-zero-sum schema of power (Li, 1998a). Conflicts arising from inadequate distribution and institutionalization of power have contributed to a situation of negative-sum power, wherein both parties perceive themselves as the loser vis-a-vis the other party. Despite the fact that substantial resources have been decentralized to the provincial level during reform, the provinces are still complaining about the mismatch between their resources and authority on the one hand, and their obligations and duties on the other. Provincial governments thus obviously would not agree to their being the 'winner' in their relations with the Centre. On the other hand the Centre sees itself being threatened by the increasing gap between central policy and provincial implementation, and by the shrinking resources at its immediate disposal. Both sides have come to see themselves as the loser in their relationship.

Mutual dependence implies that any conflict arising between the parties will be protracted. As total victory for any one party is out of question, any resolution of conflicts will involve compromise from both sides. At the same time, power from either direction is not necessarily balanced. The asymmetry of power relations, however, does not preclude the ability of the weaker party to extract concessions from the stronger. The crux is that each side to the conflict will only agree to a move when it sees benefit in so doing. In other words, a compromise will only be struck, and change ensues, when both the Centre and the provinces see gain in the change. With the move the situation changes from one of negative-sum to positive-sum.

The institution of the tax-sharing fiscal system between the central and provincial governments in 1994 serves as a good example of the shift from a negative-sum situation to one of positive sum.[8] Prior to the change both the Centre and provinces have been complaining of the dwindling resources at their disposal, and the mismatch of such resources with their increasing obligations. Under the contractual system implemented since 1980, the share of central fiscal revenue out of the total national revenue has been declining from a high at 40 per cent in 1984 to 22 per cent in 1993. As a result the central government felt increasingly impotent in face of the rising demand for macro-regulation of the economy and fulfilment of other social needs. On the other hand, provinces also complained of the inadequacy and inconsistencies of many central policies. Whilst they had been delegated more resources during the course of economic reform, they had also been made to shoulder more responsibilities, sometimes to a scale larger than what their resources could support. Both the Centre and provinces were thus dissatisfied with their situation, and sought to outmanoeuvre the other party in order to protect better their interests (Li, 1998a).

When conflicts became increasingly intense and both parties found the situation increasingly intolerable, there grew gradually the momentum and incentive for compromise, and change. In this instance the driving force of change has come more from the central government. Whilst both parties complained about their financial difficulty, comparatively speaking the Centre has had larger problems, since the provinces had by and large succeeded to bypass much of the financial control from the Centre. The budget deficits at local levels, in the final analysis, also formed the burden of the central administration. The central government thus was motivated to take the initiative and change the rules of the game to improve its own position.[9]

Despite the interest in change in the central government, the actual course of events reflected the substantial influence of the provinces. Whilst the Centre pushed through the new system, the provinces had been able to extract significant concessions and to shape

---

[8] For accounts of the fiscal system reform in 1994, see Chung (1995a) and Naughton (1997).

[9] The Centre started to show serious concern from 1988, when the Ministry of Finance and the State Planning Commission were directed to study the slide in central control over fiscal resources. The resultant study identified the decentralization programme in the 1980s as the watershed in terms of two developments. First, the share of national fiscal revenue as a proportion of national income fell. This revealed the slipping control of the state budget in societal resources. Secondly, the share of central fiscal revenue as a proportion of total national revenue fell drastically. This meant that more of the fiscal revenue had gone into local coffers. (Author's interview, Beijing, August 1994).

the content of the system in their favour. The Guangdong government, for instance, succeeded in persuading Vice-premier Zhu Rongji to change the base year for the calculation of the new revenue sharing formula under the new system from 1992 to 1993, and as a result substantially increased the revenue that the province could retain in subsequent years.[10] The tax-sharing system implemented in 1994 was, in any event, a far cry from the original conception of a uniform system in which all provinces would share fiscal revenues with the central government by means of standardized sharing ratios of taxes.[11] The revised version required the central government to refund the difference between locally retained revenue as of the base year of 1993 and local revenue of subsequent years calculated in accordance with the new tax-sharing formula, thus protecting the vested interest of provinces as of 1993. The tax-sharing system implemented in 1994 was thus a mixture of the substance of the previous contractual system and the basic framework of the new tax-sharing system.[12]

Despite the obvious provincial influence on the new fiscal system, which once caused some central officials to announce the failure of the reform,[13] subsequent developments suggest that the central government did improve its position substantially. Central revenue collections tripled and the central share of non-debt income more than doubled in one year, jumping from 22 per cent in 1993 to 56 per cent in 1994. With the share of expenditure between central and provincial governments largely unchanged (the Centre accounting for around 30 per cent), the large increase in the central share of revenue collection resulted in a substantial dependence of the provinces on central remittances. Since 1994 the percentage share of central revenue dropped slightly, but was still much higher than the average in the 1980s.[14] Despite the substantial watering down of the new system as a result of concessions to provincial demands, therefore, the original aim of the Centre in launching the fiscal reform was still by and large fulfilled.[15]

---

[10] Zhu Rongji came to Guangdong in September 1993 as part of a provincial tour to mobilize support for the impending fiscal reform. Given the robust economic performance of 1993, a shift of base year from 1992 to 1993 significantly affected the distribution of fiscal revenue in the favour of provinces.

[11] The basic principle whereby fiscal revenues and expenditures were allocated between the Centre and provinces since 1949 was always founded upon the 'base-line method'. Notwithstanding its many advantages (simplicity, and taking consideration of historical developments and past performance, for example), the 'base-line method' has faced increasing criticisms within the Centre and among some provincial governments since the 1980s. One major criticism was its tendency to aggravate the gap between the richer and poorer provinces (Song, 1992: 166-8).

[12] The State Council Document No. 85 (1993), 'The State Council's decision on implementing tax-sharing in the fiscal management system', printed in *Caizheng* 1994, 2: 18-20, explicitly stated that the existing interests of the provinces would not be affected in 1994. The compromise was intended to be temporary, but no exact timing was given in the State Council Document for the expiry of the transitional arrangements.

[13] Author's interviews, Beijing, April 1994. See also the views from the Ministry of Finance, in Lu (1994).

[14] The shares over the years are: 29.8% (1991), 28.1% (1992), 22% (1993), 55.7% (1994), 52.2% (1995), 49.4% (1996), 48.9% (1997), 49.5% (1998), 51.1 % (1999). The average for 1981-90 is 34%. See Ministry of Finance ed., *China Finance Yearbook*, 2000, p. 422.

[15] A similar assessment was made in a report by Ministry of Finance officials on the implementation of the tax-sharing system (Jiang, 1998).

To a lesser extent, provinces have also gained under the new system. Despite their lukewarm attitude initially, provincial governments also found benefits in the new system.[16] Despite its failure in imposing a clearer division of expenditure responsibilities, the new system did establish a clearer definition of central and local *revenue* responsibilities. It also prescribed a norm in the direction of a more uniform system based on factor needs. One immediate benefit for the provinces was that they were since under fewer demands from the Centre for additional 'contributions' apart from those expected under the fiscal system.[17] This reduction of central intervention allowed a stable institutional framework to cultivate new sources of local revenue.[18]

Through the institution and implementation of the new tax-sharing fiscal system we therefore see a shift from a negative-sum relationship between the Centre and provinces to a positive-sum situation. Before the change, both parties had bitter complaints and each saw herself as the loser. Afterwards, both saw *some* gains under the new system. Undoubtedly the respective gains were not equal. They were also fraught with mixed feelings. Given the structural interdependence between the Centre and provinces, it is not possible for either party to gain in all dimensions. Gains are thus bound to be 'incomplete'. Upon the initial implementation of the new fiscal system, the Centre had gained by significantly increasing its control over the flow of fiscal funds. Previously most provinces could balance their books with their own local revenue. Under the new system a substantial portion of provincial expenditure was paid by central remittances, giving the Centre potentially a larger leverage on the conduct of provincial affairs. The

---

[16]See Chung (1995a) for preliminary findings about responses by various provinces. My initial reading suggests that the principle of vested interests was also a major reason for many provinces favouring the change at the time. Most provinces were more interested in ensuring a better deal, namely more resources allocated for their use, under whatever system, than in the long-term rationality of the system *per se*. Those provincial governments that traditionally relied on central fiscal subsidies welcomed the new system because it was seen as being able to increase the share of central revenue, so that the Centre may give them more financial assistance in the future. The director of Shaanxi's Provincial Finance Bureau, for instance, had said that Shaanxi totally supported the new system, and its intended effect of centralizing more fiscal revenue to the Centre, because 'if central revenue could not be guaranteed, then everything else could not be guaranteed'. See "Director of Finance Bureaux on the tax-sharing system reform", *Caizheng* 1994, 2: 11-13, p.12. Other provincial governments, however, for example Heihangjiang, Jiangxi, Sichuan, Hebei, and Guangdong, were worried about the adverse effect of the reform on their financial position, and adopted a reluctant and lukewarm attitude towards the change. See the same source above, and the report, 'Local party and government leaders on the fiscal and tax reforms', *Caizheng*, 1994, 3: 11-13. During interviews different respondents have either made or confirmed the point that Guangdong was perhaps the strongest dissenting voice, in 1993, against the new system, not because the province felt particularly strongly about the principle of tax-sharing or was against having more uniformity and regularity in the system, but because of its immense vested interests under the previous system (Author's interviews, Shanghai and Beijing, May 1994).

[17] Author's interviews, Guangzhou, June 1996. This observation was also confirmed during author's interviews at Yichang county, Hubei, September 1999 and May 2000.

[18] This has been the major reason behind Shanghai's support for the new system, even before its adoption (Li, 1998a: ch.6). The relatively stable institutional framework also underlines local initiatives at improving fiscal management, particularly the improved local effort to implement the central policy of combating the flow of fiscal resources outside of the budget. This also largely explains the increased shares of local revenue after the initial significant drop in 1994 (Jiang, 1998: 298).

Centre accorded priority to this potential leverage from the perspective of national control and integration. This gain by the Centre did not inflict harm, or loss, upon the provinces, or at least not to the same degree of the Centre's gain, since in practice the provinces were guaranteed a level of retained revenue as of 1993 through a system of rebates. On the other hand, the normative emphasis on institutionalization in the new system has enabled the provinces to limit better the arbitrary action of the Centre, which otherwise stood to inflict greater harm due to its organisationally superior position.

At the same time, since the gains are mutual *and* incomplete for either party, both parties are bound to discover new causes for complaints. Provincial governments have, since 1994, complained about the need to wait long for central remittances to pay local bills, and that the central government has centralized too much of national revenue in the new system. They were also unhappy about the remaining ambiguity over expenditure responsibility, which allowed the central government to allocate new spending obligations to localities at will.[19] On the other hand, the central officials were weary of the downward trend of the share of central revenue in the national total after the initial surge in 1994, and some complained that the central government had yielded too much ground to provinces at the beginning of the new system, and failed to rein in local power completely.[20] As conflicts accentuate in the process of attempts to recapture lost grounds and to achieve 'complete' gains, the resultant difficult situation will force the Centre and provinces to compromise yet again. The Centre and the provinces will need to re-examine their priorities and trade off their lesser interests for their greater interests, making possible the mutuality of gain in a new round of a continuing process. Some of these complaints may then gather sufficient force to lay the ground for further change to the existing system. In fact, refinements and changes, and suggestions of changes, have been made continuously since 1994 as a result.[21]

---

[19] For instance, a central policy to raise the pay of public officials nationwide in late 1993, to be paid largely through local coffers, resulted in increased local fiscal expenditure of some 30 billion yuan in 1994 (Jiang, 1998: 301).

[20] One focal point of contention drawing complaints from both sides is the distribution of newly generated fiscal revenue between the local and central coffers. Local officials complained that the central government has excessively stripped localities of almost all new increments to fiscal revenue, and that the distribution formula on new revenue was consistently under-fulfilled, to the advantage of the central government. On the other hand, central officials claimed that the formula was misinterpreted by local officials, and that local revenue had managed to increase its share still since 1995, and that the intention and objective of the new fiscal system was always to centralize more fiscal revenue at the Centre, an objective which was only half-fulfilled (Jiang, 1998; Wang and Zhang, 1998).

[21] These include the increase in transfer payments from the central coffers to needy regions and refinements in the calculation formulae, the suggestion of giving more local autonomy in setting local taxes, and improvements to the formulation process and structure of the state budget.

## ADJUSTING THE MODERNISING AGENDA:
## THE STATE-SOCIETY BOUNDARY

The modernising Chinese state has adopted, since 1949, the socialist programme, mandating a greatly enlarged role of the state in the society. Until economic reform set in during the 1980s the spontaneous initiatives from the society were ruthlessly crushed and the state, as the representative of the working class, monopolized the privilege of effecting change in the society. The central and local governments became co-managers of state property, as well as the engines of social development on all fronts.

Having governments as managers of the economy proved to be problematic, however. One problem was that economic activities could never be neatly compartmentalised to tally with administrative jurisdictions. Under the socialist schema, state ownership became the operational form of public ownership, and the various levels of government, and their state agencies, became the *de facto* custodians of these state-, and public-, owned properties (Granick, 1990). All economic and social organisations in the society were subordinated to state agencies at various administrative levels, which were then charged with the responsibility for their development. Experience since 1949 has revealed multiple problems in this system, the most common and notable of which were issues of externalities and economies of scale. In a market economy a major role of the government would be to regulate and contain externalities. As the Chinese government itself became an active participant in the economy, it was entangled with problems that came with economic development as well. In these circumstances the original regulation function between the state and society turned into a problem of co-ordination and control among different agencies, and often even within a single state agency.

An unreasonable economic decision as viewed at the national level, for instance, often appeared entirely sensible from the viewpoint of local governments. Since the late 1980s the local governments have been increasingly criticised by the central government for being too 'narrow-minded' in their economic development strategy.[22] Local governments all concentrated their development effort on a few similar industries, it was said, irrespective of their natural and human endowments and the requirements for the efficient operation of the industries. As a result there were over-production of some goods on a national level, and under-production of others, requiring imports. From the perspective of the local governments these comments were irrelevant if not misplaced. Their role within the established system required them to be entrepreneurial. It was therefore only sensible for local governments, it was maintained, to focus their effort on industries that were likely to produce high return.[23] Rather than considering questions of, for instance, how best to develop a certain industry in the local governments asked specific questions which related directly to the circumstances of the localities. These included, for example, how best to increase the local industrial output value, and how to

---

[22] For an example of such comments, see a report on investment pattern by research officials in the State Planning Commission Investment Research Institute, Lin (1993: 327, 330).

[23] *Ibid.*, p. 331.

increase the locally retained revenue to allow for a higher level of local consumption.[24] For many local governments, any concerns which transcended their specific circumstances, and the institutional constraints they faced, were of 'academic' interest only, and should be the task of higher-level authorities rather than their own.

In compartmentalising the management of state property to its various local agents the central government had intended to include the tasks of the operation and development, as well as the regulation, of the property. In practice this was not at all possible. It was difficult for the government, whether central or local, to be simultaneously the manager and the regulator of the economy. Since local governments played a greater role in the daily management of the economy, especially since the time of economic reform, the gap between their performance as manager and regulator had become even more apparent. The local governments were thus obviously not happy when they found themselves being blamed for all kinds of economic problems which, according to their line of thinking, lay outside their domain of responsibilities. To local officials, criticisms against local parochialism were no more than the Centre unfairly attributing its difficulties (and failures) in regulating the national economy to their success in developing the local economy. Local officials regarded themselves simply doing their assigned job in the system, and considered it gravely unfair that they should be blamed as a result of performing too well.[25] In the eyes of the Centre, however, local governments have at best fulfilled only part of their duties, as they had largely overlooked their job as regulator (Lin, 1993: 332).

In summary, conflicts between the central and local governments were inherent in the encapsulation of the society by the state, and the subsequent mismatch between administrative responsibilities and economic requirements. The sheer increase in the range and quantity of state activities had a direct effect on the frequency and intensity of central-local conflict.

To a large extent the move towards the socialist market economy in the 1990s was the response of the Chinese leadership to find a way out of the increasing conflicts between the central and local governments. Administrative decentralization had been tried out in the late 1950s and in the 1980s to reduce tension and motivate better performance within the established socialist planning system. In the end it only aggravated central-local conflicts. As local governments were motivated to become a more entrepreneurial manager, the inherent potential of conflict between its roles as a manager and regulator was triggered off. A paradox then emerged: the more a local government sought to achieve as a manager and developer of the economy, the more likely it was to fail in the regulating aspect of its job. A mediocre and conservative local government avoided being blamed for creating imbalances within the national economy, but it also failed in the task of fostering development and improving productivity. Given the design of the washing basin, the baby was thrown out together with the dirty water.

Difficulties in administrative decentralization have forced the Chinese leaders to rethink the state-society boundaries. Pressures for economic decentralization, meaning

---

[24] Author's interviews, Yichang, Hubei, May 2000.
[25] See (Quan & Jiang, 1992: 30-35) for a theoretical justification of the role of local government investment.

returning decisions on enterprise management and investment to enterprises, gradually built up towards the late 1980s. In October 1992 the Fourteenth Party Congress proclaimed the direction of future reform as building the socialist market economy. The boundary between the state and society was to be redrawn, with the state gradually retreating from its previous role of production manager, and enterprises taking up the full role as a producer. There was to be a gradual 'delinking' between the state and the enterprises, which would no longer be 'administered' in the traditional sense by a state agency. By enhancing the autonomy of enterprises and thus the society as a whole, the new schema sought to avoid the previous contradiction of roles *within* the state structure, thus allowing the state to then focus on its retained role as regulator.

Along with this new definition of state-society relations the configurations of central and local relations could then be redrawn. The design of the tax-sharing system in fact reflected this new definition. One major feature of the system, if implemented in its full form, was that fiscal revenues of the central and local governments would no longer be divided according to the administrative subordination relations of enterprises as in the past. There was also a plan to reduce the role of the government in investment. The government would limit its role to infrastructure development and to the non-profit-making sector.[26] This trend of distancing the government from the competitive sector led to the adoption of the theory of 'public finance' in the design of the state budget.[27] Public money was to withdraw from the competitive sector, with government expenditure concentrating on the provision of public goods. Implementation has been slow, undoubtedly, given the weight of inertia and the resistance of vested interests. When the tax-sharing system was first implemented in 1994, for example, subordination relations remained as a principle by which the profit taxes of enterprises were divided between the Centre and provinces.[28] The embracement of public finance theory has yet to stamp out the numerous government investment activities in the competitive sector. Local officials were sceptical of the practicability of a complete government withdrawal from competitive investment, given the immaturity of market forces, at least in the immediate future.[29] Nevertheless, a new norm was being established, and complaints and

---

[26] This is in accordance with the policy recommendations drafted by the State Planning Commission in 1996. See Chen (1997: 305). For a more detailed elaboration of the thoughts underlying the proposed system change, see a report by the Investment Research Institute of the State Planning Commission in State Planning Commission (1995: 159-73).

[27] The reference to the theory of 'public finance' in state budget and fiscal management was explicit in government publications since 1998/99. See for instance (Xiang, 1999, p. 527), a publication on the historical development of public finance in China edited by the Finance Minister.

[28] In a study on the medium-long term fiscal policy of the Ministry of Finance in 1993, it was stated that 'the substantive content of the tax-sharing system resides in *ending* the practice of basing local and central revenue along the division of enterprise subordination relations'. It was envisaged that, by severing the linkage of local revenue with the administrative subordination relations of enterprises, the entrenched tendency of local governments to jealously protect local enterprises and government intervention in enterprise micro-management would be abated (Ministry of Finance, 1993). However, administrative subordination relations have remained a major principle of dividing local and central revenues in the post-1994 fiscal system.

[29] One specific measure implemented under the policy of 'public finance' is the announced abolition of fiscal credits as from 1999 - investment funds that the fiscal departments of various levels of government

reservations from both sides often served to stimulate refinements to the system that would meet better the disparate interests of the parties, and to achieve mutual gain.

## CONCLUSION

This essay argues that in order to understand the tension between the central and local governments in China since economic reform we need to look at two dimensions of state power. Central-local relations are, by nature, a question about the locus of power distribution within the state. Discussion in the literature has thus focused on the logic, principle, or evaluation of a certain mode of power distribution. This essay maintains that there is another set of questions requiring our attention. These are questions about the scope of state power within society. During this century the Chinese state has seen drastic change in this latter set of questions. With a modernising state agenda, and a socialist programme since 1949 in particular, the Chinese state has tremendously expanded its scope of activities in the society. The distribution of power within the state remained, however, highly indeterminate and unstable. As in the imperial past, the authority and formal power of the lower-level governments and agencies was delegated from the Centre. In practice, however, there has always been a lot of room for manoeuvre within the political order beneath the top. Provincial governments had abundant *de facto* autonomy within, and sometimes despite, the letters of central rules and policies. There was also a great deal of ambiguity regarding the precise jurisdiction and responsibility of each level of government and the constituent state agencies. The emperor and the Party relied primarily on moral and ideological influence to ensure compliance and co-ordination, not on organisational means of control and clear demarcation of duties. When these influences failed and conflicts occurred, there was a lack of institutional means, apart from sheer coercion, with which to resolve conflicts and re-establish order.

Given the historical continuity in the eclectic situation of power distribution within the state, the immersion of China since 1949 in a wide range of economic management activities posed a tremendous challenge. The constituent parts of the Chinese state were called upon to perform a much more demanding task, one that involved many specific and complex decisions, and accordingly more co-ordination among various agencies. The system simply was not equipped to deal with these issues, and conflicts between levels of government and among state agencies quickly snowballed. Given the structural interdependence of the Centre and its intermediaries, protracted tension resulted in change. This essay notes that, over the last few years, signs of change have emerged in both dimensions of the loci and the scope of state power in China.

operated in the past and which grew especially big in the 1990s. Fiscal departments invested the funds, themselves drawn from a variety of sources from within and outside of the state budget, in projects for a return. The funds were supposed to be circulating and the fiscal departments acted in a quasi-commercial way in the administration of the funds. In practice much of the funds became sunk-funds with little prospect of repayment let alone profits. However, local governments resisted the central policy of abolishing fiscal credits altogether, though admitting the need to improve the targeting of projects and fund management. Author's interviews, Yichang, Hubei, May 2000.

# REFERENCES

Breslin, G. Shaun. (1996). *China in the 1980s: Centre-Province Relations in a Reforming Socialist State*. New York: St. Martin's Press.

Bunger, Karl. (1985). "The Chinese State between Yesterday and Tomorrow", in Schram, ed. : xiii-xxvi.

Chang, Maria H. (1992). 'China's Future: Regionalism, Federation, or Disintegration', *Studies in Comparative Communism*, 25, 3: 211-27.

Chen, Jinhau. (1997). Ed. *1997 Nian Zhongguo Guomin Jingji he Shehui Fazhan Baogao* (A Report of the National Economic and Social Development of the People's Republic of China, 1997), Beijing: Zhongguo Jihua chubanshe.

Chung, Jae Ho. (1995a). 'Beijing Confronting the Provinces: The 1994 Tax-Sharing Reform and its Implications for Central-Provincial Relations in China', *China Information*, IX, 2/3: 1-23.

-----. (1995b). 'Studies of Central-Provincial Relations in the People's Republic of China: A Mid-Term Appraisal ', *China Quarterly*, 142: 487-508.

Donnithorne, A. (1969). 'Central Economic Control in China', in R. Adams, ed., *Contemporary China*, London: Peter Owen.

-----. (1976). 'Comment: Centralization and Decentralization in China's Fiscal Management', *China Quarterly*, 66, 328-40.

Friedman, Edward. (1995). *National Identity and Democratic Prospects in Socialist China*, Armonk, New York: M. E. Sharpe.

Ge, Jian Xiong. (1994). *Tong I Yu Fenlie: Zhongguo Lishi de Qishi* (Union and Break-up: Lessons from Chinese History). Beijing: Joint Publishing House.

Gernet, Jacques. (1985). "Introduction", in Schram, ed.: xxvii-xxxiv.

-----. (1987). "Introduction', in Schram, ed.: xv-xxvii.

Goodman, D. (1986). *Centre and Province in the PRC: Sichuan and Guizhou, 1955-65*, Cambridge: Harvard University Press.

-----. Ed. (1997). *China's Provinces in Reform: Class, Community, and Political Culture.* New York: Routledge.

-----, and G. Segal. (1994). *China Deconstructs: Politics, Trade and Regionalism*, London: Routledge.

Goldstone, Jack A. (1995). 'The Coming Chinese Collapse', *Foreign Policy*, 99: 35-52.

Huang, Yasheng. (1995). 'Why China Will Not Collapse', *Foreign Policy*, 99: 54-68.

-----. (1996). *Inflation and Investment Controls in China: The Political Economy of Central-Local Relations during the Reform Era.* Cambridge: Cambridge University Press.

Hendrischke, Hans, and Feng Chongyi. Ed. (1999). *The Political Economy of China's Provinces: Comparative and Competitive Advantage.* London and New York: Routledge.

Jia, Hao and Lin Zhimin. (1995). *Changing Central-Local Relations in China: Reform and State Capacity*, Boulder: Westview Press.

Jiang, Jung Hua. (1998). 'Fenshuizhi caizheng tizhi xunxin qingkwong fenxi yu jingqi xunce' (An appraisal of the implementation of tax-sharing system and options for improvement), in *Zhongguo Caishui Redin Wenti Yanjiu* (A Study of Hot Issues in China's Tax and Finance), Beijing: Zhongguo Caijing chubanshe: 289-307.

Lampton, D. (1987a). 'Chinese Politics: The Bargaining Treadmill', *Issues and Studies*, 23, 3: 11-41.

-----. (1987b). ed. *Policy Implementation in Post-Mao China*, Berkeley: University of California Press.

Lardy, N. (1975). 'Centralization and Decentralization in China's Fiscal Management', *China Quarterly*, 61: 25-60.

-----. (1976). 'Reply', *China Quarterly*, 66: 340-54.

Li, C. Linda. (1997a). 'Towards a Non-zero-sum Interactive Framework of Spatial Politics: the Case of Centre-Province in Contemporary China', *Political Studies*, 45, 1: 49-65.

-----. (1997b). 'Provincial Discretion and National Power: Investment Policy in Guangdong and Shanghai, 1978-1993', *China Quarterly*, 152: 778-804.

-----. (1998a). *Centre and Provinces: China, 1978-1993. Power as Non-zero-sum*, Oxford: Oxford University Press.

-----. (1998b.) 'Central-Provincial Relations: Beyond Compliance Analysis', in Joseph Y. S. Cheng, ed., *China Review 1998*, Hong Kong: Chinese University Press: 157-86.

Lieberthal, K. and M. Oksenberg. (1988). *Policy Making in China: Leaders, Structure and Processes*, New Jersey, Princeton: Princeton University Press.

Lieberthal, K. and D. Lampton. (1992). eds. *Bureaucracy, Politics and Decision-Making in Post-Mao China*, Berkeley: University of California Press.

Lin Senmu. ed. (1993). *Zhongguo Guding Zhichan Touji Touxi.* (An Analysis of Fixed Asset Investment in China). Beijing: Zhongguo Fanzhan chubanshe.

Liu, Shu-hsien, and Robert E. A. Ed. (1988). *Harmony and Strife: Contemporary Perspectives, East and West*, Hong Kong: The Chinese University Press.

Lu Wei. (1994). 'The 1994 fiscal and tax reforms is not a straight and trouble-free route', *Guangdong Caizheng*, 5: 4-6.

Lyons, T. (1987). *Economic Integration and Planning in Maoist China*, New York: Columbia University Press.

Ministry of Finance, Research Institute for Fiscal Science. (1993). 'A study of the policy orientations of medium-long term fiscal policy' *Caizheng Yanjiu*, 3: 14-24, p.19.

Naughton, B. (1997). 'Fiscal and Banking Reform: The 1994 Fiscal Reform Revisited', in M. Brosseau, Kwan H. C. and Y. Y. Kueh, eds., *China Review 1997*, Hong Kong: China University Press, 251-76.

Oksenberg, M. and J. Tong. (1991). 'The Evolution of Fiscal Relations in China, 1971-1984: The Formal System', *China Quarterly*, 125: 1-32.

Quan, Zhiping and Jiang Zuozhong. (1992). *Lun Difang Jingji Liyi* (An Analysis of the Local Economic Interests). Guangzhou: Guangdong Renmin chubanshe.

Schram, S. R. (1985). *The Scope of State Power in China*, Hong Kong: Chinese University Press.

-----. (1987). *Foundations and Limits of State Power in China*, Hong Kong: Chinese University Press.

Schwartz, B. I. (1987). 'The Primacy of the Political Order in East Asian Societies: Some Preliminary Generalizations', in Schram, ed.: 1-10.

Segal, G. (1994). *China Changes Shape: Regionalism and Foreign Policy*, Adelphi Paper 287, London: The International Institute for Strategic Studies.

Shirk, S. (1990). 'Playing to the Provinces: Deng Xiaoping's Political Strategy of Economic Reform', *Studies in Comparative Communism*, 23, 3: 227-58.

Shue, V. (1988). *The Reach of the State: Sketches of the Chinese Body Politics*, California: Stanford University Press.

Solinger, D. (1977). *Regional Government and Political Integration in South-west China, 1949-54*, (Berkeley: University of California Press).

-----. (1996). 'Despite Decentralization: Disadvantages, Dependence and Ongoing Central Power in the Inland - the Case of Wuhan', *China Quarterly*, 145: 1-34.

Song, Xinzhong. (1992). Ed. *Zhongguo Caizheng Tizhi Gaige Yanjiu* (A Study on the Fiscal System Reform in China), Beijing: Zhongguo Caizheng Jingji chubanshe.

State Planning Commission, Economic Research Institute. (1995). Ed. *Jingji Shehui Fazhan Zhongda Wenti Yanjiu* (A Study into Major Issues in Economic and Social Development), Beijing: Zhongguo Jihua chubanshe.

Tong, J. (1989). 'Fiscal Reform, Elite Turnover and Central-Provincial Relations in Post-Mao China', *Australian Journal of Chinese Affairs*, 22: 1-30.

Teiwes, F. (1966). 'The Purge of Provincial Leaders, 1957--1958', *China Quarterly*, No. 27, 14-32.

-----. (1971). 'Provincial Politics in China: Themes and Variations', in John M. H. Lindbeck (ed)., *China: Management of a Revolutionary Society*. London: George Allen and Unwin, 116-92.

-----. (1974). *Provincial Leadership in China: The Cultural Revolution and Its Aftermath*. U.S. A.: Cornnell University, China Japan Program.

Vandermeersch, L. (1985). "An Enquiry into the Chinese Conceptions of the Law", in Schram, ed. : 3-26.

Vogel, E. (1989). *One Step Ahead in China: Guangdong Under Reform*: Cambridge, Massachusetts: Harvard University Press.

Wang, Jing, and Zhang Lan. (1998). 'Guanyu gai shuisuo fanhuan wei shuiji fenxiangzhi di tansuo' (Exploring the feasibility of a transition from tax rebates system to a tax-base-sharing system), in *Zhongguo Caishui Redin Wenti Yanjiu* (A Study of Hot Issues in China's Tax and Finance), Beijing: Zhongguo Caijing chubanshe: 133-39.

Wang, Shaoguang. (1995). 'The Rise of the Regions: Fiscal Reform and the Decline of Central State Capacity in China', in Andrew G. Walder, ed., *The Waning of the Communist State: Economic Origins of Political Decline in China and Hungary*. Berkeley: University of California Press: 87-113.

-----, and Wu Angang. (1993*). Shongguo Guojia Nengli Baogao* (A Report on the State Capacity of China). Liaoning: Liaoning Remin chubanshe.

White, L., III. (1976). 'Local Autonomy in China During the Cultural Revolution: The Theoretical Uses of an Atypical Case', *American Political Science Review*, 70: 479-91.

Whitney, J. B. R. (1969). *China: Area, Administration, and Nation Building*. Chicago: University of Chicago, Department of Geography, Research Paper No. 123.

Wong, C. P. W. (1991). 'Central-Local Relations in an Era of Fiscal Decline: The Paradox of Fiscal Decentralization in Post-Mao China', *China Quarterly*, 128: 691-715.

-----. (1992). 'Fiscal Reform and Local Industrialization: The Problematic Sequencing of Reform in Post-Mao China', *Modern China*, 18, 2: 187-227.

Wu, Guoguang, and Cheng Yongnian. (1995). *Lun Zhongyang-Difang Guanxi: Zhongguo Zhidu Zhuanxing de Yige Zhouxin Wenti* (Central-Local Relations: A Central Question in the Institutional Changes in China), Hong Kong: Oxford University Press.

Xiang, Huaizheng. Ed. (1999). *Zhongguo Caizheng 50 Nian.* (Public Finance in China: the Past 50 Years). Beijing: Zhongguo Caizheng Jingji chubanshe.

Yang, Dali L. (1997). *Beyond Beijing: Liberalization and the Regions in China*. London and New York: Routledge.

Zhao, Suisheng. (1990). 'The Feeble Political Capacity of a Strong One-Party Regime---An Institutional Approach Toward the Formulation and Implementation of Economic in Post-Mao Mainland China', part 1 & 2, *Issues and Studies*, 26, 1: 47-80; 2: 35-74.

*Chapter 10*

# THE URBAN DEVELOPMENT POLITICS OF SEOUL AS A COLONIAL CITY

## *Won-Sik Jeong*

Faculty of Law and Public Administration
Kyungnam University, the Republic of Korea

## ABSTRACT

The study analyzes what forces guided the growth and development of Seoul under the Japanese colonial period, 1910-1945. Historically, it is worth emphasizing that the events of the colonial period were of fundamental importance in helping to shape present patterns of urban growth and urbanization. The emphasis is on exploring the consequences of urbanization for the colonial political system, and the impact of governmental intervention on the patterns of urban growth and housing development. The impact of colonialism on urban development in Korea is to be understood as the impact of a Japanese(i.e. culturally), capitalist-industrialist, and colonial(i. e. politically dominant) power. The extensive role of the colonial state in the urban planning through 1945 was not surprising, given the direct and often authoritarian role of the Japanese colonial administration in Korea. The developmentalist heritage of a strong and autonomous state under the Japanese colonial rule succeed to the post-independence authoritarian Korean state.

The purpose of this article is to examine the political logic behind an early capitalist urban growth of Seoul in South Korea, focusing on its changing character during the Japanese colonial period, 1910-1945. Throughout a long history as a feudal state of the Yi dynasty(1392-1910), Seoul was the symbolic place of national feeling and political power, and the distinctive premier city. This elite position of the city was further strengthened by developmentalist ideology of the Japanese colonial government.

The study analyzes what forces guided the growth and development of Seoul under the colonial rule. One dimension that is often neglected in current urban development studies in Korea is the historical. Therefore, it is worth emphasizing that the events of the colonial period were of fundamental importance in helping to shape present patterns of urban growth and urbanization. The emphasis is on exploring the consequences of urbanization for the colonial political system, and the impact of governmental intervention on the patterns of urban growth and housing development. The impact of colonialism on urban development in Korea is to be understood as the impact of a Japanese(i.e. culturally), capitalist-industrialist, and colonial (i. e. politically dominant) power.[1]

More specifically, the study is to show how the colonial urban system, focusing on urbanization and its related housing and land development, is determined by the overall social and political structure. The early colonial period of urban Korea's ideas and practices have had a lasting effect upon the planning of Korea's cities. Thus, an analysis of this period aids in understanding the origins of the modern urban system and its organization in Korea.

In theory, colonial government provides an appropriate venue for examining the state-directed urban development argument. The focus is on the policies of state regulatory and planning agencies, and the economic and class interests which the policies seek to advance in relation to patterns of private activity. It is argued that urban development policy became one of the significant menas through which the Japanese colonial government maintained their respective political legitimacy. The state influences on the urban development process through its policies are patterned by the state's relationship with social groups.[2]

Within this vein, this study will supplement the criticism that so many prevailing approaches are too focused on the state or society to explain urban development. Migdal give us a suggestive starting point for the study of the role of the state: "the state-centered approach is a bit like looking at a mousetrap without at all understanding the mouse."[3]

The interplay between the state and society has largely been derived from the political logic of the distributive effects of the state's development policies, namely who benefits and who loses.

---

[1] Support for the use of these variables in examining colonial urban development may be found in Sjoberg's *Cities: Their Origin and Growth* (San Francisco: W. H. Freeman, 1965).

[2] For a set of good analyses of this point, see Theda. Skocpol's "Bringing State Back In: Strategies of Analysis in Current Research," in P. Evans, D. Rueschemeyer and T. Skocpol, eds, *Bringing State Back In* (Cambridge: Cambridge University Press, 1985), and John. H. Mollenkopf's *The Contested City* (Princeton, N.J.: Princeton University Press, 1983).

[3] Joel Migdal, *Strong Societies and Weak States: State-Society Relations and State Capabilities in The Third World* (Princeton: Princeton University Press, 1988), xvi.

## THE EMERGENCE OF THE MODERN CAPITALIST CITY IN KOREA

During the late nineteenth century, a rapid transition to capitalism occurred in Korea. Following unsuccessful attempts by France (1866), and the United States (1866 and 1871), to open the Korean peninsula, Japan invaded Kanghwa island (located nearest to Seoul) by using the warships to demand the opening of Korean ports. The Korean government was forced to sign the first treaty of amity with Japan in 1876.[4]

To acknowledge that capitalism had its origin in this period is to suggest that the roots of the vibrant and internationally recognized capitalism of South Korea today might in some way be traceable to Japan.[5]

To block the Japanese from obtaining a monopoly on foreign invasions and receiving Western diplomats, the Korean government also concluded treaties of amity and commerce with the U. S., England, Germany, Russia, France, and other nations in the end of 1870's. These treaties seemed to offer the Western powers a break in Korea's long isolation,[6] and these nations began to take an interest in relations with the late Yi dynasty. As a result, Korea ceased to be a "Hermit Kingdom," and became a part of the modern capitalist world.

Foreign residential quarters affected the existing urban structure during the early modernization period.[7]

Characterizing the pre-industrial towns, the private handicraft industries in Seoul and other villages did not develop into factories until the late nineteenth century. Almost all the industrial activities in Korea utilizing the factory system of manufacturing were undertaken by Japanese entrepreneurs who emigrated to Korea after the Treaty of 1876.[8]

---

[4] All of the treaties of the Korean government concluded with Japan since 1876 were unequal in content. The Treaty of Amity stipulated that Korea's ports should be opened to Japanese merchants to build houses and to engage freely in commerce. In addition, no customs duties were to be imposed on trade with Japan, and Japanese merchants could engage in commercial activities with Japanese currency in the open ports. These unequal treaties provided a legal springboard for Japan's political and economic aggressions against Korea.

[5] In a country where national pride is not only very sensitive but closely connected with anti-Japanese sentiment, the idea of Japan as agency of "modernization" is psychologically wrenching. Many South Koreans would naturally much rather believe that the original impetus for capitalist growth came from within Korea itself.

[6] The isolation in Korean history engendered many obstacles on the road to modernization in Korea. According to Sang Chul Suh's *Growth and Structural Change in The Korean Economy, 1910-1940* (Cambridge: Harvard University Press, 1978), 10-19, the isolation policy prevented international contacts which, in the West, often played a vital role in modern economic growth during the nineteenth century. And it also meant a loss of the traditional source of strength for political unity of the nation by bearing a heavy burden of national defense against the frequent invasions of powerful nations (China, Japan, and Russia).

[7] The foreign settlement was first established by The Chemulp'o Foreign Settlement Rule on October 3, 1884 in Inch'on. The rule was drafted by W. G. Aston who was the first British Consul-General in Seoul and acted as the leader of diplomatic officials in Seoul. For more detail, see Inch'on-si, *Inch'on Pusa* (The history of Inch'on)(Inch'on: Inch'on-si, 1976), 135.

[8] Daniel S. Juhn, "Entrepreneurship in An Underdeveloped Economy: The Case of Korea, 1890-1940," *Ph,D. Diss.* (The George Washington University. 1965), 29-30.

Unlike the previous era, this period was shaped more by external stimulus than by internal dynamism. In other words, the advent of the modern city in Korea was closely related to its opening to foreign residents and international mercantile trade. Increasing contact with the foreign capitalists began to enhance Seoul's economic dominance over its hinterland. In particular, the commercial treaty with Japan brought about a rapid expansion of foreign trade and its complete monopoly by Japan. On the other hand, China was menaced by the Japanese penetration into the Korean peninsula and concluded the Korea-China Land and Sea Commercial Activity Treaty in 1882 in order to transform their relationship from a traditional dependent one to one based on equality with Korea. Seoul was opened by the treaty which approved the Market Establishment Right for the Chinese in both Seoul and Yanghwajin. Immediately after the treaty's signing, Seoul became the place of struggle for the great capitalist powers by opening itself to other countries such as the United States, Great Britain, Germany, Japan, and China. With the opening of Seoul, the city wall was torn down, and the boundaries expanded to include the old market towns and lower class areas outside the walled city.

Starting from the 'Korea-Japan Eulsa Treaty' in 1905, which had stolen the sovereignty of the Yi dynasty, Seoul underwent many changes and hardships. By establishing *to'nggam-bu*(residency-general) at Yongsan, on the banks of the Han River, the water front district thrived with Japanese solders and Korean workers. Thus, the old saying that anyone who dominates the Han River can dominate the Korean peninsula came true once again.

It is true that the open-door policy during the transition period in Korea, gave rise to the emergence and rapid growth of some modern sectors in the Korean urban areas and particularly in Seoul. One of the most important was the construction of the Seoul/Pusan railroad that marked the beginnings of modern urban growth in Korea.[9]

A modern urban infrastructure was installed at the insistence of foreigners and a westernized Korean bourgeoisie that was beginning to emerge. Following the completion, Japan took away even the country's nominal sovereignty and turned Korea into a Japanese colony in 1910. The Japanese government degraded Seoul's political and administrative position by changing its direct control from the central government to Kyongki province government.

## THE COLONIAL URBAN GROWTH OF SEOUL:
## DEMOGRAPHIC AND ECONOMIC CHANGE

Most Korean demographers agree that Seoul started its distinct demographic transition during the colonial era. The population of Seoul was 25,000 in 1910 but exceed 100,000 by 1944. During the same period, the city's population increased at an average

---

[9] The Seoul-Pusan railway was one of the four railway plans considered by the Japanese government and business in 1894 and established in 1906. At this time, Pusan had a large Japanese business community, and handled most of the trade between Korea and Japan. It was the construction of this line which aroused the most interest in Japan.

annual rate of 5.2 percent in comparison that of 1.6 percent nationally. Especially, Seoul's population increased by 74 percent in 1930-1936. This rapid growth was absolutely due to the expansion of administrative districts in Seoul by Ordinance no. 18 of the Government-General on Feb. 14, 1936.[10]

The demographic shifts of Seoul in the colonial era can be explained by natural increase, rural decline, and Japanese immigrants to Korea.

First, the decline in death rates was caused by the restoration of social order from the political and social turmoil in the late Yi dynasty, and by improved public health measures by the colonial government. From the early days of the colonial period in particular, Japanese authorities developed the various health policies such as the prevention of infectious disease, sanitary improvements, the rigorous inspection to public places, the introduction of vaccination, and the enactment of sanitary regulations.[11]

The crude death rate decreased from 29 births per 1,000 population in 1925-1929 to 22 in 1938-1942, falling 7 points within the two decades for which a detailed set of registration data is available. Concurrently, the colonial policies designed for the rapid growth of population produced a high growth rate throughout the colonial period.

Second, the volume of migration to the city during this time cannot be precisely measured because records of the annual figures were not maintained. However, many of rural residents had to move to the domestic urban areas, or Manchuria and Japan because of agricultural exploitation both by Japanese capitalists and by the Japanese colonial government's policies, namely the Project for Land Survey from 1910 to 1918. By 1925, nearly 30 percent of the total urban population in Korea was estimated as migrants from the rural areas.[12]

Third, Seoul's population growth at this time dues to the Japanese government's immigration policy along with the rapid urbanization and industrialization since the Meiji Reform. To the Japanese, immigration particularly was an essential part of their colonization program. By 1911, the Japanese government had instituted the Oriental Development Company that it had to send 30,000 Japanese per year and 350,000 to 500,000 Japanese to the Korean peninsula in the next eleven years.[13]

For the Japanese, it was practical and desirable to send several million emigrants from the Japanese islands to the relatively larger peninsula.[14]

---

[10] For more detail, see Seoul Metropolitan Government, *Seoul 600 Nyonsa* (The history of 600 years in Seoul) (Seoul, 1986).

[11] For a more extended discussion of the colonial health policy, see Yun-Shik Chang, "Planned Economic Transformation and Population Change," in C. I. Eugine Kim and D. E. Mortimore, eds, *Korea's Response to Japan: The Colonial Period 1910-1945* (Michigan: The Center for Korean Studies Western Michigan University, 1975).

[12] Government-General of Chosen, *Report of Population Census* (Government-General of Chosen, 1930), 23-35.

[13] According to reports of the Japanese Ministry of Foreign Affairs, Japanese emigrants totaled 640,018 in 1920; of which 275,156 went to Asia, 158,412 to North America, 139,521 to Oceania, 71,324 to South America. 3,359 to Europe and 76 to Africa. See Yoshino Nishiyama, *Tosikeiryogku Stsushigal Setsu*(The history of urban planning n Japan) (Toyko: 1978), 101-102).

[14] The population density was only 883 persons per hori(1 hori=2.4 sq. miles) in Korea as opposed to 1,886 in Japan, further facilitating population expansion.

At the same time, the Japanese government launched a policy of actively trying to assimilate Koreans into Japanese culture.[15]

The theory of assimilation was that the Koreans should be first become Japanized, after which political rights would become theirs as a matter of course. By assimilating the Koreans, Japan attempted to create its own unique empire in Northeast Asia, different from the Western imperial core-periphery structure. It can be said that this intention prompted Japan to venture to establish "the Greater East Asian Co-prosperity Sphere" in Northeast Asia. The government realized that the greater the number of Japanese migrants the greater the likelihood of success in its integration policy and therefore encouraged a larger migration from Japan.[16]

Finally, urban infrastructure is one of the important aspects of societies that has critically affected urban patterns, and a region's incorporation into a changing role within the capitalist world-system.[17]

The most significant factors for colonial urban development in Korea were the new transportation networks roads and railways which gave impetus to the large regional city, and consequently, the organization of the economy around regional marketing and financial centers. Changes in the transportation systems are considered by many to have been the single most important determinant of urban morphology and residential differentiation within city. This infrastructure shaped and/or reinforced Seoul's growth patterns just as technology has changed urban structure.

Prior to the annexation of 1910, transportation development in Korea already became a priority policy of the Japanese government. By 1894, the Japanese were already considering the construction of railways in Korea. All these would originate in Seoul, the capital, and would run approximately north-east, north-west, south-east, and south-west of the city. In 1906, the Japanese government took over all existing lines and placed them under the Railway Bureau of the protectorate, but upon the establishment of the Government-General in 1910, their control once more changed hands to the Japanese colonial government. In spite of rugged terrain, nearly 4,000 miles of rail line were completed by 1944. In short, railroad construction was intended to stimulate general economic development. Business interests saw that the railroad line was important because it opened up new markets, lowered the cost of moving Japanese goods into the interior, and facilitated rice trade.

In many theories of urban geography, urban primacy is an important characteristic of urban growth in most underdeveloped societies which experience a great degree of rural exodus and colonization.[18]

---

[15] Education programs were already established to assimilate Koreans into Japanese society by obliterating Korean national consciousness. This included the degradation of Korean history and the elimination of Korean language.

[16] Tsunataro Aoyki, *Chosen Techiron* (Conquest theory of chosen) (Seoul: Chosen Kenkyu-kai, 1923), 659. Quoted in Jong Mok Son, *Sikminji Kangjomgi Tosi Yon'gu* (The study of Korean city in colonial rule) (Seoul: Ilgi-sa, 1989).

[17] See, for example, Carol A. Smith "Theories and Measure of Urban Primacy," in M. Timberlake, ed, *Urbanization in the World-Economy* (New York: Academic Press, Inc., 1985), 209-210; C. Ward, *The Child in the City* (New York: Collier Books, 1978).

Even if the definition of urban primacy is burdened by both conceptual and practical difficulties, Table 1 shows the degree of urban primacy in colonial Korea from the notion of a three-cty primacy, regional multiple-city primacy, and national population size. The table indicates that, unlike the percentage of Seoul to the total population of Korea, Seoul's proportion to the total urban population of Korea continued to decline except for 1940, the year a few 'kun'(county) of the Kyonggi province were incorporated into Seoul. By the same token, the population distribution of the three big cities also showed a similar phenomenon. Nevertheless, the data illustrates that although Seoul's percentage to the total population of Korea decreased,[19] its urbanization pattern in the colonial era showed the characteristic of urban primacy.[20]

By 1936, Seoul's population(677,241) was more than twice the size of the second largest city, Pusan(206,386). As evidenced by the demographic trends, Seoul as a primate city continued to play the role of colonial exploitator in regards to other cities and rural areas.

**[Table 1] Trends of a Primate City and Three Big Cities, 1925-1944 (Unit: %)**

| Criteria | 1925 | 1930 | 1935 | 1940 | 1945 |
|---|---|---|---|---|---|
| Primate City(Seoul) | | | | | |
| Per Three Big Cities | 63.4 | 57.9 | 54.9 | 63.4 | 59.6 |
| Per Total Urban Areas | 40.3 | 33.1 | 27.6 | 33.2 | 29.0 |
| Per National Population | 1.6 | 1.7 | 2.8 | 4.1 | 4.2 |
| Three Big Cities(Seoul, Pyongyang, Pusan) | | | | | |
| Per Total Urban Areas | 63.4 | 57.3 | 50.4 | 52.2 | 48.6 |
| per National Population | 2.8 | 3.2 | 3.5 | 6.0 | 6.4 |

**Source:** Calculated from Government-General of Chosen, *Kokusei Chosa Hokokusho* (Report of National Power), corresponding Years.

Just as the physical structure of Seoul underwent tremendous changes during the colonial period, so did its economic base. One major area of such change was in the production of craft goods such as textiles and metal wares. There had always been industry in the city before, if only because of the great demand for manufactured products continually generated by its huge population, but it was small in scale and traditional in organization and technology. During the colonial period, however, traditional hand crafts

---

[18] For a discussion of the urban primacy, see John Kasarda and Edward Crenshaw, "Third World Urbanization: Dimensions, Theories, and Determinants," *Annual Review of Sociology*, 17(1991): Carol A. Smith, *op cit.*

[19] This pattern is strongly similar to McGee's observation in other South East Asian colonial countries. He found that despite their important political, commercial, and educational roles, South East colonial cities did not attract large numbers of rural migrants. T. G. McGee, *The Southeast Asian City* (New York: 1971), 142-150.

[20] Carol Smith defines urban primacy as a "situation in which the largest city within an urban system is overlarge; that is much larger than lower-ranking cities." Carl A. Smith, *op cit*, 90.

were seriously undermined by the effective penetration of cheaper, mass-produced substitutes from the factories of Japan.

Korea's dependence on Japan as a colonial ruler was quite different than the other colonial arrangements of that time.[21]

Whatever Japan's fundamental purpose in annexing Korea might have been, it was a necessary step to achieving complete control of the Korean economy, making it part of the periphery of Japan.[22]

As a result, the Korean economy underwent a significant change, largely determined by a colonial Government-General based on a political system of strict totalitarianism.[23]

The colonial state was not merely a dictatorship but a military dictatorship, reflecting the strategic significance that Japan had attached to the Korean peninsula. Since there was no representation of Korean interests in Japanese national policy formulation, the economic policy of the colonial period was always in line with the changing needs of Japan. The economic policy of the colonial government was primarily directed towards developing Korea as a source of raw materials and as a market for Japanese manufactured products.

In the Seoul of the 1910's, the two societies, whose physical urban forms were being juxtaposed in the early colonial city, were organized around two different systems of economic production, most simply described as industrial and agricultural. There was still a large population involved in agriculture although industrial occupations were rapidly growing in number. As a matter of fact, Japan's initial colonial policy was to increase agricultural production in Korea to meet Japan's growing need for rice.[24]

The colonial Government-General's economic policy was essentially an "Agriculture First Policy"; relatively few measures for commerce and industry were taken by the government.

Japan begun to build large-scale industries in Korea in the 1930's as part of an empire-wide program of economic self-sufficiency and war preparation. Between 1939 and 1941, the manufacturing sector represented 29 percent of Korea's total economic production. The primary industries - agriculture, fishing, and forestry - occupied only 49.6 percent of total economic production during the period in contrast to having been 84.6 percent of total production between 1910 and 1912. When industrialization was in full swing, beginning in the early 1930's, the government's programs to aid businesses

---

[21] Hyun-Chin Lim*f*s *Dependent Development in Korea* (Seoul: Seoul University Press, 1989), 36, explains two differences: (1) the experience goes beyond the exchange of primary products for manufactured goods and includes socio-cultural integration aimed at the Japanization of the Korean people; (2) because of this integration policy, both development and exploitation were too intricately intertwined to be differentiated in colonial Korea, much more so than in colonial Latin America and African countries.

[22] Sang-Chul Suh, *op cit*, 6.

[23] Japan instituted a highly sophisticated political system to rule Korea based on the Prussian model. Gregory Henderson's *Korea: The Politics of the Vortex* (Cambridge: Harvard University Press. 1968), Chap. 4, has described its nature as totalitarian in that it was harsher than any of its various European counterparts.

[24] Sok-Dam Chon and Others, *Iljehaui Choson Kyongjesa* (Korean economic history under Japanese rule) (Seoul: Choson Chohap, 1947); Ho-Jin Choi, "The Strengthening of the Economic Domination by Japanese Colonialism," *Korean Observer* 4 (1975): 234-238.

were mainly directed to benefit large factories supported by Japanese *zaibatsu*[25] capital, rather than local entrepreneurs.

A consequence of Japanese war preparation and the encouragement of Japanese *zaibatsu* investment resulted in a substantial expansion of heavy industries from 23 percent of factory product in 1930 to 50 percent in 1940. According to Keijo(Seoul's Japanese name) Chamber of Commerce and Industry, Seoul produced 41 percent of Korea's textiles, 42 percent of the machinery, 74 percent of the lumber, 47 percent of the printing, and 25 percent of the food products.

The economic development which occurred under Japanese rule, brought little benefit to the Koreans. Virtually all industries were owned either by Japan-based operations or by Japanese corporations in Korea. In 1924, the Japanese dominated Seoul's industrial establishments both in number and in value of production. It was pointed out by the *Tong-A Ilbo* (August 19, 1924) that Japanese manufacturers were mainly engaged in the production of machinery and chemistry which required large scale factories and advanced technology. Also, Japanese entrepreneurs were export-oriented, the newspaper pointed out, and were trying hard to improve their products to fit the tastes of foreign markets. The lack of export-oriented Korean entrepreneurs was lamented by the same newspaper. Table 2 was derived from data provided by the *Tong-A Ilbo* in a series of articles. Although there is no way of proving or disproving the accuracy of these data, national statistics comparing the relative position of Japanese and Korean entrepreneurs in the same period tended to support the general trend indicated in the newspaper data. At this time, both sources indicated the relatively poor showing of Korean industrial entrepreneurs.[26]

In 1941, the Keijo Chamber of Commerce and Industry reported a significant increase in the number and production of Korean factories in Seoul. As for the nationality of the owners, 39.75 percent were owned by Japanese, while Koreans owned 59.06 percent. The remaining 1.19 percent was owned by foreigners. The evidence provided by the chamber clearly shows that, in comparison to the Japanese, Korean entrepreneurial activities increased more than proportionately in response to rising economic opportunities in Seoul. In terms of the number of factories owned by Koreans, the percentage increased from 37 percent of the total number in 1924 to 59 percent in 1939, completely reversing the superior position enjoyed by Japanese in 1924.

---

[25] The term *zibatsu* has been defined as a "system of highly centralized family control through holding companies." Chitoshi Yanaga, *Big Business in Hapanese Politics* (New haven: Yale University Press, 1968), 38. Its distinct structure ingeniously combined Western concepts of corporation and Japan's traditional values.

[26] In 1939, the Keijo Chamber of Commerce and Industry conducted a survey of all industrial establishments in Seoul, and in 1941, published the book, *Keijo ni Okeru Kojo Chosa* (A study of industrial establishments in Seoul).

**[Table 2] Comparison of Japanese and Korean Factories in Seoul (1924)**

| Criteria | Japanese | Korean |
|---|---|---|
| No. of Establishments | 466(63%) | 269(37%) |
| Building Area(in py'ong*) | 64,086 | 6,429 |
| Paid-up capital(yen) | 44,686,857 | 18,685,047 |
| No. of Workers | 13,987 | 1,714 |
| Gross Value of Production | 37,860,452(86%) | 6,299,570(14%) |

* equivalent to 3.95 yards
**Source:** *Tong-A Ilbo* (August 20, 1924).

In terms of gross value of production, the achievement of the Korean entrepreneurs is even more impressive. 42 percent of the gross value of factory production, in 1939, was attributed to Korean owned establishments, compared to 14 percent, in 1924. Nevertheless, the figures still give an indication of Japanese capital. Moreover, industrial product was concentrated - a tendency toward oligopoly favored by the colonial administration - with a mere 1.2 percent of all firms producing 80 percent of all factory product in 1939.[27]

## HOUSING AND LAND DEVELOPMENT UNDER COLONIAL RULE

The issues of housing was far from social concern until the beginning of the 1920's. Housing conditions began to deteriorate with changes in colonial economic policies, such as the Program of Land Survey, the Planning for Promotion of Industrial Rise Production, and the Program of Land Ownership Expansion. All of these stimulated the increase of rural migration to urban areas and the Japanese immigration into Korea. By this time, *Tong-A Ilbo* reported the housing problem in Seoul with the title "Housing Supply To Lower Classes" - "Reside On The Road In The East Tonight And In The West Tomorrow Night."[28] The housing problem in Seoul was not just limited to cave dwellers, rather it was much more serious for urban middle classes. The newspaper describes the situation, under the headkine "6,000 Vagrants in Western Clothes," as follows.

According to the Seoul City Government's housing survey, among the salary men in public offices, public corporations, banks and other private offices within the city, 6,390 persons do not possess their own housing. Among the number, 725 live in official or private residences, 539 in inns, and 5,135 are homeless persons. (Tong-A Ilbo, December 12, 1921)

---

[27] Capital export to Korea was very profitable for Japanese business. Andrew J. Grajdanzev's *Modern Korea* (New York: Institute of Pacific Relation, 1944), 156, reports that textile corporations earned net profits of 50% in 1939-40.

[28] (December 12, 1921).

Furthermore, in 1930, the Japanese government turned Korea into a weapon depot for a continental invasion(the Manchuria War in October, 1931) and forced an industrialization policy, adding to rural-urban migration. During the two decades from 1925 to 1944, the number of households in Seoul became tripled(see Table 3). In accordance with the rapid increase of housing demand, many dwellings were supplied by private housing developers, but the housing problem remained, and moreover, it was exacerbated by the serious lack of construction materials at the end of colonial period. By 1944. the rate of housing shortage in Seoul became 44 percent.

Despite the fact that the housing problem was serious in Seoul as well as in other big or medium-sized cities,[29] throughout the whole colonial period, the General-Government never established a specific housing policy until the later 1930's. The reason was that although the housing problem was serious, as Table 3.6 shows, it was urgent problem for Korean, not Japanese.

With both the Sino-Japanese War in 1937, and the Pacific War in 1939, the Japanese colonial government had to construct many military-industrial complexes on the Korean peninsula and thus felt the importance of the enormous demand for housing by industrial employees. In the Consultation Meeting on Current Affairs on Oct. 6, 1938, the government first officially talked about the housing problem in Korea. The major plans decided were: i) an increase in public housing, ii) the establishment of the status of the housing and tenement union, iii) an improvement and increase of small houses for laborers, and iv) the establishment of the housing association for squatter improvement.

**[Table 3] Housing Distribution in Seoul, 1933**

| Nationality | Population | Households | No. of Housing | Shortage Housing | Shortage Rate |
|---|---|---|---|---|---|
| Korean | 270,590 | 54,226 | 46,012 | 8,214 | 15.15% |
| Japanese | 106,782 | 24,388 | 23,719 | 669 | 2.75% |
| Foreigner | 5,119 | 905 | 868 | 37 | 4.1% |
| Total | 382,491 | 79,519 | 70,599 | 8,920 | 11.2% |

**Source:** Keijo Nippo-Sa, Chosen Annual Report (Keijo, 1935).

First, the colonial government used land readjustment techniques in order to obtain housing sites. The Land Readjustment Project(LRP) - which originated from the Law Concerning Land Transfer(Lex Addicks) adopted by Frank-am-Main Land Readjustment Act in Germany in 1902 to consolidate fragmented agricultural land holdings,[30] is a

---

[29] The housing problem even extended to small/medium cities such as Chinju, P'ohang and Wonsan. The *Tong-A Ilbo* reported the housing deterioration in national major cities every week for a year since April 21, 1930.

[30] William A. Doebele, *Land Readjustment Project* (Lexington: Lexington Books, 1979).

method of converting land from non-urban use, using site planning, and the installation of infrastructure and public facilities.[31]

The objective of the Project in Germany was not only to reapportion land holdings but also to sell off some of the land to provide capital for the construction of the roads and public facilities that were required for the sale as a whole.

The basic ideas were picked up by Japanese planners at the end of the First World War and incorporated into legislation designed to control urban development. In Japan, The LRP began with The Act of Cultivated Land, which was used as the official instrument for urban housing site adjustment with the rapid increase in the demand of land for factories and housing following the rise and development of capitalism at the end of the nineteenth century in Japan. In Korea, since it was first enforced in Seoul, in 1928, it has been used as one of the important tools for urban development until now.[32]

Kyongsong(Seoul) Urban Replanning Report, in 1928, shows that the five old central districts of Seoul and the underdeveloped peripheral areas of the city were planned by the land readjustment technique. The LRP at that time was interpreted in a broad sense, which includes simultaneously redevelopment of the old districts, like the urban renewal project today.

The housing policy of the colonial government was closely related to island Japan's insular war policy. The Japanese urban scholar, Tosida effectively notes that the Japanese government began to regard housing as labor power's maintenance and a means of its reproduction throughout the Sino-Japanese War period.[33]

At this time, the Japanese government strongly emphasized the need of housing for laborers so as to increase the production of military equipments. There was no exception in its colony, the Korean peninsula. It was natural to use the Korean peninsula as a supply base for the war because Korea was located near the battlefield, mainland China. With the accomplishment of the Electric Network Plan after 1931, an abundant and cheap supply of electric power on the Korean peninsula promoted the penetration of Japanese *zaibatsu* into the country,[34] which increased the housing demand by urban laborers. The Japanese government's motive by using housing policy as the instrument for the

---

[31] Historically, public urban renewal is similar with the land readjustment in that it "has usually taken the form of developing new areas outside the cities, rather than reconstructing obsolescent areas within them." C. A. Doxiadis, Urban renewal and the Future of the American City (Chicago: Public Administration Service, 1966), 15. However, within the Korean context, the concepts are different in that the former only aims to reshape the existing urban configurations, while the latter focuses on developing new urban areas, by converting rural lands into the urban sphere. The most distinctive characteristic of land readjustment is that it does not place any substantial financial burden on the part of the developers (usually local governments). At present, use of the LRP is practiced in Germany, Korea, Japan, Australia, Canada, Taiwan, and Hawaii in the United States. Its methods and procedures, however, differ from country to country.

[32] Myong-Chan Hwang, "Tojiguhoekjongnisaop P'yongga" (The evaluation of land readjustment project in Korea), 368-369, in Myong Chan Hwang, ed, *Togijongch'aeknon* (Land policy) (Seoul: Kyongmunhwasa, 1985).

[33] Tokuei Tosida, *Gendaitisiron* (Urban study) (Tokyo: 1975), 231-232.

[34] Moro Kobayasi, *Daitoakyoeikenno Keiseito* (Development and destruction of pacific co-properity Network) (Tokyo: 1965), 79-85.

maintenance and preservation of labor power, was to change the classical economic view that housing is just one of the durable consumer goods such as clothes or furniture. By this time, Japanese scholar Kamamoto in the journal, *Social Policy Review* writes,

> Housing is absolutely short in Japan today. Low-income housing is especially true. . . Laborers reproduce their own labor power by consuming the living materials in each household. Accordingly, housing for laborers is a place where they can maintain and preserve their own labor power, and by doing so, stimulate its reproduction.[35]

The colonial government established the Housing Committee composed of each director of bureaus within the General-Government by Imperial Ordinance No.38, July 12, 1939.[36]

> However, the committee never held a meeting during the next three months. Rather, the Japanese government took actions which exacerbated the housing problem by announcing the Regulation Act of Land and Housing Rent by the Japanese Royal Ordinance 704. The Act states that further increases of land and housing rent were frozen. This Act, together with other acts such as the Price Control Act(the Ordinance No. 703), and the Temporary Measure Act of Wage(the Ordinance No. 705), was to control price and curb inflation during the war period.[37]

Nevertheless, prices continued to go up, and even essentials were marketed by an underground economy. To add to the economic recession, a shortage of building materials prevented the construction of the private rental houses.

In this economic recession, the active intervention of the colonial government was immediate. As an alternative for promoting housing development, the colonial government created the Chosen Housing Corporation(CHC) on June 14, 1941. The CHC was directly influenced by the Japanese Housing Corporation established on March 6, 1941, in order to solve the serious housing problems at that time.

By 1942, the CHC constructed 500 houses in Dorim Complexes, 1,000 houses in Sangdo Complexes and 500 houses in Simdaebang Complexes.[38]

Clarence Perry's neighborhood unit[39] was first introduced in these new complexes. Useful facilities, such as hospitals, public baths, and shops in every block were located within the complexes. This method was used as an effective mechanism for reproducing and protecting the labor power, and for controlling and drafting Koreans during war time period. The Government-General intended to construct the housing style which added a

---

[35] This argument is quoted in Tokuei Tosida's *Gendaitisiron* (1975), 231.

[36] The Official Gazette 3742, July 12, 1939 and the Official Gazette3743, July 13, 1939.

[37] Kenjo Yamauchi, *Chosenkeizaitoseihozensho* (Chosen economic regulation act) (Toyko: 1964), 19-22.

[38] The housing complexes changed to high quality residential areas in today. But only few dwellings built at that time still remain in those complexes. During the period of 1941-1945, the CHC produced 12,184 houses in Korea and 4,488 houses in Seoul. See Korean National Housng Corporation, *KNHC Samsipnonsa* (The history of thirty years in KNHC) (Seoul), 64-65.

[39] Clarence Perry, *Housing for the Machine Age* (New York: Russell, 1939). Actual planning with the neighborhood unit has been used, mostly unintentionally, to segregate racial and ethnic groups into distinct location.

Korean style home to a regular Japanese style home: only one room was indeed built with the Korean under-floor heating system which is congenial to the Korean people's living condition. By doing so, the government advertised its intention of assimilation even in the housing production.

In the process of land acquisition, the government was not in serious conflict with native Koreans. With the reorganization of landownership in 1915, a large portion of the idle-land in urban areas was already transformed to Japanese possession or colonial government property. In fact, the process of urban renewal and municipal district reform in Seoul, from 1912 to 1927, was a bitter experience for the colonial government because of the readjustment work compensation. For example, the total expenditure during the period was 11,250,000 *won*(the Korean unit of currency) and 64 percent of this amount, 7,170,000 *won* was disbursed in the name of land compensation.[40]

Although the exact acreage is unclear, according to newspaper, governmental officers and persons of that time, if government property is included, the Japanese may have controlled more than two-third of the land.[41]

For the Government-General, the LRP was the most rational approach because it could be accomplished at a minimum public expenditure. The most important task of the land adjustment was to secure as much land as possible for public facilities after applying the *chongbo*[42] reduction rate of land for landowners within the target areas. As a result, the Government1-General usurped 20-25 percent of the capital gain from every landowners in the name of the land adjustment. Most importantly, the reduction rate was only to obtain the land gratuitously for public facilities and never included the substitutive land for construction cost. Instead, the authority appropriated the beneficial rates for the work. The Kyongsong Street Subdivision Ordinance obviously shows the benefit principle system which was introduced from the Japanese Act: Article 48 of the ordinance notes, "The public authorities for the LRP could appropriate the total or limited costs for the work to the landowners within the work target areas under the control of the Government-General" (Article 48).

When the LRP was almost completed, the landowners began to sell their lands. In the process of transfer and acquisition of the lands, the government created The Land Advice Office(LAO) in the Department of Urban Planning, and gave the office the authority to play the role of realestate agent. According to Sang-Hoon Youn, who was the vice director of the General Affairs in Kyongsong City Government during that time, noted in an interview that "one of the most important roles of the LAO was to decide a conventional price which was lower than the market land-price in its day." In spite of the grand advertisements and public lectures, however, actual land transactions were minimal. Moreover, the economic recession added to the transaction difficulties for

---

[40] Kyongsong-bu (Seoul), *Kyongsong Sigaji Chegaebal* (Town replanning report) (1934).

[41] According to Yo-Song Lee and So Yong Kim's work, *Sutja Chosen Yon'gu* (The study of Korea in figures) (Seoul: Kuk'hakjarouwon) 97-99, based on a few materials about the announce of the Chosen Municipal District Planning Act, they estimate that the rate of Korean land-wnership in the major cities was 42% in Seoul, 38% in P'yongyang, 23% in Taegu, 25% in Pusan, and 22% in Inch'on.

[42] *Chongbo* is an acreage unit and it is equivalent to hectare. One *chongbo* estimates 9,917.4 square meters while one hectare does 10,000 square meters.

citizens. Under this slack land market, the only customer was The Chosen Housing Corporation established in 1941. By this time, the CHC planned to secure housing sites for future use and purchased an enormous number of housing sites at the low prices. Many of these sites were transferred to the Chosen Housing Administration after the 1945 Liberation.

## THE LOGIC OF COLONIAL URBAN DEVELOPMENT

Previously, there were various schools of thought regarding how to define Korea's relationship to Japan.[43]

Given present evidence, there can be little doubt that Korea was a colony under dictatorial Japanese rule and the country was developed, not as an autonomous unit, but as part of the Japanese empire. The changes in urban Korea during this period closely reflect Japanese colonial policy, which was deliberately planned and effectively carried out by the imperial regime. Compelling evidence of Korea's colonial character is that "the military-bureaucratic power"[44] of the Government-General occupied outstanding positions in every walk of life. Its ultimate objective was to maximize the benefits which would accrue either directly or indirectly to Japan.[45]

The main logic of the impact of colonialism on urbanization would be one of dominance-dependence where the ultimate source of social, economic, and political power rests in the colonizing metropolitan society, with physical force being the ultimate sanction in the colonized society. As described in the previous section, during the first two decades of colonial rule, Japan saw Korea mainly as a source of agricultural products which could be exported to Japan, and most of the investment went into agricultural development and the construction of transportation facilities necessary to get farm produce to ports, particularly, Pusan and Inch'on.

In a similar context, the economic structure of urban Korea was being changed through the influence of Japanese entrepreneurs and the imperialist activity of the Japanese government. Predominantly manual manufacturing activities gradually became factory-directed. A uniform and centralized monetary and banking system was

---

[43] Paul Reinsch's book, *Colonial Government*(New York: Macmillan, 1924), distinguishes a colony from a dependency on the grounds that the latter is more inclusive than the former. Such a distinction may have some geographical significance, but in the political and economic realm the terms are practically indistinguishable.

[44] This can be inferred from the fact that the Governor-General was appointed directly by the Crown from army or navy officers to command the forces in defense of Japan and to exercise supreme control over the administration. He was authorized to memorialize the Throne and receive the Imperial Sanction through the Prime Minister, and to issue general ordinances in virtue of his delegated or discretionary power. In practice the Governor-General was the lawgiver, the chief executive, the commander-in-chief of army and navy, and the highest tribunal. See Henry P. Chung, *The Case of Korea* (New York: Fleming H. Revell Company, 1921), 61; Edward Chen, "Attempt to Integrate the Empire," in Ramon H. Myers and Mark R. Peattie, eds, *The Japanese Colonial Empire* (Princeton: Princeton University Press, 1984), 259.

[45] Shannon McCune, *Korea's Heritage* (Toyko: Tuttle Company, 1967), 30.

established. The major cities were rebuilt and new cities were further developed with the aid of the development of new systems of transportation and communication. However, as Yun-Sik Chang has argued, most Korean cities were developed in response to the new industrial requirements of the Japanese expansionist movement of the late 1930's.[46]

Moreover, the manufacturing growth which occurred under colonial rule was determined by the requirements of Japanese industrialization rather than Korean needs. The contemporary observer George McCune commented(well before dependency theory had appeared), "The Korean economy was Japanese-owned and Japanese-directed and in no sense an entity in and of itself, but rather the geographical location of a portion of the wider configuration of the economy of Japan."[47]

The colonial administration carefully controlled capital investment in Korea, through the *zaibatsu* and the Japanese Overseas Department. This policy was aimed at creating the Korean economy's total dependency on Japan. The Japanese owned 90 percent of the total paid-up capital of all corporations in Seoul in 1938 and 85 percent of all manufacturing and industrial facilities in 1944, as well as, controlling all major banking, insurance, and so on. Korean capital was limited in most industrial sectors and confined to small-scale industry.[48]

If there was any indigenous influence on the city's economic achievement, it was made possible by an effective coalition with the colonial ruling power groups including government elites and Japanese capitalists. Accordingly, local entrepreneurs had to gain the support and recognition of the state ministries and state-controlled financial institutions to survive and compete with their Japanese counterparts. The close working ties they formed with the strong colonial state defined business-state relations, as the several studies of major local entrepreneurs has documented.[49]

The Japanese government also foisted upon Koreans an ideology of incorporation emphasizing a structural family principle and an ethical *filiale*. This influence remains strong. As Korea industrialized in the postwar period, she has fostered *zaibatsu*-like conglomerates, with extensive family inter-penetration, and ideologies of familial hierarchy and filial loyalty(e.g., the New Spirit movement in the 1970s in South Korea, corporate familism in North Korea).[50]

Immediately after the official annexation, the colonial government implemented the Land Project to establish a modern private land owning system. This was crucial for control of the Korean economy. Upon the completion of the Project, the Japanese

---

[46] Yun-Sik Chang, o*p cit*, 291-300.

[47] George A. McCune, *Korea Today* (Cambridge: Harvard University Press, 1950), 37.

[48] ". . . it was the Japanese who constituted almost the entire middle and upper classes of Chosen." See Gregory Henderson, o*p cit*, 97.

[49] See, for example, Dennis McNamara, *The Colonial Origins of Korean Enterprise, 1910-1945* (New York: Cambridge University Press, 1990); Bruce Cumings, "The Origins and Development of the North East Asian Political Economy," in F. D. Deyo. ed, *The Political Economy of the New Asian Industrialism* (Ithach: Cornel University Press, 1985).

[50] Bruce Cumings, *Op cit* (1987), 56

government was successful in its initial attempt to utilize Korean landowners' capital by encouraging the formation of several Korean-owned banks.[51]

As members of *yangban* class, The Korean landowners, willingly or unwillingly, cooperated with the Japanese authorities. Close ties with the Japanese government were essential to Korean business success. Forms of political coalition by Korean indigenous elites were more salient within the structure of the colonial administration, such as through the Central Advisory Council(Chungch'uwon)[52] advisors, or provincial governors.

From this point of view, it may be noted that the coalition between the colonial state, Japanese capitalists, and the pro-Japanese clique including both the indigenous aristocratic *yangban* and new entrepreneurial class, played a central role in the early colonial urban process.[53]

Nevertheless, Korean entrepreneurs faced difficulties in gaining support from the colonial state. The few who gained its favor were then able to gain extensive support for various urban infrastructure projects, again contributing to concentration of capital among a few established local entrepreneurs.[54]

In fact, some business elites won at least a consultative role in policy making in Seoul's economy through participation on the boards of larger Japanese combines, or *zaibatsu*, prominence in business-policy associations, and their position in the local economy as corporate owners.[55]

The colonial state was the critical actor in the coalition. During Japanese rule, the colonial government abolished the existing feudal class distinctions and subordinated all classes to the colonial state bureaucracy. This pattern persisted into the post-independence period, and provided a model for state-directed development in South Korea, based on the political culture such as strong centralism and authoritarianism inherited from the colonial period.

There was no possibility, however, of a return to pre-colonial Korea. Japanese colonialism had introduced capitalist social relations on a wide scale, it had destroyed the traditional legitimacy of the landlord-tenant relationship in the popular consciousness and had ruined the authority of the old aristocratic ruling class. The Korean people began to

---

[51] Han wrote in his autobiography that many Korean landowners became banking officers or prominent Korean businessmen in later years. For example, all of the top executives of the Korean Life Insurance Company established in 1921 were members of the *yangban* class. see Sang Yong Han, *Kan Soryo Kun wa Kataru* (Reminiscences by Han Sang Yong) (Keijo, 1941). 54.

[52] In this time, the council's primary purpose was to reward with sinecure some seventy former pro-Japanese high officials of Korea.

[53] The colonial Korean society during the colonial period marked the decline of the *yangban* class as a ruling and privileged entity with the disappearance of the traditional class. But it is not doubtful that some members of the formal *yangban* class, especially the pro-Japanese groups, became social leaders and leading commercial and industrial enterprises in leading the Korean economy at that time.

[54] Carter J. Eckert, *Offspring of Empire: The Kochang Kims and the Colonial Origins of Korean Capitalism* (Seattle: University of Washington Press, 1986).

[55] For example, Pak Yong Hyo, a director of the Chosen Bank, and Pak Yong Chol, a vice president of Oriental Development Company, played prominent roles in the middle decades of Japanese rule as advisors and consultants. Dennis L. McNamara, *op cit*, 114-125.

accept such concepts as capitalism and entrepreneurship as important ingredients for economic improvement. As a result, in many ways, concepts and the way of life of the people became non-traditional as they maintained a delicate balance between traditional and modernity. Urban Korea had irreversibly entered a period of profound change.

The major line of colonial urban planning in Korea was often focused by capitalist theories, considering housing and land development as an instrument of reproducing labor forces for the effective achievement of the imperial Japanese government's political goal. This follows Castells' argument that capital's interest in "reproducing labor power" provides the motive for state intervention in the field of urban planning.[56]

Nevertheless, the role of the government is particularly important because of its control over the patterns and conditions of provision of 'collective consumption' like housing and land. This logic also directed the Land Readjustment Project for housing site development by the colonial government. The Japanese scholar, Nishiyama criticized that "the land readjustment approach is used as the cheap instrument of urban development through which the lands for public facilities were obtained not by direct purchase but free of charge from the powerless Korean landowners."[57]

Focusing on policy instruments, the state's economic responsibility will be growth-oriented, and its political responsibility will be distributive in modern capitalist societies. In most of underdeveloped countries, the former is emphasized more than the latter, but the distributive policy would be stressed in the situation where there exists social and political instability. Plausible evidence is found in the LRP used to decrease the Korean's resistance derived from the uneven development between the Korean village, Pukch'on, and the Japanese village, Namch'on. Also, the construction of housing complexes within Seoul in both the Sino-Japanese War and the Pacific War period was an important political tool of the colonial government.

During the colonial period, the LRP was a firm and powerful state-directed program in which state power completely blocked the power of private developers or corporations. Based on the concept of centralized government power, the government-directed land readjustment work under colonial rule was succeeded by, and developed into, the popular instrument for urban development under the post-independence authoritarian government. Most of the LRPs today, big projects in particular, have been implemented by the public authorities such as local governments, Korea National Housing Corporation, or Korea Land Development Corporation.[58]

Colonial heritage was largely maintained even after independence, and recognition of the basic and lasting changes under the colonial rule in the direction of capitalistic concepts of urban development, as well as modernization are a first step in the intellectual exploration. In particular, the zeal for rapid national economic development of post-independence Korea has called for a large measure of centralized planning and

---

[56] Manuel Castells, *The Urban Question* (Cambridge: MIT Press, 1977), 431.

[57] Yoshino Nishiyama, *op cit*, 109.

[58] Based on a few materials from the Department of Urban Planning in the Ministry of Construction, among 395 land adjustment works until 1985 since colonial period, only 70 programs have been implemented by private corporations.

government interventionism. As Eckert notes, the model shared a number of elements with its contemporary Japanese archetype: the pivotal economic function of the state, the concentration of private economic power in the hands of a small number of large business groups or *Jaebol(zaibatsu)*, and the emphasis on exports.[59]

It is by no means an exaggeration to say that this political and ideological factor has contributed to a certain imbalance between urban and rural areas, and has accelerated urbanization in the post-independence Korean society.

## CONCLUSION

The manner in which the urban structure of Seoul was shaped during the colonial period furnishes clues, not only to the nature of early urban development, but to the character of colonial life in larger terms. In the end of nineteenth century, foreign penetration of the Korean Peninsula proved to be irresistible, and the Japanese emerged as the dominant economic force. This is not to suggest that economic gain was the primary motivation behind the Japanese imperialist thrust into Korea. Indeed, it seems quite clear that, initially at least, Japanese interest in Korea was more political and strategic rather than economic.

The primacy of centralized authoritarian state in the colonial era has been emphasized throughout this study. The political and institutional forces allowed the development of broadly interventionist policies to deal with the issues related to Seoul's urban growth. Throughout this process, the state existed as an independent, identifiable entity, with its own functions and objectives; and, at the same time, it was clearly situated as a constituent element of a wider set of power relations within society. In the colonial period, Seoul showed its dependence on the state with urban growth policies and market regulation, which enhanced capital accumulation and consequent urban growth. This study argues, however, that Koreans shared neither the direction of this development nor its benefits. The wealth of Korea had increased, but not the wealth of the Korean. No significant effort was made by the Government-General to aid small industries and the mass of people. The urban planning progress under Japanese direction was solely for the war effort, and brought neither political stability nor social welfare to Korea. Capitalistic classes, including Japanese and Korean entrepreneurs, exclusively participated in the urban development projects and made great economic gains. Not surprisingly, this evidence combined the interconnected logic between the independent state theory and the capital logic theory of structuralists. The authoritarian colonial state was seen as playing to stimulate and maintain capital accumulation. Nevertheless, what should be stressed is that the colonial state has acted as an independent arbiter of the class struggle, and not as a subordinate. The Japanese colonial state has been aptly characterized as growth-oriented and interventionist in economic affairs, promoting the peninsula as a base of Japanese economy. The state tried to incorporate Korea into the Japanese empire, not just

---

[59] Carter J. Eckert, *op cit*, 249-260.

as a colony but as a new territory, to avoid the negative aura of patronization and exploitation that had become the hallmark of disrepute for European colonialism. Nontheless, the structuring role of the colonial state far exceeded what Stepan has observed more generally: "The administrative, legal, bureaucratic and coercive systems of the state attempt not only to structure relations between civil society and public authority in a polity, but also to structure many crucial relations within civil society as well."[60]

The very opposite of Myrdal's "soft and weak state"[61] constrained by anxieties over domestic political consensus, the Japanese administration on the peninsula proved itself as a strong state primarily concerned with military security and economic productivity. The extensive role of the colonial state in the urban planning through 1945 was not surprising, given the direct and often authoritarian role of the Japanese colonial administration in Korea. The developmentalist heritage of a strong and autonomous state under the Japanese colonial rule succeed to the post-independence authoritarian Korean state.

---

[60] Alfred Stepan, *The State and Society: Peru in Comparative Perspective* (Princeton: Princeton University Press, 1978), xii.

[61] Myrdal wrote that "soft states" are ones in which "governments require extraordinary little of their citizens" and "obligations that do exists are enforced inadequately if at all." Gunnar Myrdal, *Asian Drama: An Inquiry into the Poverty of Nations*, vol. 2 (New York: Twentieth Century Fund, 1968), 896.

*Chapter 11*

# GOOD GOVERNANCE, DEMOCRACY AND CIVIL SOCIETY IN BANGLADESH

## *Samiul Hasan*
The University of Technology, Sydney

## ABSTRACT

In the recent years many countries in the developing world have been passing through a transitional phase from autocracy to democracy. These countries are said to be aiming to achieve good governance or a pluralist polity where public, private, and the non-government sectors can cooperate with each other in an enabling environment to achieve development through the existence of political and civic pluralism. The system calls for a freely and regularly elected representative legislature, and free and neutral judiciary. All these can be achieved through the establishment and proper functioning of different types of civil society organisations: economic, cultural, informational, educational, etc. Democratic governance thus requires more than free and fair elections. In many newly democratising countries, however, a free and fair election becomes synonymous to democratic governance.

Bangladesh has been one of the countries passing through this transitional phase of autocracy to democracy. Since 1991 in the 'transitional zone' two governments have been formed in Bangladesh through free and fair elections held under neutral caretaker administration. In this essay an effort is made to analyse how far these elections and the political parties have taken Bangladesh towards good governance through the establishment of civil society. Why? Why not?

## INTRODUCTION

In the recent years many countries in the developing world have been passing through a transitional phase from autocracy to democracy. More and more countries are entering this 'third wave' of 'transition zone' (Huntington, 1991) due to an improvement in the levels of urbanisation, education, and resultant "decline in the size and importance of the peasantry, and the development of the middle class and an urban working class" (Huntington, 1997). This also has been the result of globalisation ensuring free flow of technology, capital, and information about the openness and liberalisation and their impacts, and a subsequent evolution of a social force to challenge the authoritarian regimes. Bangladesh has been passing through this transition.

Achieving democracy in these countries is a vehicle of establishing good governance. Good governance relates to "institutional performance and the relations between state and society" (Crook and manor, 1995). It also refers to the government's capacity to discharge governmental functions by formulating and implementing policies with the inputs and involvement of different stakeholders (World Bank, 1992; Moore, 1995). Governance is thus seen as a process of interaction between the public sector and the various actors in 'civil society' (Paproski, 1993)- or in the "public life of individuals and institutions outside the control of the state" (Harpham and Boateng, 1997: 66). Thus the political meaning of good governance denotes a political and economic structure, a pluralist polity with a freely and regularly elected representative legislature, with the capacity at least to influence and check executive power, and a clear separation of legislative, executive, and judicial powers (Leftwich, 1994). Democratic features can ensure favourable interrelationships among stakeholders in policy process and good governance. For these reasons, there has been a push from the donors and an advent of democratisation process in the developing countries.

Democratization, according to OECD (1994), integrates participation into the political life of the country and requires the "development of a pluralist civil society comprised of a range of institutions and associations which represent diverse interests and provide a counterweight to the government" (cited in Nunnenkamp, 1995). Civil society, a public realm located between the family and the state, consists of a plurality of civil associations (Robinson, 1995). Linz and Stepan (1996) provides a detail explanation of civil society referring it to "that arena of the polity where self-organising groups, movements, and individuals, relatively autonomous from the state, attempt to articulate values, create associations, and solidarities" (p. 7).

Civil society organisations can be varied depending on goals, activities, and membership characteristics. Diamond (1994) classified these civil society organisations into seven categories: a) economic; b) cultural; c) informational and educational; d) interest-based; e) developmental; f) issue-oriented; and g) civic. The last category of organisations aim at strengthening the political system and imparting democratic values (Robinson, 1995). Stepan (1988) however opines that civil society is distinct from political society that includes political parties, legislatures and elections, through which organised interests compete for political power (cited in Robinson, 1995). Interestingly enough, however, in most newly emerging democratic polities election is seen as the only requirement for democratic governance, and not the institutionalisation of the functioning of civil society. Free and fair election thus becomes synonymous to democracy or even good governance. In this essay an effort is made to look at these aspects in one of the newest democracies- Bangladesh, and to analyse the achievements it has had towards good governance through the establishment of civil society.

## BANGLADESH IN TRANSITION

Bangladesh got independence in 1971, following a nine-month-long liberation war and, incurring immense economic and infra-structural losses. Massive work of reconstruction and rebuilding required a strong and politically committed democratic government. It never became real- the government failed in delivering the promises the liberation brought the people. The failure of the government in providing even the minimum necessities of life resulted in unrest among people within just a year of the independence. The government, formed by the Awami League (the party that struggled for justice and democracy and led the Liberation War), took the shape of an authoritarian regime, and the military intervention in the political process followed.

Within its first ten years (up to March 1982) Bangladesh experienced nine known attempts at coup-d'etat (*Defence Journal*, 1986) four of which were successful and resulted in changes in government. In the last twenty-eight years military generals have ruled the country for more than fourteen years. These military generals captured power through unconstitutional means, later legalized their rules with the help of some political parties, leaders, and elections. But elections have not been regular events in Bangladesh. In the 25 years until 1996 (the year the last election held) seven general elections were held, but five of these elections were held in ten years between 1986 and 1996. Most of these elections were, however, not free and fair.

Since 1991 in the 'transitional zone' two governments have been formed in Bangladesh through free and fair elections held under neutral caretaker governments, but the major aspects of democracy are yet to be achieved. In the next sections an attempt is made to look at the political party and election system in Bangladesh to examine the success it has had in achieving good governance through the establishment of civil society in a democratic polity. Before moving to that discussion a brief attempt is made to identify the essential aspects of good governance and establishing their relationship to civil society.

# GOVERNANCE, DEMOCRACY AND CIVIL SOCIETY

Governance is a governmental structure or form dictating or determining interrelationships among subsystems, the functioning process of the system, and the capacity of the 'system' in exercising authority in the management of the country's economic, social, and environmental resources to achieve the 'goals' with the involvement of the beneficiaries. Thus good 'governance' is a form that ensures political plurality and economic liberalism, a process that is conscientious and transparent, and a government's capacity to ensure accountability and develop an enabling system (Hasan, 1999).

An enabling system in democratic governance requires a favourable structure and a process to empower the people in policy formulation as well as implementation process. According to Przeworski (1988: 64) democracy is a system of power under which no group can guarantee that its interests will automatically or always prevail. In a democratic system everyone must subject his or her interests "to competition and uncertainty" (cited in Leftwich, 1993).

Democracy can be defined in behaviourist terms as well as in structural terms. While competition, participation and effective civil freedom are emphasised in behaviourist definition of democracy, a free election system, political institutions appropriate to a multi-party system and independent legislation and judiciary are essential for structural aspect of democracy (Rijnierse, 1993: 653; Bratton, 1989). Democracy requires all these to function and ensure a rule by the elected majority.

The facilitation of a majority rule requires an open and inclusive political system where the people can make free choices regarding the policy makers as well as the policy, through a free and fair election process. Thus, a fair political system should also have a responsible political opposition. Parties in position and in opposition all have important roles to play in democratic governance. The five key opposition functions are: resisting integration into the regime; guarding zones of autonomy against; disputing its legitimacy; raising the costs of authoritarian rule; creating a credible democratic alternative (Stepan, 1990: 44). Stepan, however, refers this to opposition in an authoritarian system of government. In the case of a democratically elected government the first two could be the most important function of the opposition. It is true that a government's likelihood to "tolerate an opposition increases as the expected cost of suppression increases" (Dahl, 1971:15). But the opposition has to think about a political cost to the government, not material cost to the country through destruction and violence. Thus when a democratic system is already in place the opposition can endeavour to create an alternative policy regime without disrupting the continuity of the political and economic systems in the country. But that again through an accepted process- free and fair election- and not by violent means.

A free and honest election has long been seen as an essential precondition of democracy (Schumpeter, 1954). Elections are essence of democracy (Huntington, 1997), and still is regarded as an essential criterion of democracy (Huntington, 1991). Democracy, however, is not just a matter of a decision or "of hastily organised elections", "it requires a long process of political development" (UNDP, 1993). In many recent democracies a free and fair election seem to be regarded as its only criterion. Diamond (1996) however, tends to call this, election-only democracy, an 'electoral democracy', and makes a distinction between an 'electoral' and a 'liberal' democracy. Liberal democracies need more than free and fair elections. It requires the absence of "reserved domains" of power for non-accountable forces, 'vertical' as well as 'horizontal' accountability, and provision for political and civic pluralism (Diamond, 1996). Specifically, liberal democracy should have the following features:

- Vesting of real power on elected officials and their appointees.
- Constitutionally limited executive power accountable to other institutions: judiciary, parliament etc.
- Uncertain electoral outcome, and an open and inclusive electoral system.
- No disadvantaging of any body in the electoral process or in the expression of interests due to cultural, ethnic, religious or other background.
- Multiple and continuous means of interest articulation and aggregation.
- Independent media and other sources of information with easy and equal access for all citizenry.
- Freedom of belief, opinion, discussion, speech, publication, assembly, demonstration, and petition.
- Equality in the eye of law administered by an independent and impartial judiciary.
- Protection of all citizen under rule of law and also from organised anti-state forces (Diamond, 1996).

All these criteria can only be achieved if all the seven types of civil society, mentioned earlier, can be established in the polity concerned. "Civil society's capacity for free organisations and of its vitality" is actually expressed through the third sector organisations (Frantz, 1987:123). The third sector organisations also contribute to re-democratisation process of the country concerned, maintaining or expanding existing forms of democracy. A third sector organisation may help maintain democratic spaces even under dictatorial rules by creating and supporting spaces for people's participation at least within their own sphere (Padron, 1987). But the question is can this sphere be expanded to embrace the whole polity in an 'electoral democracy'?

It will be interesting to see if the democratic process in Bangladesh starting from a free and fair election has been able to create an independent space for civil society development and functioning to ensure the consolidation of democracy aimed at good governance in the shortest possible time. Before looking at the election and its outcome we will first add a brief on political parties in Bangladesh.

## Political Parties in Bangladesh

In late 1980s there were 160 political parties in Bangladesh (Hasan, 1988). In the recent past, some old parties have become inactive, however, more new parties have been formed. Thus, the total number of political parties in Bangladesh is still around 160. There has been a lack of a definite governmental policy, and a slack or politically motivated implementation of the measures, related to political party registration, party politics and functioning. Thus a large number of political parties are formed by people having interests in making personal gains through poly-tricks and not having any interest in achieving democracy ensuring 'government by the people' or influencing policy. These political parties were not formed to establish any political ideologies or to achieve specific political agenda. Most political parties in Bangladesh are 'one-man' with no supporters, and came into being mainly for five reasons:

♦ Frustration with the existing political system or parties;
♦ Struggle for power and benefits;
♦ Conflicts of opinion and personality among the party leadership;
♦ To enjoy (legal as well as illegal) benefits available to the political parties; and
♦ To help the military rulers gain a 'civil character (Modified from Hasan, 1988).

This excessively high number of political parties helps different regimes in different ways. These 'one-man' political parties help unconstitutional activities of different regimes, and nobody has much intention to solve the problem. General Zia, in 1976, tried to address the problem with the introduction of Political Party Regulation (PPR). The PPR, among other things, stated that any party that fails to win 10% of the cast votes in an election would automatically cease to function as a political party.

In the election in 1979, two parties, out of the thirty-four that participated in the election, won more than 10% of the votes. Some of the parties that failed to poll the required percentage of votes to survive as political parties, as a survival strategy (or due to a 'carrot and stick' trick of the government), supported programmes of General Zia. For General Zia the acceptance of the support was more beneficial to himself and his group than to impose the PPR regulation on to these parties. So these parties (and all the other parties, as a result) were allowed to continue to function as political parties. The PPR regulation finally became inoperative and the problems of burgeoning political parties and their use by different regimes continued.

A party in power creates problems on the functioning of the other political parties or the leadership until the other political parties or the leaders decide to support the government. When they do that they receive good returns from the government. The other two governments formed in the early 1970s and 1980s also used the same trick.

In 1972 Sheikh Mujib tricked all the other parties. The disgruntled Awami League that suffered oppression in the hands of the neo-colonial government formed the government in independent Bangladesh. Nevertheless, the AL leadership, from the day one, showed least interest in cooperating with the other parties or in listening to different views within the party. A group of young leaders splinted out of the Awami League to force their demand for modified socialism labelled as 'scientific socialism', and became a main opposition force in the election held in 1973. The government wanted to restraint the activities of the other parties, and changed the multi-party parliamentary system to a one-party presidential form through a constitutional amendment (fourth amendment) in 1975. The party leaders who wilfully joined the new one-party were given rewards.

General Ershad, the army general who came to power through a military coup d'état also tried to use these one-man political parties to survive the political agitation and external pressure of conducting free and fair election in the country. All the major political parties in the country boycotted the parliamentary election held under General Ershad in 1988. The Ershad government, however, received support from seventy-six of these 'one-man' political parties, grouped as Combined Opposition Parties (COP) (Rahman, 1989), and tried to convince the aid donors that it had the support from a 'huge' number of 'political parties'. This strategy, however, did not work. A major donor, the US, insisted the government of General Ershad arrange for a free and fair election with the participation of all the major political parties (Rahman, 1990). On the backdrop of the ongoing political agitation in the country, General Ershad did not dare to lose the power by arranging a fair election with the participation of all the parties. Following a massive political upsurge in the country he was forced to resign from the Presidency any way in December 1990 and pave the way for a fair election under a neutral caretaker government.

A free and fair general election was held in Bangladesh in 1991, and the ineffectiveness of the support of these 'parties' provided to the government of General Ershad became evident. None of these seventy-six parties won a parliamentary seat in the election. Nevertheless, the major partner of the COP, JSD (Rab) won only one seat (the party leader) in the election held in 1996, and managed a cabinet position in the AL government with that. The AL government, formed in 1996, did not need support to form the government, but wanted to weaken the opposition.

## POLITICAL PARTIES AND POLLING POLITICS: SETTING THE SCENE

After independence, Sheikh Mujibur Rahman, the leader of the Awami League and the war of independence, formed the government based on the results of the elections held in East Pakistan. The liberation war was participated by various groups under the *Mukti Bahini* (Freedom Fighters or FF) along with the members of the Awami League (Jahan, 1973). Sheikh Mujib, however, did not form a multi-party government nor did he arrange a fresh election to renew his mandate as demanded by the other political parties and ignored the sacrifices and contributions of other parties. The AL went to the election in 1973, and polled 73% of the votes, but faced opposition to its policies in the following months. To suppress the opposition political parties and their democratic activities and concentrate more power in his own hands, Sheikh Mujib introduced a presidential system with a single-party blaming the "divisive activities of the opposition parties" to justify his actions (Khan, 1983). The democratically elected government of Sheikh Mujib misread the people's mind and misused the mandate given to them in the general election held in 1973 and deceived the citizens to favour his own party and party-men.

A military coup in August 1975 removed the Awami League from the office, and banned all political activities in the country. In 1977, General Ziaur Rahman, the chief of the military government, planned to form a political party mainly with some retired military officers and a few political leaders who gathered around him for a give-and-take purpose (Rashiduzzaman, 1977; Rashiduzzaman, 1979; Khan and Zafarullah, 1979). During the civilianisation process members of the Awami League and communist radicals like the National Awami Party (different factions), and on the other extreme Muslim fanatic groups along with the Muslim League gathered around him (Franda, 1982). The leaders who had divergent beliefs and interests "hastily assembled under this multi-dimensional umbrella party" (Haque, 1980).

In the wake of the revival of political activities again in 1983, following the military coup in 1982, factionalism increased to an unprecedented degree and affected most major political parties. Some leaders from various political parties left their previous parties in groups and gathered around General Ershad. The weaknesses of the political parties were manifested "not only in their intense factionalism but also in their individual susceptibility to the government's 'carrot-and-stick' policy and their tenuous links with the grass-roots" (Rahman, 1984: 242). A political front emerged as a single political party, the Jatiyo (National) Party, in 1985 comprising of elements from most major parties: AL, BNP, Muslim League, and the radical leftist parties like the United People's Party (UPP), and the Gano (People's) Front. The so-called political leaders thus shop-around for privileges and pay allegiance according to the benefit gained. They hardly ever work for the establishment of democracy or framing policy and programs to fulfil the constitutional responsibility of the government in development.

The main purpose of the Jatiyo Party was to consolidate military's power by suppressing the other parties and their activities. The suppression by the military regime, following the military takeover in 1982, forced the political parties to come out in the street to call for the establishment of democracy. In 1986 the opposition groups' 15 party alliance led by the Awami League, a 7-party alliance led by the BNP, and some other opposition parties demanded the establishment of a neutral caretaker government to arrange a free and fair election, and the resignation of the military government. The government issued an ultimatum to the political parties, to decide on participation before midnight on the 21st of March 1986. As the opposition demands were not met, all the opposition parties took a unanimous decision not to submit to the government's 'trick'. To an utter surprise of all the other opposition parties the Awami League, after a few hours, changed its stand and unilaterally announced its decision to participate in the general election. It appeared to some that the Awami League had already reached some understanding with the government (Islam, 1987). In addition, the Awami League rightly understood that if it participated in the election without the BNP, Sheikh Hasina (daughter of Sheikh Mujib), President of the AL could become the leader of the opposition, and regain lost status for the Awami League. In fact, the AL and the BNP sought each other's destruction as much as they sought the downfall of the Ershad regime (Islam, 1987), and the AL resorted to this 'trick' to gain an upper hand.

This decision of the Awami League in 1986 was a blow to the joint efforts of the opposition parties that had been active since 1983. The behaviour of the Awami League proofs that the political leaders can resort to any trick to further their own narrow interests. This move benefited Ershad, who had been looking for ways to divide and defeat the opposition movement. This act of the Awami League helped the government regain a second life that endured until 1990.

The Ershad government finally arranged a parliamentary election in May 1986. The Awami League polled 26% of the votes in the election- just one percent more than what it polled in 1979 election. This one percent more vote won the AL 36 more seats than the 40 seats it won in 1979. In the following days, the AL realised that participating in the election was a mistake, because it failed to show that its support among the general people has gone up, and also there were signs that the BNP was gaining popularity due to its constant stance against the authoritarian regime. The AL finally came out on the street and joined the 'out of the parliament' opposition groups in demanding a free and fair election under a neutral care taker government. Instead of accepting the demand of the major opposition parties, the government staged another election in 1988 without the participation of major political parties. Finally, however, the Ershad government succumbed to a strong agitation by combined opposition and resigned. A free election under a neutral caretaker administration was held in 1991.

## ELECTION AND 'NATURAL SELECTION'

So far, parliamentary elections participated by all the major parties in the country have been held in Bangladesh in 1973, 1979, 1991 and June 1996. All the major parties boycotted the elections held in 1988 and February 1996.The election held in 1986 was not participated by a major group of political parties. The following analysis is thus based, mainly, on the elections participated by all parties.

Many people participate in the general elections, but only a few receive a reasonable endorsement from the electorates. In the elections held in 1991 and 1996, there were 1,786 (including 424 independents) and 1,827 (including 350 independents) contestants, respectively for three hundred parliamentary seats (Khan, 1997). Many political parties participate in the elections, but most do not have any contact with the people they wish to represent and serve. This fact is proved from the results of the parliamentary elections.

On an average six candidates contest in every constituency, but in some constituencies the number, sometimes, goes up to as high as twelve. Thus, the percentage of votes polled by the winning candidate remains very low. This phenomenon always has been existent in elections in Bangladesh. In some seats the winning candidate poll as low as 23% of the cast votes. Only in a few seats the winner polls more than 50% of the cast vote (Hasan, 1988). Overall nationwide only 0.73% votes made the major difference between the two main parties in 1991. The BNP received only 0.73% (30.81%) more votes than did the AL (30.08%). However, this fraction of a percentage point won the BNP 17% or 52 seats more than the AL (Table 1), due to the division of votes among different candidates in every constituency. The election results of 1996 is even more interesting. A swing of just 7% of popular votes in favour of the Awami League in 1996 won it 19.3% (or 58) more seats than it won in 1991. The popular votes polled by the BNP also increased by 4%, but it lost 24 or (8%) seats.

In all the fair parliamentary elections held in the recent past the party winning the government polled only a small percentage of the votes. The major problem occurs in the political scenes in the country when the party in power forgets that most voters voted against the government party. In the elections held in 1991, the BNP formed the government receiving only 31% of the cast vote, and failed to reckon the fact that 69% of the voters favoured other candidates against them. The party took many political and economic measures ignoring the opposition parties that enjoyed more than double the support among the general voters enjoyed by the government. Thus the government antagonised the people and finally succumbed to the latter's agitation. Eventually for their arrogance the BNP failed to come back to the power. In 1996 the Awami League with the support of only 37% of the cast vote formed the government. If the Awami League forgets the 'number' and ignores the opposition it might face the same consequence in the next election.

The recent election results are also a proof of the fact that the political parties lack maturity, but the people in Bangladesh through the political struggle under the authoritarian regimes have achieved some maturity. The election results showed that on the face of the government's failure to limit the number of political parties, the people have made their choices. There is a trend that the parties without much people base, or policies contradictory to the aspirations of the most people will be wiped out very soon. In 1991 Jamate Islami (JI) won 18 seats with 12% of the popular votes, in 1996 its portion of cast votes decreased by 25% but it lost 15 seats or 83% of the seats it won in 1991. In 1991 the Jatiyo Party also polled 12% of the popular votes, but unlike JI it won 35 seats. In 1996 it polled 4% more votes, but lost three seats. These results also suggest that the smaller parties are being regionalised. Instead of polling votes all over the country, the small parties, are polling votes in a few 'pockets'. JP and JI fielded candidates in all the seats, but polled votes only in some specific constituencies. This trend is the result of the voters' lack of interest in minor parties due to, mainly, their selfish or anti-people activities in the past. There are signs that the smaller parties will eventually lose all their grounds.

Table 1 depicts that while in 1991 twelve parties won any seats, in the election held in 1996 only six political parties managed to win any seats. Even then, only three major political parties won 294 seats, while three other parties won only five seats (one seat was won by an independent candidate). Also the Jamate Islami, known for their subversive activities against the war of liberation and fanatic ideologies, though won 18 seats in 1991 managed to win only three seats in 1996. This reflects the disapproval of the people of the Jamate Islami's activities between 1991 and 1996, including the reinstitution of Golam Azam (known for his opposition to an independent Bangladesh) as the party chief.

## Table 1: Bangladesh Parliamentary Election Results

|  | 1973 | 1979 | 1986 | 1988 | 1991 | 1996 June |
|---|---|---|---|---|---|---|
| **No of Parties Participated** | 14 | 34 | 18 | 3+76** | 63 | 76 |
| **No of Candidates** | 1075 | 2125 | 1527 | 764 | 1786 | 1827 |
| **Vote Cast (% of total)** | 55 | 48 | 60 | 52*** | 57 | 74 |
| **Number of Parties Won Seats** | 4 | 11 | 11 | 4 | 12 | 6 |
| **Number of Parties Polled 10%+ Vote** | 1 | 3 | 2 | 1 | 4 | 3 |
| **% Cast Vote Polled by Different Party** |  |  |  |  |  |  |
| Awami League | 73 | 25 | 26 | Abstained | 30 | 37 |
| BNP | -- | 41 | Abstained | Abstained | 31 | 34 |
| Jatiyo Party | -- | -- | 42 | 68 | 12 | 16 |
| Jamate Islami | -- | 10* | 5 | Abstained | 12 | 9 |
| Other parties (+ independents) | 27 | 24 | 27 | 32 | 15 | 4 |
| **No of Seats Won** |  |  |  |  |  |  |
| Awami League | 291 | 40 | 76 | Abstained | 88 | 146 |
| BNP | -- | 205 | Abstained | Abstained | 140 | 116 |
| Jatiyo Party | -- | -- | 153 | 251 | 35 | 32 |
| Jamate Islami | -- | 20* | 10 | Abstained | 18 | 3 |
| Other parties (+ independents) | 8 | 35 | 61 | 49 | 19 | 3 |

The election held in February 1996 was not participated by most parties, thus is not included.
**Source**: Z. R. Khan, "Bangladesh's Experiment With Parliamentary Democracy", *Asian Survey* 37: 575-89, 1997; A. S. Huque and A. Hakim, "Elections in Bangladesh: Tools of Legitimacy", *Asian Affairs* 19: 248-61, 1993. Samiul Hasan, "Political Parties in Bangladesh: A Study of Alienation" (in Bangla), Conference Paper, Fifth Bangladesh Political Science Association Conference held in Rajshahi, Bangladesh, June, 1988.

* Jamate Islami contested this election as Islamic Democratic League and jointly with Muslim League.
** JSD (Rab) gathered 75 other small parties to participate in the election as Combined Opposition Parties.
*** Main parties that did not participate claims only 1% voters voted, see A. S. Huque and A. Hakim, "Elections in Bangladesh: Tools of Legitimacy", *Asian Affairs* 19: 248-61, 1993.

There are increasing signs that the voters have been moving away from smaller parties. In 1991, minor parties won seventy-two seats, while in 1996 only thirty-eight seats went to these parties. In the recent past, on the one hand, the rate of election participation has increased on the other the consciousness of the people during the election have changed their electoral behaviour. In the general election held in 1979 only 48% of the voters cast ballots. In the election held in 1991 under a neutral government 57% of the eligible voters cast their ballots. The number rose to 74% in the election held in 1996. The voters now understand and feel that their ballots can make a difference because there is no chance of massive vote rigging. Due to the presence of a large number of voters in the polling stations the scope of giving proxy votes favouring the strategically and economically strong candidates has diminished significantly. This success can also be attributed to the consciousness raising and motivational works undertaken by civil society organisations, especially development agencies functioning in rural areas of Bangladesh. The situation is vividly manifested in the local elections. In the local elections held in 1998, 83% of the women voted in the election. A surprising number of 44,134 women participated in the elections- 90% of them were members of different voluntary organisations (*Dhaka Courier* 27.11.98 cited in Shehabuddin, 1999).

Interestingly enough, only four parties in 1991 and three parties in 1996 polled more than 10% of the cast vote. The ratios of success by the political parties in polling 10% of the cast votes to the number of parties participating in the elections were 1:14 in 1973, 1:11 in 1979, 1:16 in 1991, and 1:25 in 1996 (Table 1). Had some control mechanisms like the Political Party Regulation of General Zia (discussed earlier) been in place, the parties without much support would have been abolished by now. It would, on the one hand, end the ill motivated use of the smaller parties by the major parties or regimes, on the other hand would pave the way of the establishment of a two or three party healthy political system in the Country. Even without the regulation, it seems, if the free and fair elections are held regularly under neutral caretaker governments, the voters will make it happen anyway. The question is will the 'electoral democracy' in Bangladesh eventually lead to a 'liberal democracy'?

## 6. Discussion and Concluding Observation

Bangladesh is a homogenous country with a geographic, constitutional, and political legitimacy. In such a country, following Leftwich (1993), three pre-conditions must be ensured in order to consolidate a democratic polity. First, a secure and broad-based consensus about the rules of political game, because democracy requires all-round loyalty to the democratic process itself. Losing parties in elections must accept the outcome and embrace the status of 'loyal opposition'. Second, governmental restraints on the extent of policy change undertaken by the winning party or parties. Third, existence and functioning of a rich and pluralistic civil society (Leftwich, 1993: 615-6).

In Bangladesh, military as well as civil governments in the past have shown disregards to the importance of having an opposition and failed to consider the opposition with civility, and to achieve, respect, and implement a broader consensus. It is seen that in Bangladesh in the 1970s and 1980s:

- The opposition parties were either tricked out of the political scenario (1972);
- Lured or forced into dilution (1975);
- Forced into factionalism (1979);
- Succumbed to 'carrots' offered (1985, 1988) by the regime/party in power or,
- Engaged in each other's destruction (1986).

Since 1991, following the fall of the authoritarian regime, a space and scope have been created for the political parties to be involved in constructive and restrained activity, and thus support development in the country. Due to stubbornness and inconsistent behavior, the political parties have not been very successful in nurturing that 'space'. The first general election under a neutral caretaker administration was held in 1991. It is true that the AL went to the poll as the preferred party of the people, but still the people were interested in hearing specific policy measures and programs. Sheikh Hasina, the president and the leader of the party, being over-confident about the election win, started to talk about revenge- emphasising on actions to be taken against all the oppressions it had faced between 1975 and 1991 (including the killing of Sheikh Mujib etc.). At the end, the election result in 1991, came as a surprise to all. AL failed to achieve the main purpose of defeating the BNP and gaining back its lost status in the political arena.

The parties in government cannot restrain their behavior, either. For example, the BNP government, elected by the people in free and fair election, wanted to trick out the Awami League from the election in 1996. Finally, however, the BNP lost the game. One major reason for the loss of BNP in the election in 1996 was its leader's (the Prime Minister, Khaleda Zia) "haughty, proud, overbearing, vindictive and inept" (Kochanek, 1997) attitude. When the opposition parties raised demand for the formulation of a neutral caretaker government to hold the general election, Khaleda Zia ignored that and, arrogantly, tried to trick out the political opposition from the election, and held a general election in February 1996. The opposition parties and the people began a strong agitation against the government. Finally, the BNP government was compelled to accept the demand and leave the Office after amending the constitution to include the provision of holding parliamentary elections under a neutral caretaker government. The BNP resisted the formation of a neutral caretaker government to conduct the parliamentary election, thus when the election was held under a neutral caretaker government the BNP succumbed to its own arrogance.

Since August 1999, the BNP and other parliamentary opposition parties have been boycotting the present parliament protesting against the 'bullying tactic' of the AL inside the Parliament. The AL took this opportunity to hastily pass the Public Safety Bill, essentially to curb the opposition. These are the major characteristics of the present political system in Bangladesh.

In the transitional form of democracy in Bangladesh, the political parties and the political leaders are persistently unrepentant and stubbornly resisting or insensible to moral influence. The *Oxford English Dictionary* terms the situation as obduracy. We can thus, for its characteristics, term the transitional democratic form or the first phase of democracy in Bangladesh as 'obducracy'. In the system the political parties, by trying to constrict the government in achieving any success, for fear of losing its own ground, are actually constricting their own future. On the other hand, the deprivation is augmenting determination among the people to push for the scope of their own development. While democracy is a fair game, the transitional form, obducracy, seems to be an unfair game, so far the relationships among the political parties are concerned.

The major features of obducracy in Bangladesh are:

- Failure of the political groups in nurturing the prospective political 'space';
- Unfair and hostile relationships among political parties;

- Failure of the political parties in becoming institutions, instead the parties are being 'demonised' by the omnipotent leaders and the irresponsible sycophants;
- Absence of accountability in the government as well as within the political parties;
- Constrictive activities of opposition ;
- Use of 'poly-tricks' by the political parties to knock out each other;
- Civil society's overbearing activities in hindering the 'political course', and not in consolidating it;
- Emphasis is on political society and election, and not on a sound development of multi-faceted civil society;
- Absence of democracy within the political parties striving to establish democracy in the country (cf. Hasan, 1998).

The opposition political parties during the political agitation of 1986 to 1990 against the Ershad government and also again between 1993 and 1996 during the BNP government insisted that the general election be held under a neutral caretaker government. In the past the incumbencies in Bangladesh have generally "undermined a free and fair electoral process' by misusing "public resources in order to remain in power" (Khan, 1997). In order to institutionalise the process after its success in 1991, the Bangladesh Parliament in 1996 enshrined the provision of holding parliamentary election under a neutral care taker administration in the constitution (Ahmed, 1998).

A major jewel of obducracy in Bangladesh is thus the provision of a neutral caretaker administration to hold and oversee the parliamentary elections. The elections are being free and fair, and people are taking more interest now in the elections than they did in the past, with the hope of influencing the result due to the absence of any unfair means. The proof is the voter turnout in 1996 was 76%, as opposed to 48% in 1979 and 57% in 1991 (Table 1). There is, as a result, re-emergence of people's power overriding the 'political regimes'. In course of time, thus 'civil society' is assuming a greater role in influencing the 'political process'. But the problem is, civil society can destroy a non-democratic regime, but efforts for democratic consolidation "must involve political society" or the institutions including "political parties, elections, electoral rules, political leadership, interparty alliances, and legislatures- by which society constitutes itself politically to select and monitor democratic government" (Linz and Stepan, 1996: 8). In Bangladesh, monitoring aspect is really ignored because the politicians are involved in varied unscrupulous activities. Thus the politicians, irrespective of their position in the parliament, keep on diverting the people's attention from that to the aspects of election and its fairness. Monitoring cannot be effective or even existent unless there is accountability.

A major aspect of good governance is accountability. One of the major reasons of the absence of accountability in the administrative system is the lack of political accountability in the Country, with no chance of influencing the government. The scope of ensuring accountability increases when politics is able to produce socially desired outcomes. When parties are "no more than vehicles to enable an individual or group to capture power, accountability for policy outcomes is blurred" (Root, 1996). Bangladesh is a good example of this. Instead of looking for people with skills and experiences, in the elections in 1991 and 1996, the two major political parties nominated, mainly, those people for elections who either did have the capability to pay a large sum to the party coffer or a large thug-base to control the constituency, or both. The political parties in power or in opposition need those 'politicians' as their survival strategies, because "in Bangladesh paid 'mercenary' demonstrators and armed activists, hired by both the opposition and pro-government groups, made up the 'street mobs' and 'foot soldiers' who drove processions, rallies, blockades, arson, violence, and other form of civil disobedience" (Rashiduzzaman, 1997: 257). As a result, though the voting was fair the constituencies did not get the best people, because the good party stalwarts did not win the tickets in the first instance.

Democratic governance requires a liberal, transparent and accountable political system in the form of freedom of interest articulation and expression, and the existence of an independent legislature that allows participation in legislative process and make the administration answerable to the people. The principle of democracy calls for responsible and accountable rule, and not tyranny, of the majority. There could be two types of accountability vertical and horizontal (Sklar, 1996). The leaders must be accountable to the followers, rulers to the ruled, and office-holders to the citizenry or the mass. Horizontal accountability "consists of the obligation of office-holders to answer for their action, or decisions, to one another" (Sklar, 1996: 27). In the Bangladeshi system neither is existent. The second type of accountability may sound very simple, but the Leader see this as an intrusion in his/her authority because the political culture requires the party members or the office-holders to be subservient only to the Leader. The Leader can ensure this control with his/her omnipotent power in distributing positions or offering party tickets. Further, in the recent past due to the existence of a number of groups and interests in the party the members of a party themselves do not feel obliged to the fellow party men. Rather at occasions they work to discredit each other to receive the maximum favour from the omnipotent leader. If not any thing more this obedience ensures a permanent seal on a party ticket for the incumbent in the future elections. All these are the results of the absence of democracy within the political parties struggling to establish democracy in the Country.

One main objective of all the political parties, in Bangladesh, is to struggle to uphold democracy in the country. It is very interesting that none of these political parties has ever practised democracy within their own parties. The party leader, who happens to be the chief of the party, distributes the offices- national as well as sub-national levels. The large political parties hold regular convention to 'choose' their leadership, but in practice the positions are distributed among the party 'yes men' by the chairperson. The convention is convened merely to endorse them formally. In some occasions the leader takes a long time to nominate 'compromise' candidates to key positions. For example, the Chairman of the BNP (government party at the time) took almost six months after the convention was held in 1994 to fill in the position of the party general secretary. The compromise candidate normally does not deserve the positions nor do they try to improve their credibility. Thus they fail to help the party or the country, but they help the leaders.

Lack of democracy in and the existence of varied interests in the party are compromised by the personal symbol of the party leader who is the key player in election strategies and party nominations for the elections.

Democracy is not only "a matter of election", but regular elections are required to achieve democratic governance through a transition from obducracy. Obducracy may retard development, at the initial stage, in different ways. However, it is self-correcting. The changes in the government's as well as in the opposition's attitude have the potential to ensure true political pluralism in the country. "Free, fair, and competitive elections are only possible if there is some measure of freedom of speech, assembly, and press, and if opposition candidates and parties are able to criticise incumbents without fear of retaliation" (Huntington, 1997: 7). In Bangladesh all these are reasonably possible during the general election under a neutral caretaker government. The proliferation and functioning of a 'robust civil society' has been instrumental in this regard. The existence and activities of the third sector have boosted the peoples' understanding of the developmental reality and their roles and responsibilities in development, and also the importance of participating in the election because the voluntary sector emphasises on consciousness raising programs as an essential method of achieving development.

Huntington (1997) comments, analysing 39 countries in Africa, Asia, and South America, that have governments produced by reasonably open and fair elections, that they are not necessarily taking the right steps towards liberal democracy, because they lack many criteria of liberal democracy and the willingness to achieve those. The Bangladesh case is not different. Democratic development occurs only when "political leaders believe they have an interest in promoting it or a duty to achieve it" (Huntington, 1997). The Bangladesh government or opposition leaders still do not subscribe to this, because democratic development will cut the benefits they are enjoying in a pseudo-system.

Bangladesh government comprises of people from different interest groups, having pecuniary interests in government decision systems, who have bought their ways into politics and depend on local thugs for mobilising resources and votes for the party. The civil society thus has become a prisoner of these narrow interest and fail to work for common good. A vibrant civil society is, however, more "essential for consolidating and maintaining democracy than for initiating it" (Diamond, 1994).

Przewoski et al (1997) after observing "survival and death of political regimes" in 4,318 country-years contends that five conditions are required to be fulfilled if any country wants to establish a democratic regime. These are: democracy, affluence, growth with moderate inflation, declining inequality, a favourable international climate, and parliamentary institutions. They are, however, taking a minimalist definition of democracy as proposed by Dahl (1971): having elections in which the opposition has some chance of winning and taking office (Przewoski et al, 1997: 39). In Bangladesh, however, none of these conditions exists now except the holding of free and fair elections in 1991 and 1996. Per capita income in Bangladesh is only about $200/capita with a very slow growth and high increase in inequality, unfavourable business environment seeing not much FDI movement. Parliamentary institutions have become vehicles of self-fulfilment by the ruling party, or of opposition bashing, or dishonouring the democratic system by the opposition parties who often prefer agitating on the streets through *hartals* (complete halt of any type of economic activity) than to face the elected government head-on at the parliament. 1995-96 was the peak year for hartal in Bangladesh with 170 days wasted in just a year (Rashiduzzaman, 1997). In 1999, there were 30 hartal days costing more than \$2 billion to the economy (Shahriar, 2000).

Election is a tool of achieving aspects of good governance, like planning has been a tool of achieving development. But like planning, 'elections' have become the 'end' in many countries. In the post-War period in the newly independent countries, economic growth was an objective and the governments expected the growth to trickle down to the poorer section of the community and ensure equality. It did not happen. Now the same countries are trying to achieve democracy starting with free and fair election hoping that it will cross-over to or join-together other characteristics of good democratic governance, eventually or 'trickle-in'. There are, however, signs that the endeavour may fall apart and not achieve the objectives. A trickle in approach to liberal democracy will not succeed. Bangladesh will thus require a consciously framed program to develop and allow all the other aspects of civil society to grow, survive, and function, and not just to emphasise on election or even political society. The civil society organisations must reconsider their positions now before it is too late. It is true that government has to give leadership in this regard. But the achievement of a free and fair election was a result of the agitation by the civil society organisations, and not by a conscious and concerted effort by the government. The onus is on the civil society organisations now to wake up and enlighten the people about the importance of improving and getting different aspects and types of civil society perform. Too much emphasis on the election, and not at all on the other aspects of civil society, will jeopardise the scope created by the free and free elections of establishing good governance in Bangladesh.

## REFERENCES

Ahmed, N. (1998). 'Reforming the Parliament in Bangladesh: Structural Constraints and Political Dilemmas' *Commonwealth and Comparative Politics* 36: 68-91.

Bratton, M. (1989). 'Beyond the State: Civil Society and Associational Life in Africa', *World Politics* 41(3): 4-1

Crook, R.C. and J. Manor (1995). 'Democratic Decentralisation and Institutional Performance: Four Asian and African Experiences Compared', *Journal of Commonwealth and Comparative Politics* 33:309-34.

Dahl, R. A. (1971). *Polyarchy: Participation and Opposition* (New Haven: Yale University Press).

*Defence Journal* 12, 4 (1986), 44-5.

Diamond, L. (1994). 'Towards Democratic Consolidation', *Journal of Democracy* 5(3)????

Diamond, L. (1996). 'Is the Third Wave Over?', *Journal of Democracy* 7(3):20-37.

Franda, M. (1982). *Bangladesh: The First Decade* (New Delhi: South Asian Publishers Private Limited).

Frantz, T.R. (1987). 'The Role of NGOs in Strengthening of Civil Society', in A.G. Drabek, ed., *Development Alternatives: The Challenges for NGOs* (New York: Pergamon Press), pp. 145-60.

Haque, A. (1980). 'Bangladesh in 1979: Cry for A Sovereign Parliament', *Asian Survey* 20: 217-30.

Harpham, T. and K.A.Boateng (1997). 'Urban Governance in Relation to the Operation of Urban Services in Developing Countries', *Habitat International* 21:65-77.

Hasan, S. (1988). 'Development Administration Through Local Government: Recommendations for Bangladesh' Master degree thesis, University of Waterloo, Canada, 1988.

Hasan, S. (1988). 'Political Parties in Bangladesh: A Study of Alienation' (in Bangla), Conference Paper, Fifth Bangladesh Political Science Association Conference held in Rajshahi, Bangladesh, June.

Hasan, S. (1998). 'Obducracy, Opposition, and Development in Bangladesh' Paper presented in The State of the Asia-Pacific Region Conference, City University of Hong Kong, June 6-7.

Hasan, S. (1999). 'Governance, Politics, and Development Management in Bangladesh', in M.Alauddin and S. Hasan, eds. *Development, Governance, and the Environment in South Asia: A Focus on Bangladesh* (London: Macmillan), pp. 195-205.

Huntington, S. (1991). *The Third Wave: Democratisation in the Late Twentieth Century* (Norman).

Huntington, S. (1997). 'After Twenty Years: The Future of the Third Wave', *Journal of Democracy* 8(4): 3-12.

Huque, A.S. and A. Hakim (1993). 'Elections in Bangladesh: Tools of Legitimacy', *Asian Affairs* 19: 248-61.

Islam, S.S. (1987). 'Bangladesh in 1986: Entering A New Phase' *Asian Survey* 27: 163-70.

Jahan, R. (1973). 'Bangladesh in 1972: Nation Building in a New Nation' *Asian Survey* 13: 199-210.

Khan, M.M. and H.M. Zafarullah (1979). 'The 1979 Parliament Election in Bangladesh' *Asian Survey* 19: 1023-36.

Khan, Z.R. (1983). *Leadership in the Least Developed Nation: Bangladesh* (New York: Syracuse University).

Khan, Z.R. (1993). 'Bangladesh in 1992: Dilemmas of Democratization' *Asian Survey* 33: 150-56.

Khan, Z.R. (1997). 'Bangladesh's Experiment With Parliamentary Democracy', *Asian Survey* 37: 575-89.

Kochanek, S.A. (1997). 'Bangladesh in 1996: The 25th Year of Independence' *Asian Survey* 37: 136-42.

Leftwich, A. (1993). 'Governance, Democracy and Development in the Third World', *Third World Quarterly* 14: 605-24.

Leftwich, A. (1994). 'Governance, the State and the Politics of Development', *Development and Change* 25:363-86.

Linz, J.J. and A. Stepan (1996). *Problems of Democratic Transition and Consolidation: Soitherns Europe, South America, and Post-Communist Europe* (Baltimore: The Johns Hopkins University Press).

Moore, M. (1995). 'Promoting Good Government by Supporting Institutional Development?' *IDS Bulletin* 26(2): 89-96.

Nunnenkamp, P. (1995). 'What Donors Mean by Good Governance: Heroic Ends, Limited Means, and Traditional Dilemmas of Development Cooperation', *IDS Bulletin* 26(2):9-16.

Padron, M. (1987). 'Non-Governmental Developmental Organisations: From Development Aid to Development Cooperation', in A.G. Drabek, ed., *Development Alternatives: The Challenges for NGOs* (New York: Pergamon Press), pp. 145-60.

Paproski, P. (1993). 'Urban Governance System- Another Unanalysed Abstraction?' *Development Planning Unit No 28*, University of London (cited in Harpham and Boateng, 1997).

Przeworski, A. (1988). 'Democracy as a Contingent Outcome of Conflict', in J. Elster and R.Slagstad, eds., *Constitutionalism and Democracy* (Cambridge: Cambridge University Press), pp. 59-83.

Przeworski, A. et. al. (1996). 'What Makes Democracies Endure?', *Journal of Democracy* 7(1): 39-55.

Rahman, A. (1984). 'Bangladesh in 1983: A turning Point for the Military', *Asian Survey* 24: 239-45.

Rahman, S. (1989). 'Bangladesh in 1988: Precarious Institution Building Amid Crisis Management', *Asian Survey* 29: 216-22.

Rahman, S. (1990).'Bangladesh in 1989: Internationalisation of Economic and Political Issues', *Asian Survey* 20:150-57.

Rashiduzzaman, M. (1977). 'Changing Political Patterns in Bangladesh: Internal Constraints and External Fears' *Asian Survey* 17: 793-808;

Rashiduzzaman, M. (1979). 'Bangladesh in 1978: Search for A Political Party', *Asian Survey* 19: 191-97.

Rashiduzzaman, M. (1997). 'Political Unrest and Democracy in Bangladesh', *Asian Survey* 37: 2554-38.

Rijnierse, E. (1993). 'Democratisation in Sub-Saharan Africa? Literature review', *Third World Quarterly* 14:647-64.

Robinson, M. (1995). 'Strengthening Civil Society in Africa: The Role of Foreign Political Aid', *IDS Bulletin* 28(2): 70-80.

Root, H. (1996). *Small Countries, Big Lessons: Governance and the Rise of East Asia* (Hong Kong: Oxford University Press).

Schumpeter, J. (1954). *Capitalism, Socialism, and Democracy*, 4th ed (New York, 1954).

Shahriar, H. (2000). 'Fighting Crime or Each Other?', *Newsweek International* 21 February, p.25.

Shehabuddin, E. (1999). 'Bangladesh in 1998: Democracy on the Ground', *Asian Survey* 39: 148-56.

Sklar, R.L. (1996). 'Towards a Theory of Developmental Democracy', in A. Leftwich, ed. *Democracy and Development: Theory and Practice* (Cambridge: Polity Press).

Stepan, A. (1988). *Rethinking Military Politics: Brazil and the Southern Cone* (Princeton: Princeton University Press).

Stepan, A. (1994). 'On the Tasks of Democratic Oppositions', *Journal of Democracy* 1(2): 41-9.

UNDP (1993). 'People and Governance' in *Human Development Report 1993* (NY: Oxford University Press).

World Bank (1992). *Governance and Development* (Washington D.C: The World Bank).

*Chapter 12*

# THE POLITICS OF REFORM IN VIETNAM, 1986-2000

## *Zachary Abuza*
Simmons College

In 1986 Vietnam embarked on a radical course of economic reforms to revive its moribund, war-torn economy. The reforms, known as *doi moi*, saw very positive initial results as the country courted foreign investment and began a development strategy based on export-led growth; the country seemed ready to become the next tiger economy. Yet the initial reforms were running out of steam by the mid-1990s and Vietnam became stuck in a transitional system of market socialism. The leadership, deeply divided into ideologically based factions, exacerbated by the collapse of socialism across Eastern Europe, was unable to come to a consensus on how to proceed with the reform program. Deadlocked, they were unable to effectively respond to a series of crises: a faltering economy, rampant corruption, the Asian economic crisis, and a wave of peasant rebellions. Being a one party state, the Vietnam Communist Party is fraught with factionalism (*bung di*) based both on ideology and patron-client ties. The factional nature of Vietnamese politics, compounded by generational rifts, as well as an overwhelming fear of losing ultimate control has hampered Vietnamese decision-making. Until the next party congress is held when there can be a large-scale leadership transition and generational change, bold policies that will rejuvenate the reform program are unlikely to be implemented. Instead, the Vietnamese leadership will continue to implement piecemeal policies that will allow them to muddle through.

# 1. THE ERA OF *DOI MOI*: THE 6<sup>TH</sup> PARTY CONGRESS THROUGH THE 7<sup>TH</sup> PARTY CONGRESS (DECEMBER 1986 TO JUNE 1991)

At the 6th Party Congress, the newly elected General Secretary of the Vietnam Communist Party (VCP), Nguyen Van Linh, embarked on a radical reform economic program known as *doi moi*. *Doi Moi* was launched in the context of a terrible economic malaise. Decades of war, including the costly 11-year occupation of Cambodia, had left the country on the brink of bankruptcy. Despite over $1.2 billion in annual Soviet military assistance, over one-third of the state budget went to security. The centrally planned economy, which favored heavy industry at the expense of agriculture and light manufacturing was faltering. The rapid socialization of the southern economy had caused terrible dislocations and agricultural out put had declined sharply after the land had been collectivized. Inflation was running in the triple digits. In short, war communism was threatening the regime's legitimacy.

*Doi moi* sought to remedy these imbalances. Chinese styled agricultural reforms were implemented, giving farmers "land-use rights," and contracts, while small-scale private enterprises were legalized. The role of central planning diminished, and prices, except for a few key commodities, were set by market forces. Many inefficient and loss-making state-owned enterprises (SOEs) were merged in an attempt to make them profitable. And finally, Vietnam sought to join the world economy, by courting foreign investment, and accepting its position in the global division of labor, exporting goods in which it had a comparative advantage in producing.

In addition to *doi moi*, there was a loosening of politics and debate, especially for intellectuals and the press. General Secretary Nguyen Van Linh knew that the party and government bureaucracies were unwilling to implement his economic policies, as much of their power came from their ability to control the distribution of goods, services and resources. Market forces would strip that power away from them. In order to cajole the recalcitrant bureaucracy, Linh employed the press and intellectuals to ferret out corrupt officials and cadres who were abusing their power. . As he told a group of journalists on 6 October 1987,

> On the days when our party was fighting for power, it depended on the people for support. Now, the possession of power is likely to lead to alienation from the masses, arrogance and high-handedness, greed and embezzlement, bureaucratism and authoritarianism in economic and ideological leadership. All this must be strongly criticized and condemned. [1]

In order to win the support of the intellectuals and journalists, he had to agree to an overall loosening of ideological constraints; this became known as *coi moi*. Journalists and writers were urged by Linh to not "bend their pens," and to report truthfully. Liberalization also occurred in the literary and visual arts, and for the first time

---

[1] Nguyen Van Linh, "Let Writers and Artists Actively Contribute to Renovation," 6 October 1987, in *Vietnam Courier*, No. 1 (1988), 12.

Vietnamese artists and writers were no longer constrained by the tenets of "socialist realism." Writers such as Duong Thu Huong, Nguyen Huy Thiep, Bao Ninh and Le Luu became a voice of a generation in Vietnam and won international acclaim.

The reform program experienced fantastic results. Economic growth soared. In just a few years, Vietnam went from being a net importer of food, to the world's third largest exporter of rice. Foreign investment began to enter the market, industrial output resumed, and inflation was brought down to the low double digits.

Despite its obvious successes, the reform program was in jeopardy due to events in Eastern Europe and the former Soviet Union. The lively political and intellectual debates of the late-1980s, were curtailed as the party became overwhelmed in protecting its monopoly of power. Newfound press and literary freedoms were curtailed as censorship and party interference returned. Leading advocates of political reform were silenced and purged, as conservatives, who had all along argued that the pace and scope of *doi moi* was to great, regained the upper hand. What little freedom the press had won since 1986, was stripped, as journalists were ordered to toe the party line, and to not "report solely on negative events." The VCP was determined to not let the forces of counter-revolution get a toe-hold as they did in Eastern Europe. The military was called on to reiterate its loyalty to defending the socialist regime and publicly announced that "revolutionary violence," as had been applied in China in the Tiananmen Square Massacre, was justified. At the 9th Plenum, in March 1990, a leading advocate of political reform, Tran Xuan Bach, was sacked from the Politburo, the country's 13-man ruling body, while a leading ideologue was promoted to the body, giving the conservatives a clear upper-hand.

This majority was important for two reasons: First, the current Politburo selects the incoming members of both the Politburo and Central Committee, as well as the General Secretary of the party. Second, the majority would allow the conservatives to select the member responsible for drafting the *Political Report*, the key document presented at the forthcoming party congress that sets the political and economic tone for the next five years. Yet despite this majority, the Politburo was still sufficiently divided to really hamper effective decision-making.

The 7th Party Congress was clearly a compromise for both the conservatives and reformers. On the one hand, the economic reform program was acknowledged to be a success, and the party vowed to continue on with the economic policies of *doi moi*. On the other hand, *coi moi* and any attempt at political or intellectual liberalization was deemed to dangerous and abandoned. The party emphasized that it would do all that it had to in maintaining its monopoly of power and leading role in society.

There was a significant turnover in the leadership: eight of the thirteen members of the Politburo stepped down, while 46 of the 146 member Central Committee (31.5 percent) were newly elected. The party also went to great lengths to ensure a balance in its leadership. General Secretary Nguyen Van Linh stepped down and was replaced by the northerner and conservative Prime Minister Do Muoi, while the southerner and leading reformer, Vo Van Kiet, took the premiership. The Presidency, was assumed by the former Minister of Defense, Le Duc Anh, a staunch conservative from the central region of the country. The regional balance is important in Vietnamese politics, as southerners tend to be stronger advocates for economic liberalization. At the 7th

Congress, five of the thirteen members of the Politburo were southerners. And the average age fell from 71 to 64. For the first time, power was truly shared. Though *primus inter pares*, General Do Muoi had to contend with two other top officials who had significant power bases, patronage networks, and reputations as decisive leaders.

## 2. THE POLITICS OF NEAR TIGERDOM: THE 7TH THROUGH THE 8TH CONGRESSES (JUNE 1991 TO JUNE 1996)

Despite the Congress and the overhaul in the party leadership, the party remained terribly divided and in a constant state of stalemate, crippling much of the country's policy-making in the early-1990s. Vietnam's hasty normalization of diplomatic ties in November 1991 following the 7th Congress seemed to reaffirm Vietnam's socialist identity. At the mid-term Party Congress in January 1994, the conservatives again tried to regain the upper-hand in the run-up to the 8th Party Congress to be held in June 1996, by promoting four more people to the Politburo, three of whom were very clearly opponents of the radical reform program.

Conservative maneuverings, not withstanding, the liberal economic reform program continued with steady results. The average annual growth rate was 8 percent between the 7th and 8th Congresses. Foreign trade expanded rapidly, from a paltry $2.94 billion in 1986, to $12.7 billion in 1995. Between 1991 and 1995, exports increased from $2.04 billion to $5.20 billion. The percentage of manufactured exports also rose, in that same period, from 10 percent to 17 percent.[2] Foreign investment poured into the country. Between 1987 and 1996, $23.4 billion was pledged for 1,615 projects, by some 56 countries. In 1996 alone, Vietnam received $2.3 billion in actual investment, up 30 percent from 1995. Staples output increased from 18.38 million tons in 1986 to 27.5 in 1995.[3] Inflation was curbed from its triple digit figures in the mid-1980s, including a high of 774 percent in 1986, to 12.7 percent in 1995. The number of SOEs was cut from 12,296 in 1989 to 5,962 in mid-1995.[4] Yet, the percentage of industrial output to GDP has increased from 36.5 percent in 1991 to 41.9 percent in 1995. From 1991-1995, industrial production increased 88.4 percent, an annual average of 13.5 percent.[5] Vietnam was set for "tigerdom."

Vietnam's foreign policy reflected this outward economic trend. Once the Paris Peace Accords were signed in November 1991, formally ending the Cambodian conflict, Hanoi charged out of diplomatic isolation. It quickly normalized ties with the ASEAN states, Japan and Korea. A fiercely unilateral state, Vietnam resumed ties with

---

[2] UNDP, *Catching Up*, 30; World Bank, *Viet Nam: An Agenda for Financial Sector Development* (Hanoi: World Bank, 1995), 4.

[3] Le Van Toan, "An Overview of Vietnam's Economy After 10 Years of Renovation," *Tap Chi Cong San* (*Communist Review*) (February 1996): 25-30, in Foreign Broadcast Information Service, *Daily Reports-East Asia* (hereafter *FBIS-EAS*), 4 June 1996, 77.

[4] Vietnam News Agency (hereafter VNA), 23 June 1996, in *FBIS-EAS*, 25 June 1996, 102.

[5] Toan, "An Overview," 77.

multilateral lending institutions, such as the World Bank, IMF and Asian Development Bank. In 1995 Vietnam joined its former adversary, ASEAN, becoming the 7th member of the regional grouping. For the first time Vietnam displayed a willingness to resolve differences in multi-lateral settings. That same year, Hanoi normalized ties with both the United States and the European Union. Vietnam seemed committed to an economic development policy based on global integration and interdependence.

But there were already many underlying problems in the economy that Hanoi was unwilling to confront: 90 percent of joint ventures took place between foreign firms and SOEs. Though not illegal, the government curbed private domestic firms from entering into joint ventures, hoping that if SOEs had foreign partners, they would get a cash injection, be able to export goods, and turn a profit, all without privatization. Although the single fastest growing sector of the economy, SOEs only added 90,000 jobs in that five-year period, despite tax advantages, better access to land and capital. Moreover, the commitment to creating a multi-sector economy was weak. By 1996 only ten SOEs were equitized. Their continued receipt of preferential taxes, access to cheap capital, land, power, and other benefits prevented private sector competition from developing; the firms that are responsible for employing the surplus labor. Rather than privatization, Vietnam attempted to merge and reorganize SOEs in an attempt to make them profitable. This had the net effect of "further reinforcing and expanding existing monopoly powers and inefficiencies."[6] Although Vietnam agreed to meet AFTA rules and tariff levels by 2006 when it joined ASEAN, Vietnam continues to offer very high rates of protection to its SOEs. In addition to tariffs, Hanoi continues to employ quotas, monopoly trading companies, and import licenses in order to protect its ailing state sector.

Although the average annual growth of 8-9 percent was spectacular, it was clearly not sustainable unless Vietnam pushed through some major reforms. These included the equitization of and the cessation of government subsidies to the 6,000 inefficient state-owned enterprises, banking sector reform, improving the investment climate by eliminating red tape and corruption, furthering rural reforms, ending discriminatory policies towards the private sector, and liberalizing the foreign trade system. Fearing instability, conservatives in the VCP have prevented the government from implementing these necessary reforms that would lead to a period of economic hardships, increase unemployment and socio-economic inequalities, and thus potentially a challenge to the VCP's rule. Concern for stability is paramount and the idea of implementing reforms that will cause a further loss of jobs is unappetizing in a country that already has some of the highest unemployment in the region. Vietnam acknowledged that it has 3.7 million unemployed workers, over 7 percent of the workforce, and that the number will climb to 8.5 million by 2000.[7]

Vietnam's slowing economy was compounded by the Asian economic crisis. GDP growth, fell from its record high in 1995 of 9.5 percent to 2 percent and has now recovered to just over 4 percent in 1999. Export growth rates also fell dramatically, from 30 percent in 1996, to 20 percent in 1997 but only 5 percent in 1999. Foreign investment

---

[6] UNDP, *Catching Up*, 25.

[7] Reuters, "Vietnam Plans to Prevent Unemployment Crisis," 29 November 1997.

fell by 60 percent, and was under $1 billion in 1998. Meanwhile, inflation entered double digits, 9-10 percent while the currency lost 20 percent of its value, yet still remained over-valued. Declining farm prices, have led to drastic declines in rural revenue, while the urban sector is simply not creating enough jobs. The Asian economic crisis also had a devastating effect on the Vietnamese economy, as much of its foreign investment comes from and 70 percent of its trade is with other Asian states. Moreover, Vietnam's competitiveness dissolved in the face of devalued currencies throughout the region, which fell between 30 to 80 percent of their value. In sum, the *zeitgeist* that Hanoi enjoyed between 1994-1996 is gone, which is very alarming as Hanoi has acknowledged that it needs some $45 billion in investment, much of which will come from abroad. Yet, foreign investment in 1997 was $4.5 billion, nearly half the amount of 1996's figure of $8.6 billion. For the first time, former backers such as the World Bank became critical of the speed and scope of the reform program and downgraded Vietnam's growth potential. The Bank's Vietnam Country Director, Andrew Steer warned that although

> Since launching its ambitious reform program in 1986, Vietnam has achieved unprecedented levels of growth. . . However, recent trends showing a slowdown in foreign direct investment, stagnating domestic savings, increasing problems in the banking sector, deteriorating state enterprise performance, and a regional financial crisis that has hurt competitiveness, clearly indicates the need for Vietnam to embark on a greatly deepened economic reform program and speed up progress on its long and difficult transition to a successful market economy.[8]

The economic downturn was not the only crisis confronting the leadership, and because of the political stalemate the regime was unable to effectively deal with any of them. The first crisis was the peasant protests in Thai Binh Province, the cradle of the revolution. Peasants began protesting throughout the north protesting arbitrary fees and taxes from land usage to "teacher fees" for their children's schooling, to corvee; an amount that one Vietnamese researcher calculated to total 40 percent of peasants' income.[9] In all, the total amount of taxes and levies collected between January 1994 and July 1997 were more than dong 176 billion (about $16 million) more than had been authorized by the central government. At the same time, loans to local farmers and businesses in the province fell by 40 percent compared to 1996 and unemployment was skyrocketing, already at 200,000. In addition, there were concerns regarding corruption, abuse of power, land seizures, forced contract renegotiations and "commandism." As local party secretaries tended to also be the chairmen of the local people's committee's they were in a position of absolute power. Because of this power, the village leaders were

---

[8] World Bank, "Vietnam: Deepening Reform For Growth," News Release No. 98/1534EAP, 17 November 1997.

[9] See Dang Phong, "Aspects of Agricultural Economy and Rural Life in 1993,"in Benedict J. Tria Kerkvliet, and Doug J. Porter, eds., *Vietnam's Rural Transformation* (Boulder: Westview Press, 1995), 182-183. A 1996 Oxfam study found in one province 8 types of tax imposed by the central government, including land use rights, fishing, salt-making and slaughter, as well as 6 other local "contributions," including corvee. See Oxfam UK and Ireland, *Report on the Financing and Delivery of Basic Services at the Commune Level in Ky Anh, Ha Tin* (March 1996). Peasants, on a nationwide average, must contribute 10 days of labor annually to the state.

able to redistribute communal lands, which averaged between 10 and 25 percent of a village's land area. Legally, this process is supposed to be conducted through auction, but in reality it is often conducted out of the public's eye, so that the village chief can distribute the land to his family and friends. Although the proceeds from the lease of these "second land use rights" are supposed to be used for social welfare programs, they are often embezzled.[10]

Something had to be done as the protests truly threatened the regime: its legitimacy has always come from the support of the peasantry. As Pham Van Khai warned: "If rural areas remain stable and farmers are happy with their livelihood, our country will be able to ensure stability however serious the difficulties. Therefore, rural stability is the key to national security." The party acted quickly, dispatching 1,200 police and several Politburo members to investigate. In the end, some 1,800 officials were "disciplined," but only 84 party members were expelled and only 30 were sentenced to prison; 62 peasant protestors were arrested for jeopardizing public safety. The Politburo later issued decree 89/CP that authorized military and police units to set up temporary pre-trial detention centers, in which suspects could be held for up to two years without trial.[11]

The second crisis was the rampant corruption and smuggling, much of it conducted by government officials and party cadres. Major drug smuggling operations were discovered to be run by senior members of the Ministry of Interior. Meanwhile, in two major show-case trials, a total of 77 defendants from two state owned enterprises, EPCO-Minh Phung and Tamexco, were investigated for fraud, embezzlement and $280 million in losses; a staggering figure in a country where the average annual income is less than $400. Corruption allegations even reached the highest levels as Politburo member Pham The Duyet was accused, though later exonerated in an internal party investigation.[12] On top of these show-case corruption trials, there continued to be the systematic abuse of power and petty corruption by low-level bureaucrats, such as that which caused the Thai Binh protests, that really called the regime's legitimacy into question.

On top of this, the regime has to contend with a very youthful population; 60 percent of whom were born after 1975 and have no memory of the war. The party is clearly losing touch with the people in whose name it rules.

In short, despite some remarkable achievements, there were real limits to sustained economic growth without some major new policies. But the political stalemate, crippled any chance that a new impetus for reform could be implemented. Between the 7th and the 8th Congress, the leadership experienced some of its worst infighting. This was fundamentally a debate over how to strengthen and develop the nation. Reformers argued that the way the country could overcome its perpetual poverty and for once no longer be ranked amongst the world's poorest nations was to become fully integrated into the

---

[10] Phong, "Aspects of Agriculture," 181.

[11] *Cong An Thanh Pho Ho Chi Minh*, No. 689, 10 November 1998.

[12] Faith Keenan, "Dishing the Dung," *Far Eastern Economic Review* (hereafter *FEER*), 13 August 1998, 28. After a three month-long investigation, the State Inspector, Ta Huu Thanh, announced that he had found no wrong doing by Duyet. See Dean Yates, "Hanoi Probed High-Level Graft Cases," Reuters, 4 November 1998. Members of the Inspectorate subsequently intimidated the accusers.

global economy. This meant accepting everything that Lenin railed against: Vietnam would have to accept the liberal neo-classical notions that ruled global economics. Vietnam would have to accept its place in the global division of labor, produce what it had a comparative advantage in. Vietnam would have to rely on agriculture and low-tech, manually intensive products. Vietnam would have to follow the model of the Asian Tigers and adopt an export led growth strategy, which would entail imports. Vietnam would have to borrow from abroad, and court foreign investment. All this meant that the Vietnamese economy would no longer be insulated. And the government would have to stop propping up the public sector and especially SOEs with soft budget constraints. The private sector would have to be freed up so that it could employ the surplus labor force.

Conservatives argued that the way that Vietnam could strengthen itself and become a tiger, was through socialism. State owned enterprises had to be strengthened. To do so, conservatives argued that Vietnam should emulate the south Koreans. They looked at these huge conglomerates, the *Chaebul*, which had diversified (we now know to disastrous degrees), and catapulted South Korea into becoming a industrial powerhouse. Could not Vietnam do the same with its SOEs? Could not the more efficient SOEs take over the less efficient ones so that the Vietnamese economy be run by a few giant all-encompassing *Chaebul*?

The party, which has always prided itself on its unity and consensus style approach to decision-making, was so divided on how to proceed, that there was no attempt even to hide the huge rifts in the party. In late 1995, Prime Minister Vo Van Kiet's "Letter to the Politburo," which was leaked to the press, argued that "in order to mobilize the genius of all within the party and promote transparency within the party, there must be uncompromising democracy." Kiet went on to lambaste conservatives. He called for shrinking the state-owned sector and increasing private industry, forsaking ties with the remaining socialist states, getting the party out of government affairs, putting national affairs ahead of government affairs. In response, the conservatives dispatched Politburo member Nguyen Ha Phan to lead meetings around the country to attack Kiet's "deviation from socialism." By the 9th Plenum (November 1995), the conservatives seemed to have the upper-hand. Draft resolutions stated that the main lesson of *doi moi* was "to maintain the stalwarthy the leadership role of the Party and to consider the development of the Party as the primary responsibility."

But attacks were no longer merely rhetorical. When the army's Chief of Staff, General Dao Dinh Luyen, gave a long speech in support of Vo Van Kiet and continued economic reforms he was sacked from the Politburo and lost his army post in January 1996. Then the conservative Nguyen Ha Phan was expelled from the Politburo, stripped of his party membership and placed under house arrest for treason in April 1996. Phan, who led the charges against Tran Xuan Bach in 1991 and Vo Van Kiet, was very close to the leading candidate to become the next party general secretary. If Dao Duy Tung was elected, Phan was a leading candidate to become the prime minister. But then Tung, reportedly fell into a coma following the Party's 10th Plenum (April 1996) where he was criticized for "abusing power" and "anti-democratic behavior," as he managed to get unprecedented control of both the personnel appointments and the drafting of the *Political Report* for the 8th Congress. At the Plenum, only 10 percent of the 164 members voted to reelect him to the Politburo, yet until the plenum, he was the leading candidate to replace Do Muoi. Reformers were euphoric as Tung had completely disregarded their position in the *Political Report* and in their personnel selections, both of which were rejected. The party was back at square one, and nearly had to delay the 8th Congress because of a lack of consensus. A compromise to maintain the status quo was reached on 26 June, two days before the start of the 8th Congress: the top three leaders would remain in their posts; a blow for the regularized transition of power since 1986.

## 3. THE EIGHTH CONGRESS (JUNE 1996)

While this political maneuvering maintained the status quo among the top three leaders, it did not resolve all personnel issues to be discussed at the congress. A 170 member Central Committee was elected, of which 92 (54 percent) were incumbents. Yet the central-level party apparatus saw a loss of power. Only seven, a humbling 8.9 percent of the 72 new members, were center-level cadres, while 67 percent of the Central Committee was made up of provincial and government officials. Center-level party officials and top ideologues fared even worse on the Politburo. Do Quang Thang, Director of the Central Committee's Control Commission and Secretariat member, Le Phuc Tho, Director of the Central Committee's Organization Department, Dao Duy Tung, a top ideologue and Secretariat member, and Vu Oanh, the former Director of the Central Committee's Economics Department were all forced out of the Politburo. In total, three-fourths of the remaining 16 members were either forced out or asked to resign, yet, for the sake of stability, the Central Committee requested that the 8th Politburo keep at least 8 members from the preceding body. In the end, 10 of the 19 now members were incumbents, including, Do Muoi, Le Duc Anh, Vo Van Kiet, Nong Duc Manh, Nguyen Manh Cam, Nguyen Duc Binh, Doan Khue, Phan Van Khai, and Pham The Duyet.

**Politburo of the 8th Central Committee**

| Name, Age, and Region | Concurrent Posts |
| --- | --- |
| 1. Do Muoi (79) N | General Secretary |
| 2. Le Duc Anh (75) C | President & Chairman National Defense Council |
| 3. Vo Van Kiet (73) S | Prime Minister |
| 4. Nong Duc Manh (55) N | Chairman, National Assembly |
| 5. Le Kha Phieu (64) N | Lt. General, Director, General Political Department |
| 6. Doan Khue (72) C | Lt. General, Minister of Defense (Died on 1/16/99) |
| 7. Phan Van Khai (62) S | Vice-Prime Minister |
| 8. Nguyen Manh Cam (66) C | Minister of Foreign Affairs |
| 9. Nguyen Duc Binh (68) N | Director, National Ho Chi Minh Academy of Politics |
| 10. Nguyen Van An* (58) N | Deputy-Director, CC Organization Department |
| 11. Pham Van Tra* (60) S | Lt. General, Vice-Minister of Defense, VPA Chief-of-Staff |
| 12. Tran Duc Luong* (59) C | Vice-Prime Minister |
| 13. Nguyen Thi Xuan My*(56) N | Deputy-Director, CC Control Commission |
| 14. Truong Tan Sang* (47) S | Secretary, Ho Chi Minh City Party Committee |
| 15. Le Xuan Tung* (60) N | Secretary, Hanoi Party Committee |
| 16. Le Minh Huong* (59) N | Lt. General, Vice-Minister of Interior |
| 17. Nguyen Dinh Tu* (63) N | (died on 6/28/96) Director, CC Science, Technology and Education Commission |
| 18. Pham The Duyet (59) N | Director, CC Mass Mobilization Commission |
| 19. Nguyen Tan Dung* (47) S | Vice-Minister of Interior |

* Denotes new member

Although the Vietnam People's Army (VPA) and other security personnel only held 20, or 11.7 percent, of Central Committee seats, the military received the highest number of Politburo seats it has had since the reform program began at the 6th Congress in 1986. Of the 18 members (Nguyen Dinh Tu died during the congress), six were either in the VPA or Ministry of Interior. Aside from the growing role of the "security bloc," the makeup of the 8th Politburo, as expected, was a careful ideological and geographic balance: there was a fairly equal distribution of reformers, conservatives, and moderates while there were ten northerners, 5 southerners, and 3 members from the center. The average age of the new Politburo was a sprightly 62.2. Two members were in their 40s; 5 in their 50s; 7 in their 60s; and only 4 in their 70s. The average age of Central Committee members fell from around 65 to 55.

The *Political Report* differed greatly from Dao Duy Tung's draft that emphasized that "Leadership without control is tantamount to no leadership."[13] In the redraft, state-

---

[13] The *Political Report* was carried in *Quan Doi Nhan Dan*, 30 June 1996, 3,6, in *FBIS-EAS*, 11 July 1996, 71-100.

owned enterprises and cooperatives were called on to make up only 60 percent of GDP by 2020. New paragraphs were inserted which stated that "profit" was an important criterion in evaluating state owned enterprise performance. There were far fewer references to "hostile forces" and "peaceful evolution," clear victories for the reformers and pragmatic moderates.

In sum, the Eighth Congress failed to conclusively address the nagging issues on which the country's economic development hinge. In striving to balance both factions, the party sowed the seeds of future deadlock. And without a change in leadership, there would be no change in policies. What came out of the Congress was a commitment to continued party control and an unwillingness to push through radical economic reform, i.e., stability and caution. As Do Muoi told reporters during the Congress, "I think we will have to accelerate our development. Slow development means hunger, don't you think? But as the same time I want to see efficiency and stability. If reform is too fast we will make mistakes. If you run too fast and there is something in the road you may fall down." Even moderates such as Foreign Minister Cam toed the party line, arguing that "our task is to maintain social and political stability and order. Past experience has shown that we can only have economic development with social and political stability."

## 4. THE LEADERSHIP TRANSITION: THE 8TH CONGRESS TO THE 4TH PLENUM (JUNE 1996 TO DECEMBER 1997)

Following the conservative's attempted ouster of the Vo Van Kiet at the 8th Party Congress the reformers went on the attack. The opportunity for the reformers first availed itself in November 1996 when President Le Duc Anh suffered a serious stroke. With a leading conservative incapacitated, Kiet actively pushed the reformist agenda. In his 12 March 1997 address to the National Assembly, Kiet advocated for a greater role for the private sector, while calling for more enterprise autonomy and accountability. He spoke of the importance of amassing of wealth and the establishment of a simple and open tax system. But the reformers were not powerful enough to change the party's top leadership in their favor.

The first movement towards a leadership transition came at the June 1997 Plenum. Do Muoi, Le Duc Anh and Vo Van Kiet all removed their names from candidacy for National Assembly seats. Constitutionally, the president and the prime minister, though not the party general secretary, must be National Assembly members, so it confirmed their resignations at the 9th National Assembly in September 1997 were forthcoming. Muoi, who technically could have remained in office until the 9th Party Congress in 2001, seemed determined to stay in office in order to ensure a smooth transition of power.

The Central Committee overwhelmingly approved Vo Van Kiet's protege Phan Van Khai to become the next Prime Minister. Although Khai had originally been slated to become the Prime Minister back at the Eighth Congress, Kiet apparently would not step down without concurrent moves by Le Duc Anh or Do Muoi. But his election was a clear victory for the reformers. Khai, an ardent supporter of reforming the state-owned sector, stated that he would further the reform program. But there was less consensus regarding the presidency; hotly contested by the moderate Foreign Minister, Nguyen Manh Cam, and conservative Minister of Defense, Lieutenant General Doan Khue. Keeping the regional balance in mind, both are from central Vietnam. Cam was able to take credit for a string of diplomatic successes since 1995, but as a career diplomat, he is neither charismatic, nor does he have any military experience which is important as the president is constitutionally responsible for defense issues. Due to these drawbacks, at the June Plenum, only half of the 170 members voted for Cam; not enough for a political system based on "consensus."[14]

As the president is constitutionally the commander-in-chief of the Vietnam People's Army and concurrently the Chairman of the National Defense Council, the highest national security decision-making organ in the country, the post is the natural position within the ruling triumvirate, one might assume, that the military would want to assert itself. President Anh's protege, Minister of Defense Doan Khue trailed closely behind Cam, despite Anh's campaigning. What prevented Khue from becoming President was not so much the effectiveness of the lobbying by the reformers for Cam, but an odd alliance and a slip of the tongue. First, during a trip to France, Doan Khue told President Chirac that after his "promotion" he would welcome the French president in Hanoi. As one commentator noted "Such bragging is frowned upon in a system that stresses modesty and consensus."[15] The second reason was perhaps the strange alliance between the reformers and the VPA's top political commissar, Le Kha Phieu. If a military man became the president, it would diminish Phieu's chances for becoming General Secretary, as the Central Committee would never agree to two of the top three position being held by military personnel. To that end, Phieu and the reformers were united in their opposition of Khue. In the end, it was neither man, but a relative unknown who became president, Tran Duc Luong (60). Luong, a Russian-educated geologist, a Vice-Premier since 1992 and a member of the Politburo since 1996, had remained a little-known technocrat. Though allied with Do Muoi, he was clearly a compromise candidate, as neither the reformers' or the conservatives' first choices had enough of a majority.

The transition left several nagging questions: was there really a transition of power as Vo Van Kiet and Le Duc Anh not only kept their positions in the Politburo, but also on the Politburo's Standing Committee, thus outranking their successors? Could the new president make decisions regarding national security if Le Duc Anh was still around? If the Politburo Standing Committee was indeed the "highest leading nucleus" in Vietnam, what were the implications of the president and prime minister not serving on it? The face saving solution was that Kiet and Anh joined the Central Committee's Advisory Board, originally created to accommodate Pham Van Dong and Nguyen Van Linh in their retirements. Clearly they continue to be powers behind the throne; in Putnam's terms, even without positional power, they continue to have reputational and decisional power. Although Kiet indicated that he would like to retire altogether he would not step down

---

[14] Faith Keenan, "Wait and See," *FEER*, 3 July 1997, 26.

[15] Faith Keenan, "New Crop," *FEER*, 2 October 1997, 16.

unilaterally and it was clear that Anh wanted to stay on despite his stroke. Kiet warned that he would continue to use his influence if he had to, especially if the less-powerful Khai was under attack from conservatives: "I don't think my work is finished," he told the daily *Thanh Nien*. "If I can do something to contribute to the new cabinet then I will try."

It was publicly agreed upon that for the sake of stability and a smooth transition of power the Standing Committee would remain unchanged, thus Muoi, Anh and Kiet would maintain their power. But in reality no one would step down until it was decided who would become the next party general secretary.

Between September and December 1997 the factions campaigned intensely for their respective candidates for the post of party general secretary. The conservatives fought very hard for they felt that they were being edged out of the ruling troika. For example, although Tran Duc Luong was thought to be allied to Do Muoi, he called for greater reform in his acceptance speech: "The way to overcome all trials and limits and to make the best of our opportunities to build our country and take it forward should be through continuing the policy of renovation systematically, comprehensively, and in a far-reaching way."[16] Luong's pragmatism, coupled with the radically reformist Prime Minister Phan Van Khai, alarmed the conservatives.

If one looks down the Politburo roster, it is clear that there were really few realistic and acceptable choices for General Secretary, for both the reformers and conservatives. The reformers, for their part, initially backed Nguyen Tan Dung, the former Deputy Minister of the Interior. Dung was elected to both the Politburo and its Standing Committee at the Eighth Congress and was considered to be a rising star within the party. But at 47, he was the youngest member of the Politburo, and was felt to have not enough experience to be general secretary, though he is clearly being groomed.

The conservative's problem was that there were very few like-minded people on the 18-member Politburo from whom to chose and whom could win a majority of votes. Doan Khue was unacceptable to most and weakened after his failed bid for the Presidency; Nong Duc Manh, it was already agreed, would remain Chairman of the National Assembly; Nguyen Duc Binh, the Director of the party school was too old and too ideological; a woman was not acceptable, so Nguyen Thi Xuan My was out of the running; Le Minh Huong and Le Xuan Tung were too inexperienced; and Pham The Duyet, though experienced, was not seen as capable enough.

The only credible and acceptable candidate to the conservatives was Nguyen Van An, the Director of the Central Committee's Organization Department. At 59, An was the right age. Heading the Organization Department also put him in control of the party's patronage networks. Russian educated, he had some foreign experience. Although many in the military were concerned that the election of An would leave them out of the ruling troika, Le Duc Anh and Doan Khue did not want Le Kha Phieu to get the position perhaps not for ideological reasons, but for personal ones. The animosity and rivalry towards Phieu dates back to the occupation of Cambodia; when Doan Khue was Le Duc Anh's assistant, while Phieu was the chief commisar, ostensibly second in command. As

---

[16] Reuters, "Vietnam's New President Backs Reforms, Strong Party," 25 September 1997.

a result, they campaigned hard for An, even convincing Do Muoi to postpone his retirement until the 5th Plenum in December 1997 so that they would have more time to build-up support. An could have appealed to the reformers, as well, as he was reported to be "reform minded" by the Western press. The question, then, is why was he not elected?

Despite intense lobbying, it appears that An's stature was still too small and he could not win enough supporters, especially within the military. Although Le Duc Anh supported An, it was evident that his power over the VPA was waning and he could not get the military to unite behind his candidate. Indeed, the VPA closed ranks behind Phieu. Although considered a "party man" rather than a soldier, perhaps the VPA thought him to be more conservative and willing to look out for the military's interests than An. More importantly, An's election would leave the military without a voice in the top leadership. A commissar, in the VPA's eyes, was better than no one.

Le Kha Phieu, himself, did not have the necessary backing in the Politburo to get elected even when the military began to support him. He continued to need the support of the reformers, as he did when he blocked Doan Khue's nomination for president. The reformers were willing to back Phieu in return for a greater commitment for economic reform. Phieu toned down his rhetoric and had to publicly call for greater "equitization"-- though not privatization-- of state owned enterprises as well as a greater role for small and medium sized private firms. He stated that despite "differences," socialism and capitalism could "be resolved in a world of peaceful co-existence;" a far cry from his 1996 comments that capitalism was "obsolete" and "would soon be replaced."[17] He tried to assuage foreign investors by arguing that the development of a "socialist market economy" would strengthen the Vietnamese economy and that "Only by doing so will cooperation with foreign partners be effective and successful, and only then will the growth in foreign investment be maintained without sacrificing national independence and socialist orientation. . . The door will never be shut."[18] Likewise he said that he was committed to diversifying the economy, although the "leading role has to be played by the state sector." In another move to appease the reformers, the "stability-minded" Phieu met with a leading dissident, Hoang Minh Chinh, in Hanoi.

With the reformers apprehensively behind him, Phieu began to have the numbers he needed. But what really helped him was the anger that many Central Committee members felt towards Do Muoi's apparent refusal to step down. Phieu, who had already taken over of much of the party's day-to-day affairs from Muoi, could now count enough support to force Do Muoi into retirement. Thus General Le Kha Phieu became the VCP's sixth general secretary in December 1997 the first time a military man has ever held that post.

The difficulty in finding a suitable heir to Do Muoi reflects more than personal rivalries, ideological differences and factional politics. The problem is really systemic as Carlyle Thayer succinctly summed up: "Vietnam lacks men of talent" which has enormous consequences as the top leadership positions "require more than party

---

[17] Greg Torode, "Party Leader Faces Tough Baptism," *South China Morning Post*, 3 January 1998.

[18] See Le Kha Phieu's speech to foreign investors at the Tan Thuan EPZ, "Party Commitment," *Vietnam Economic Times* (February 1998), 9.

experience."[19] As cited above, Vo Van Kiet acknowledged that the party is not producing the competent leadership that is needed to develop the country. The 18 months that it took to find a suitable and acceptable person to fill the post of general secretary drove this point home.

### Politburo of the 4th Plenum of the 8th Central Committee

| Name, Age, and Region | Concurrent Posts |
|---|---|
| 1. Le Kha Phieu | General Secretary |
| 2. Tran Duc Luong | President, Chairman National Defense Council |
| 3. Phan Van Khai | Prime Minister |
| 4. Nong Duc Manh | Chairman, National Assembly |
| 5. Pham Van Tra | Lt. General, Minister of Defense |
| 6. Doan Khue | Director, Internal Political Defense Commission |
| 7. Nguyen Manh Cam | Minister of Foreign Affairs |
| 8. Nguyen Duc Binh | Director, National Ho Chi Minh Academy of Politics |
| 9. Nguyen Van An | Deputy Director, CC Organization Department |
| 10. Nguyen Thi Xuan My | Director, Central Control Commission |
| 11. Truong Tan Sang | Secretary, Ho Chi Minh City Party Committee |
| 12. Le Xuan Tung | Secretary, Hanoi Party Committee |
| 13. Le Minh Huong | Minister of Interior |
| 14. Pham The Duyet | Director, CC Mass Works Commission |
| 15. Nguyen Tan Dung | First Vice-Prime Minister |
| 16. Pham Than Ngan * | Lt. General, Deputy Minister of Defense, Director General Political Department |
| 17. Phan Dien * | Director, CC General Office |
| 18. Nguyen Minh Triet * | Deputy Secretary, Ho Chi Minh City Party Committee |
| 19. Nguyen Phu Trong * | Editor, *Tap Chi Cong San*, Deputy party chief of Hanoi |

* Denotes new member

---

[19] Cited in Keenan, "Wait and See," 26.

## 5. REJUVENATING THE ECONOMY

The new leadership made some initial attempts to rejuvenate the economy, but the effects of the Asian flu were too great and the leadership too divided to make the hard policy choices needed to reform the economy. On the one hand, the new General Secretary, Le Kha Phieu, was indebted to the reformers, and made some overtures to their economic policies: "We understand that the way ahead is full of thorns so we have no choice other than continuing the acceleration of the *doi moi* course in a comprehensive and concerted way in he orientation to socialism of we want to bring our country further forward."[20] Likewise he stated that he would carry-through economic policies in order to double 1996's GDP by the year 2000. Warning that "We should not indulge in self-satisfaction and sleep on our laurels," he said, "the only chance for the country to move forward is comprehensive, uniform renovation along the socialist line."[21] A few weeks later, he gave a speech at the country's most successful export processing zone in Ho Chi Minh City where he tried to reassure investors that there would be no conservative-led retrenchment and that Vietnam would continue to court foreign direct investment: "We must persist and push ahead with the renovation cause. That is a consistent policy."[22]

Prime Minister Phan Van Khai also went out of his way to ensure foreign investors, by hosting a public meeting and issuing a series of new foreign investment reforms. "Your loss is our risk and our loss," he told the foreign investors, reiterating that, "Enterprises with foreign investment are integral parts of the Vietnamese economy."[23] Khai attacked bureaucratic red tape and corruption, and announced a hotline for foreign investors to call when confronted with corruption. But these were not enough.

Vietnam's reluctance to reform clearly played a part in the 60 percent reduction in foreign investment in 1998, and by October 1999 60-70 percent of foreign firms reported losses from their Vietnamese operations.[24] Vietnam's future economic growth is dependent on continued and deepened reform, but these reforms, such as privatization of state-owned assets, will challenge the authority of the state as well as its ideological underpinnings. The Asian economic crisis also had a devastating effect on the Vietnamese economy, as the leadership responded in piecemeal fashion; liberals promising reform while conservatives argue that Vietnam can weather the storm without changing. Indeed, the Central Committee's 5th Plenum, in July 1998, emphasized the mobilization of $7 billion in domestic capital to supplant the fall in foreign investment. Conservatives within Vietnam's leadership blamed the Asian economic crisis on capitalism, and believed that Vietnam's lack of integration was a blessing in disguise.

---

[20] Kyodo, "Vietnam Party Leader Says Renewal Only Choice," 5 January 1998.

[21] "Party Chief Le Kha Phieu on Significance on Fourth Plenum Meeting," VNA, 5 January 1997, in *FBIS-EAS*, 14 January 1998.

[22] AFP, "Party Chief Says Vietnam Welcomes Foreign Investment," 23 January 1998.

[23] Nguyen Ngoc Chinh and An Dao, "Your Loss is Our Loss," *Vietnam Investment Review*, 9-15 February 1998, 1; and Nguyen Ngoc Chinh, "Pledging Sweeping Reforms For Investors," *Vietnam Investment Review*, 9-15 February 1998, 4-5.

[24] Reuters, "Majority of Foreign Firms Report Losses in Vietnam," 13 October 1999.

Reformers, on the defensive, blamed the crisis on "crony capitalism," imperfect markets and too much government intervention. For two and a half years, there has been no major decision by the Politburo, which has been completely deadlocked since the 8th party congress in 1996. There is tremendous resistance to implementing these necessary reforms from within the conservative-dominated politburo.

By all measurable accounts the Vietnamese economy is in poor shape. It is growing too slowly to create jobs for the million new entrants to the workforce each year. Exports are falling, though imports have leveled off, Vietnam is not importing capital equipment, FDI has fallen off, the dong is overvalued, the banks are indebted, 46 percent of SOEs are in the red and being subsidized at huge public expense, foreign debt is still high, unemployment is already a problem, government expenditures are already in the red and inflation is on the rise. It is time for some drastic action. Foreign investors have been fleeing, and those that have stayed have raised the alarm. Even the World Bank and IMF have held up some $500 million in loads until Hanoi adopted a "more comprehensive approach to reform." The Prime Minister, Phan Van Khai has raised the alarm, but the Politburo has been unable to come to a decision.

It is in this context that Hanoi's unwillingness to conclude a trade agreement with the United States must be seen.

## 6. REJECTION OF THE TRADE DEAL

In October 1999, the Politburo of the Vietnamese Communist Part (VCP) rejected a trade deal with the United States; an agreement in principle that had been reached in July 1999. In the context of diminished exports and foreign investment since the onset of the Asian Economic Crisis in 1997, the Politburo's rejection of a deal that would have paved the way for the doubling of exports to the United States is surprising. Indeed, ever since the United States lifted its economic embargo on 4 February 1994 and the two sides normalized diplomatic relations in 1995, the Vietnamese requested a trade agreement that would give them MFN status instead of having to go through the annual Congressional approval process. The Vietnamese looked for a deal that would give them the same degree of market access that America's Asian allies enjoyed during the Cold War. The Americans, however, refused as trade deficits have become a charged political issue and American firms have demanded equal access. Trade talks, which began in 1995, went through nine rounds. The Vietnamese demanded special treatment, which they felt America was morally obliged to give them, both because of the war and because of their developing country status. American negotiators refused, and indeed got their Vietnamese counterparts to agree to a very inclusive trade deal that included investment, intellectual property and services. Only with the intervention of several liberals on the Politburo who felt that the trade deal, even with concessions to the Americans, was necessary to revive the moribund Vietnamese economy, was the agreement in principle reached. But the full Politburo rejected it. To understand the deal you must understand that the Politburo debate has little to do with tariffs and trade with its former foe the

United States. It must be seen as part of a much larger debate regarding the future of the Vietnamese reform program.

And it was because the agreement would start to undermine the socialist economic foundations and end subsidies to state-owned enterprises that the Politburo was so unhappy with the agreement and deadlocked from the start. Though inefficient, the 6,000 state-owned enterprises are the cornerstone of the socialist economy, despite the fact that between one-third to one-half operate in the red. The leadership cannot fathom any policy that would limit subsidies or subject them to increased foreign competition because unemployment rates in Vietnam are already near 10 percent, and even by April 1998, over 8 percent of the 1.8 million SOE employees had been laid off. In addition, at current population growth rates, Vietnam must create between 600,00-700,000 jobs per year.[25] Whereas reformers want to scrap the inefficient SOE system and free up the private sector, conservatives believe that the collapse of the SOE system will lead to mass unemployment and political unrest. The SOE system is at the heart of the regime's legitimacy and must be defended at all costs. As one Vietnamese diplomat was quoted as saying, "If the agreement improves trade, that's one thing, but it also pushes reform. That's what makes us hesitate. We must determine the steps of reform."[26]

The VPA, which has vast industrial and commercial holdings to augment its diminished budget, was also against the trade deal. Increased competition would threaten its market share and competitiveness, that is so critical to the military's overall budget.[27] By 1998, total revenue of the military's 164 enterprises surpassed $600 million,[28] and one estimate is that 100,000 of the military's 572,000 troops are engaged in full-time economic activity.[29] Since 1989, VPA firms have entered into approximately 30 joint ventures capitalized at $302 million, involved in industrial areas such as ship repair and construction, car assembly, building materials, hotels and entertainment centers, and food stuffs. The military operates an airline and its trying to establish a rival telecommunications service to challenge the Ministry of Post and Telecommunications' monopoly.

---

[25] Ari Kokko, "Vietnam: Ready for Doi Moi II?" *ASEAN Economic Bulletin*, Vol. 15, No. 3 (December 1998): 319-327, esp. 325.

[26] Keenan, "Opening Doors."

[27] With the withdrawal from Cambodia and the loss of all Soviet subsidies beginning in 1989, the VPA was significantly downsized in both size and budget. Once over 1 million men and commanding over one-third of the national budget, in addition to an average annual $1 billion in Soviet aid, the military's size and budget was slashed by 50 percent. The military's budget fell annually hitting a low of $800 million (5.7 percent of GDP) in 1994, before rising to $1 billion in 1999 (3.7 percent of GDP), a far cry from the $2.3 billion (18 percent of GDP) in 1989. Per capita military expenditure was only $12 per soldier, the lowest in a region experiencing unprecedented growth in military budgets and acquisitions. As 70 percent of the Vietnamese military budget goes to salaries, only 30 percent is left for maintenance and upkeep of existing weapons systems as well as new acquisitions. As many of Vietnam's weapon systems are at the end of their service life, the military feels that it needs a major refurbishment of its arsenal.

[28] Hanh Dung, "Military Enterprise," *Viet Nam Economic Times* (December 1999). The Military's 300 enterprises were reduced to 164 through closures and mergers in late-1997 through early-1998.

[29] Huw Watkin, "Proud Military Slips into Decline as Aid Dries Up," *South China Morning Post*, 7 July 1999.

The second reason that the trade deal was rejected has to do with the current deadlock in the Politburo. There are several aspects to this. First, the top three leaders, General Secretary Le Kha Phieu, Prime Minister Phan Van Khai and President Tran Duc Luong, really don't have the authority (and more importantly the patronage networks running through the party, government, and military) that their predecessors did. The Vietnamese political system is based on patron-client ties: the relationship between two or more individuals of unequal rank or stature. In return for support and protection, the client owes his patron unquestioned loyalty and support. Because Do Muoi, Le Duc Anh and Vo Van Kiet came to power during the war years, they all wore party, military and government hats. The party-military-government elite at that time really was an elite. There were ideological and strategic differences and personal rivalries to be sure, but it was a small group, who went through a formative period together. And they all had very broad experience. The current leadership, the fourth generation, came of political age during a period of stagnation when their predecessors refused to give up power- most importantly their patronage networks- the nomenklatura. They were brought up through the ranks because they were "clients" who never had enough authority or opportunity to really be "patrons" in their own right. What gave Le Duc Anh authority and power as president, was not his positional power, in Putnam's terms, but his decisional power. As a senior general and former Minister of Defense, he had vast patronage networks throughout the military. Though constitutionally as powerful as his predecessor, Tran Duc Luong has little power over the military that he technically commands because he does not control any of the patronage networks throughout the military. He has never promoted anyone or done anything to ensure unwavering loyalty to him. Similarly, because Le Kha Phieu was a compromise candidate, and came in without patronage or clear support. He is a weak leader who needs to appeal for the support of both reformers and conservatives. He tends to sit on the fence, weighing in at the last moment, and trying to build consensus between these disparate factions. Because of this he is perceived as a weak leader. He endears himself to neither faction.

Moreover, this generation of leaders was brought up in "line," i.e., Phieu was just a military political commisar, nothing else, his entire career. Tran Duc Luong was a geologist, and though a well connected one, simply a line ministry geologist. Phan Van Khai, again, rose through the economic ministries and commissions. In short, their experience is deep but not wide. Their predecessors' experience was wide not deep. They rotated through different positions across different branches of government-party-military during the war years. Do Muoi, for example, served as a labor leader, in various economic ministries, as prime minister, and in various party positions. Vo Van Kiet served as a top communist official in the south, a long-time member of the Central Committee, head of the State Planning Commission, and various other posts before becoming Prime Minister. These long and varied careers introduced them to a lot of people. And power in Vietnam is nothing but personal. The current leadership had no such broad experience, and it shows.

In short, the current top leadership does not have the leverage or personal pull over their colleagues. And they cannot pressure or influence their colleagues from below- because they do not know those underlings. At the 4th Plenum, in December 1997, the top three leaders, Le Duc Anh, Do Muoi and Vo Van Kiet, resigned from the Politburo; yet they were appointed "advisors" to the Central Committee. To this day, they use that position to make their presence known. Former General Secretary Do Moui casts a long shadow over Le Kha Phieu, weighing in when he feels like it, and he has always been against the trade deal with the Americans. Likewise, Phan Van Khai, continues to rely on the support of his patron Vo Van Kiet.

One also has to look at the composition of the Politburo to explain its current deadlock. The politburo is carefully chosen with one factor in mind: balance. Balance between regions (especially north and south), age, ideological proclivities, sector, job or career path, and incumbency. The politburo includes a diverse range of opinions and views, factored by regional, generational and bureaucratic politics. By this very fact, new policies are hard to implement as the stability and the status quo are the paramount concern.

The current Politburo has some real reformers, but also some real hardliners, and clearly the tilt is in the conservatives' favor. Though there are a few reformers, they're young and don't have too much political capital. They seem unable or unwilling to act in the face of older, more entrenched conservatives. This younger group of reform minded leaders include Prime Minister Phan Van Khai (3), Vice Prime Minister Nguyen Tan Dung (14), Truong Tan Sang (10) and Nguyen Minh Triet (17), the new Ho Chi Minh City Party Secretary. This group is very well educated, they have considerable experience- especially in economic issues. And they also have some cross-sector experience. For example, Nguyen Tan Dung is a 20-year veteran of the army and a former Vice Minister of the Interior, who has served as Central Bank Governor and Vice Prime Minister, responsible for the economy. Phan Van Khai held a large number of posts in the various economic ministries including the umbrella, State Planning Commission. Truong Tan Sang served as the Party Secretary in Ho Chi Minh City before being brought to Hanoi to run the Central Committee's Economic Commission in early 2000.

The reformers are young, and clearly going places, but they do not have the power base or political capital to take on the conservatives at present. Phan Van Khai, who has real liberal credentials, has been a terrible disappointment. Not just because he cannot get his policies through the conservative dominated Politburo, but because he must play up his conservative credentials to mollify them. He is very vulnerable to appearing too liberal, too reformist, because conservatives see a direct correlation between reform and corruption, and a cloud of corruption hovers over Khai because of his son's misdeeds. To be sure, after conservatives launched a major anti-graft campaign at the 6th Plenum (January-February 1998) the first major purge was of Khai's own Vice Minister Ngo Xuan Loc.[30] The reformers are very vulnerable.

The conservatives are powerful and there are more of them. But they are also much older, nearing the age of retirement, and many have questionable staying power past the next party congress in 2001, because of mismanagement in their sector, or because their patrons have passed on. The fact that so many of them- perhaps seven- are lame ducks is

---

[30] Adrian Edwards, "Closed Minds," *FEER*, 9 December 1999, 26.

very important in understanding the current impasse. For example, General Scretary Le Kha Phieu (70) may be held responsible for the country's current economic malaise. He has been far more pragmatic than anyone expected him to be, but as he has sat on the fence on many issues, conveying the image of a weak leader. He has endeared himself to neither faction. President, Tran Duc Luong (65) lacks charisma and leadership, and is moreover, very close to the aging Do Muoi. That relationship could hurt Luong when Muoi passes on. Nguyen Manh Cam's (72) star is fading, now that he has retired as Minister of Foreign Affairs. Cam most likely will not be reelected to the next Politburo, unless the Central Committee feels it needs a party elder for "stability." It is likely that Cam will be appointed Vice President to replace the outgoing Madame Nguyen Thanh Binh. Nguyen Duc Binh (74) is as hard core an ideologue as they come, and as head of the party school he controls one of the most powerful patronage networks. He's getting old and a lot of people want him off the Politburo because he is too ideological. Nguyen Thi Xuan My (61), the party disciplinarian, is obviously not doing a great job. She has been disciplining more than she is deterring. Her continued presence will have more to do with how successful the current anti-corruption drive goes in regaining some of the party's lost legitimacy, than with the token presence of the Politburo's first and only woman. She is in her late-50s and could be on the next Politburo, but only if some of the graft is dealt with. Le Xuan Dung (65) has taken some heat for the economic slowdown in the capital- including the mass exodus of foreign investment. He is also rumored to be in poor health. Pham The Duyet (65) is the only true proletarian on the Politburo, a former union leader. Despite being acquitted of corruption charges, in 1998, he's been under a cloud. Duyet has been the Politburo member in charge of dealing with the peasant protests in Thai Binh. Supposedly, few officials have been arrested or punished. If peasant protests resume or spread to other provinces, Duyet could be held accountable. Moreover, like Tran Duc Luong, he is one of Do Muoi's protégés; this relationship could hurt him when Do Muoi passes on.

In short, of the 18 Politburo members, there are quite a few definite and potential vacancies, many of whom are conservative. Because the Politburo tends not to newly elect more than 50 percent of its members, seven or eight new members is foreseeable. This will really be an opportunity for the balance of power to tilt towards the reformers. Until the new congress, there will be few substantive decisions coming from the Politburo. Without a change in personnel, there cannot be a fundamental shift in policy. At present, there are simply enough conservatives who can block the deal- and more importantly- the continuation of the reform program and a commitment to greater economic globalization.

In the meantime, the reformers have attempted some damage control as they do not want to lose the initiative to the conservatives. If they cannot move the reform process forward, they know that they have to prevent conservatives from reversing the gains that have been made since 1986 until the 2001 Party Congress. First, Hanoi has continued the tariff waiver of US imports. In an attempt to force the American hand to conclude the trade deal, in 1998 Hanoi passed a law that would increase all tariffs by 50 percent on imports from countries that did not accord MFN trade status to Vietnam. Then, as a gesture of good will, Hanoi waived the tariff hike for American imports in 1999. The tariff, which would have been dropped with the signing of the trade agreement, legally will take affect in 2000. When the Politburo did not sign the agreement, Vietnamese Ministry of Finance officials were quick to go on the record and announce that although no decision had been made, "The principle now is to maintain good trade relations between Vietnam and the US."[31] Second, senior Vietnamese leaders, such as First Vice Prime Minister Nguyen Tan Dung, have assured their American counterparts that the Politburo would eventually sign the agreement. Dung, who has overall responsibility for economic issues on the Politburo, is a leading reformist and a contender to become the next party General Secretary. He met with Assistant Secretary of State Stanley Roth at the APEC summit where President Clinton was hoping to sign the agreement with Prime Minister Phan Van Khai.

There will be a lot of infighting and jockeying between conservatives and reformers to see who will be responsible for the drafting of the Political Report of the 9th Congress and controlling the nomination lists for the Central Committee and Politburo membership. There is always a lot of politicking behind these issues. To be sure, the Politburo still has not been able to reach any consensus regarding who will fill Doan Khue's seat, now vacant for almost two years. Not much will happen until the next party congress in late 2001. It is possible that they move the congress up if urgent issues are at hand, but more likely, it will be delayed like the last one because they will not have been able to agree on the political report, policies, personnel changes on the Central Committee and Politburo beforehand. This was the case, for example, with the 7th Plenum in August 1999, which was delayed five times because they could not reach a consensus.

Likewise, at the 8th Plenum, in November 1999, which was scheduled to discuss the rejected trade deal and the future course of the reform program, economic integration and the trade deal were never even discussed because they are simply too divisive at present. The VCP is terrified at the idea of being divided. If one analyzes the VCP's reaction to the events in Eastern Europe in 1989, it was the collapse of communism in Hungary that most concerned Hanoi. In Hungary it was not exogenous forces that pressured the party to step down, such as the Catholic Church or independent labor unions, or intellectuals, but "reform circles" within the Hungarian Communist Party. These circles eventually became independent parties. As Hanoi does not have to worry about large student movements, a large and independent Church presence, and independent unions, it does worry about intra-party dissent and division. The leadership, at present, is unwilling to take on major ideological policy issues that could jeopardize the unity of the party.

# 7. Conclusion

The economic reforms of *doi moi* revived Vietnam's moribund economy and poised the country to become the next tiger economy in Southeast Asia. No longer

---

[31] Reuters "Hanoi Yet to Discuss U.S. Tariff Waiver for 2000," 25 October 1999, and Reuters, "Vietnam Undecided on U.S. Tariff Waiver for 2000," 12 October 1999.

diplomatically isolated, the Vietnamese embarked on an externally-oriented development plan, seeking to develop through export led growth and by courting foreign investment; to do so, Hanoi revamped its confrontational foreign policy, normalizing ties with Japan, the United States, the ASEAN states and China. The collapse of socialism across Eastern Europe and the Tiananmen Massacre in 1989, however, alarmed many in the VCP's leadership that the reform program was going too quickly. While economic reforms were allowed to continue and the country enjoyed high growth rates in the early to mid-1990s, all debates over political liberalization were silenced as the party sought to ensure its leading role in society. Yet the initial reforms were running out of steam by the mid-1990s and Vietnam became stuck in a transitional system of market socialism. The leadership, deeply divided into ideologically based factions, was unable to come to a consensus on how to proceed with the reform program. In short, there was no consensus on what economic course the country should pursue. Deadlocked, they were unable to effectively respond to a series of crises: a faltering economy, rampant corruption, the Asian economic crisis, and a wave of peasant rebellions. The factional nature of Vietnamese politics, compounded by generational rifts in the leadership, as well as an overwhelming fear of losing ultimate control has really hampered Vietnamese decision-making. The Politburo's rejection of the trade agreement with the United States magnifies the weaknesses in the system; that the party leadership is so deadlocked over an issue that will bring such tangible results and will help to rejuvenate the economy that has been in a down turn since 1996.

Until the next party congress is held when there can be a large-scale leadership transition and generational change, sometime in 2001-2002, bold policies that will rejuvenate the reform program are unlikely to be implemented. Instead, the Vietnamese leadership will continue to implement piecemeal policies that will allow them to muddle through. Vietnam currently has very weak leaders at a time when the country desperately needs bold measures.

Ironically, the next generation of leaders will probably have more power and authority than the current leadership, for two reasons. First, they were promoted and hand picked not by the current leaders, but by the past group. They have had a lot of support and patronage. Second, and more importantly, as they are all relatively young, they will have been in top positions for a long time, and rotated through many different postings and bureaucracies; they have both depth and breadth of experience. This gives them a long time to promote and train proteges- a cadre of loyal supporters across many different bureaucracies. Only with stronger leaders, will Vietnam have the political will to make the hard policy choices to reform the economy and get it back on track to becoming the next "tiger" economy.

# INDEX